ORTHODOXY & WESTERN CULTURE

A Collection of Essays Honoring
Jaroslav Pelikan on His Eightieth Birthday

D1565970

Orthodoxy & Western Culture

A Collection of Essays Honoring
Jaroslav Pelikan on His Eightieth Birthday

Edited by

Valerie Hotchkiss and Patrick Henry

st vladimir's seminary press
crestwood, new york
2005

Library of Congress Cataloging-in-Publication Data

Orthodoxy & Western culture : a collection of essays honoring Jaroslav
Pelikan on his eightieth birthday / Valerie Hotchkiss and Patrick Henry, eds.
     p.   cm.
   Includes bibliographical references
   ISBN 0-88141-271-6 (alk. paper)
     1. Pelikan, Jaroslav Jan, 1923–   2. Orthodox Eastern Church.   I. Title:
Orthodoxy and Western culture.   II. Pelikan, Jaroslav Jan, 1923–   III.
Hotchkiss, Valerie R., 1960–   IV. Henry, Patrick, 1939–

BX395.P44O78 2005
270 — dc22

2005022068

COPYRIGHT © 2005
ST VLADIMIR'S SEMINARY PRESS
575 Scarsdale Rd, Crestwood, NY 10707
1-800-204-2665
www.svspress.com

ISBN 0-88141-271-6

PRINTED IN THE UNITED STATES OF AMERICA

Table of Contents

Jaroslav Pelikan:
The Living Legend in Our Midst

John H. Erickson*

*I*t is entirely appropriate that this volume in celebration of
Jaroslav Pelikan's eightieth birthday be published by St Vladimir's Seminary Press. Jary—as his friends at the seminary are
pleased to call him—is a Trustee of St Vladimir's, and in the summer
of 2003 was the keynote speaker for the seminary's Institute of Liturgical Music and Pastoral Practice, which had "Living Tradition" as its
theme. The goal of Jary's career has been "the vindication of tradition," as the title of one of his books puts it, and he exemplifies living
tradition, particularly for those of us whose homes are in the West.

Jary traces many of his academic and religious interests to his Slovak
background. His grandfather, Jan Pelikan, was born in Slovakia—that
remarkable meeting place of cultures and religious traditions—and
after coming to the United States was one of the founding fathers of
the Slovak Synod of Lutherans. Jary's father, also a Slovak Lutheran
pastor, said that his son "combined German Lutheran scholarship and
Slavic orthodox piety—and fortunately not vice versa."

In this volume, there are references to Jary's exemplary academic
career, the awards he has received, and his prodigious output of publication. One honor not mentioned elsewhere was bestowed in 2000,

---

*This testimony to St Vladimir's Orthodox Theological Seminary's esteem for its
Trustee Jaroslav Pelikan, by the dean of the seminary, John Erickson, is adapted from
"Jaroslav Pelikan: The Living Legend in our Midst," *SVS News* (Spring 2003): 2–3;
http://www.svots.edu/Events/Summer-Institute/2003/readings.html.

in the course of celebrations for the 200th anniversary of the Library of Congress. Jary was officially named a Living Legend, along with General (subsequently Secretary of State) Colin Powell, publisher Katharine Graham, violinist Isaac Stern, and—as Jary notes with a twinkle in his eye—Barbra Streisand, Gloria Steinem, and Big Bird.

For us who are Orthodox, the fact that Pelikan's magnum opus, *The Christian Tradition*, was the first—and to date still the only—major history of Christian doctrine to take the Orthodox East seriously, made him a Living Legend long before he became formally a member of our community. And Jary credits another of our legendary scholars with teaching him the most important lesson of his career.

He describes Fr Georges Florovsky (1893–1979) as "the last of my mentors and the one to whom I owe the most." On the wall of Jary's study there are two portraits, one of Florovsky, the other of Adolf von Harnack. Both Harnack and Florovsky wrestled with a question that anyone who tries to be both a historian and a Christian must confront: What is the relationship between universal truth and its particular embodiments? The answer, Jary suggests, is to be found not in reductionism (e.g., Harnack's attempt to identify "the essence of Christianity") but rather in a living tradition that mediates between past and present. "Harnack showed me what it is to be a scholar. Florovsky showed me what it is to be a scholar and a Christian at the same time."

In *The Vindication of Tradition* (1984) Jary develops, as a clue to the universal/particular conundrum, the distinction between icon and idol that developed in Byzantium in the course of the iconoclastic controversy of the eighth and ninth centuries. An icon "does not present itself as coextensive with the truth it teaches, but does present itself as the way that we who are its heirs must follow if we are to go beyond it . . . to a universal truth that is available only in a particular embodiment." An idol, on the other hand, is "the embodiment of that which it represents, but it directs us to itself, rather than beyond itself." Thus, when tradition becomes traditionalism, it becomes idolatrous; "it makes the preservation and the repetition of the past an end in itself." The truth is at once universal and particular; it refuses to choose between these two alternatives, "knowing that an authentic icon, a living tradition, must be both" (pp. 55–57).

In addition to recalling his debt to Florovsky, Pelikan likes to speak of his friendship with two former Deans of St Vladimir's Seminary, Fr Alexander Schmemann (1921–83) and Fr John Meyendorff (1926–92). Jary was invited to give the 1975 commencement address, in which he spoke on "Continuity and Creativity" (available online at *http://www. jacwell.org/articles/1998-SPRING-Pelikan.htm*). In introducing him, Fr Schmemann noted, "the hardest thing for me to say about Professor Pelikan is why he is not Orthodox." But that was to change. On March 25, 1998, the feast of the Annunciation, Jary was chrismated by Metropolitan Theodosius, primate of the Orthodox Church in America (OCA), and received into the Orthodox Church. His wife Sylvia joined him in embracing Orthodoxy a few months later, and together they worship regularly in the seminary chapel.

In a conversation shortly after his entrance into the Orthodox Church, Jary likened his path to Orthodoxy to that of a pilot who kept circling the airport, looking for a way to land. Orthodox Christians can be thankful that he landed before running out of fuel.

Dr Jaroslav Pelikan receiving the 2004 John W. Kluge Prize for Lifetime Achievement in the Human Sciences from the Librarian of Congress Dr James H. Billington, December 8, 2004. (Photo by John Harrington)

Was wir ererbt haben

*F*AMILY LORE SAYS that when little Jaroslav Pelikan did not yet have the manual dexterity to form letters with a pen, he learned to use a typewriter. He was two and a half years old when he typed his first words. This eagerness to express himself has not waned over the years. He is the author of nearly forty books and editor of over a dozen multi-volume reference books that have become standard historical works.

Another family story locates the origin of his passion for tradition and its transmission early in his life. As a teenager, he had to decide whether his vocation was as scholar or concert pianist. One day at home in Chicago he was practicing a Beethoven sonata. A guest of the Pelikans was Jan Masaryk—son of Tomas Masaryk, the first president of Czechoslovakia, and Charlotte Garrigue Masaryk, an American pianist who had met Tomas when she went to Europe to study piano with Franz Liszt. Suddenly Jan Masaryk shouted, "No, that should be an F-natural!" "But right here in the score it's an F-sharp." "That's wrong. I heard from my mother that there's a mistake in the printed score, and she heard it from her teacher Liszt, who heard it from his teacher Carl Czerny, who heard it from his teacher, Beethoven."

Jaroslav Pelikan's writings have focused on the entire history of Christianity, from its beginnings to the present day. He is recognized as the foremost church historian of the twentieth century—or as one reviewer recently put it, "the premier historical theologian of our time."[1] It is a position he has held for nearly fifty years, a reputation built upon such monuments as his *Riddle of Roman Catholicism*, the fifty-five volume English edition of Martin Luther's work, his magisterial five-volume *The Christian Tradition*, and his most recent work on

Christian creeds. To say he is the "premier" or "foremost" scholar in this field is an understatement, for he is the only scholar recognized as the authority for the immense field of all of Christian history. One might name a runner-up for the patristic period, another for medieval history, or an equally worthy Reformation scholar, for example, but there is no one else who covers *all* of this and more with such consummate skill.

Pelikan's books are used in universities and seminaries and by clergy of every denomination. His books reach a broader audience, however, thanks to his erudition, skill as a writer, and knack for choosing compelling topics. For example, *Jesus Through the Centuries* (1985) and *Mary Through the Centuries* (1996) are popular bestsellers. Other examples include his *Bach Among the Theologians* (1989), which is required reading for musicians, and several of his books that began as public lecture series, including *Imago Dei* (1990), *What Has Athens to Do with Jerusalem?* (1997), and the latest on *Interpreting the Bible and the Constitution* (2004).

Many of Pelikan's writings deal with the interrelation of Christian tradition and the history of culture, including philosophy, music, the visual arts, literature, rhetoric, political and legal theory, and the natural sciences. His books cross disciplinary boundaries. Pelikan's research on Dante, Goethe, and Tolstoy makes theological connections that literary critics tend to overlook in their interpretations. His knowledge of music history and his appreciation of its practice have led not only to his important book on Bach, but also to provocative work on Olivier Messiaen and many presentations at public concerts, notably with Yo-Yo Ma and the late Robert Shaw. He also served as Director of the Summer Humanities Institute for the Bellingham Music Festival.

In addition to his own writings, Pelikan has used his remarkable linguistic abilities to edit and translate primary texts from the biblical, classical, medieval, Reformation, and modern periods. There is no other historian in America who knows as many languages as Jaroslav Pelikan. He reads—and in several cases is fluent in—every single

European language except Finnish and Hungarian. In addition, he knows all the ancient languages required for biblical and patristic studies, and is well versed in most Western medieval languages. Pelikan is a very close and careful reader of documents. This is his strength; he knows so much primary literature and understands it so well, that he is able to compare, analyze, synthesize, and interpret large periods of intellectual history with a mastery that no other historian matches.

Indeed, the idea of "interpreting" is central to Pelikan's approach. His most recent work deals with the fundamental issue of interpretation, whether literary, historical, religious, or political, by looking at the history of interpreting the U.S. Constitution and the Bible. As he says, in both cases "you have a text that's hundreds of years old—200 or 20-hundred, as the case may be—which is assumed to be able to speak to situations and problems that its writers could not have foreseen. And that means that there's got to be some way to tease out of the text a meaning for these new situations." This is simply the latest in his lifetime's series of commitments to what he identifies as the scholar's creed, words spoken by Goethe's Faust: "What you have inherited from your Fathers, take now as task in order to make it your own!" ("Was du ererbst von deinen Vätern hast, / erwirb es, um es zu besitzen." *Faust*, 682f).

Tradition matters greatly to Pelikan, but he has never tried to make himself a tradition. That there is no "Pelikan School" is, in fact, one of his greatest achievements. His students have learned from him how to proceed with their own research, not simply to build upon the work of their master. Pelikan's doctoral students and their work have taken diverse paths—from Byzantine churchmen to cross-dressing monks, and from Anglo-Saxon homilies to Erasmus's prayers to Orthodoxy in imperial Russia. He has inspired us to be responsible scholars, always taking our inheritance, both from primary sources and the scholarly tradition, as task and as foundation for new interpretations. What Pelikan once said of his own mentor, Wilhelm Pauck, holds true for our view of him: "none of us will call himself his disciple, even as he . . . has refused to be the disciple of any."

To our brief description of Pelikan's scholarly accomplishments we must add his work on the Reformation, particularly Martin Luther, on Saint Augustine, on Søren Kierkegaard, on medieval philosophy, and on Eastern Orthodoxy. His bibliography demonstrates the scope, depth, and sheer volume of his scholarly output. The fact that Pelikan has received forty-two honorary degrees speaks to the high esteem in which he is held by so many. And he is not merely an American phenomenon. He has been invited to many other countries to teach and lecture, delivering the prestigious Gifford Lectures, for example, in Aberdeen and the Gilson Lectures in Toronto. He also served as Chairman of the U.S.-Czechoslovak Commission on Joint Research in the 1980s and 90s and has received several honors from the Czech Republic, Slovakia, Ukraine, Poland, and Germany.

Pelikan has not produced this impressive oeuvre in scholarly solitude. It is astonishing that he finds time to produce so much, given his busy schedule as an academic administrator, consultant, traveling lecturer, and nurturer of younger scholars. The breadth and depth of his expertise have taken him far beyond the confines of church history. He served on commissions of the World Council of Churches. He has long been active in university administration—Dean of the Graduate School at Yale University (1973–78) and Chairman of the Publications Committee, Vice President, and on the Board of Governors at Yale University Press from 1980 to the present. He has also held numerous positions of distinction outside of universities, including that of President of the American Academy of Arts and Sciences (1994–97), the international learned society of the world's leading scientists, scholars, artists, business people, and public leaders. As Founding Chairman of the Council of Scholars at the Library of Congress (1980–83; 1988–94), Councillor of the American Philosophical Society (1984–87), and Judge for the National Book Awards (1990), he has led organizations dealing with issues and ideas in disciplines other than his own. Likewise, while serving on the U.S. President's Committee on the Arts and the Humanities he spoke for broader issues from his eminent place as perhaps *the* leading humanities scholar in the nation. He served as

Chairman of the Board of the American Academy of Political and Social Science in 2003–04, after having served as its President from 2000–01—a position in which one would not expect a church historian, but Pelikan is no ordinary church historian. He has recently accepted a post as the Scholarly Director for the "Institutions of Democracy Project" of the Annenberg Foundation, a multifaceted national project that will involve conferences, publishing, grant making, media presentations, and the production of educational materials.

All these extra-curricular duties illustrate Pelikan's lively engagement with all aspects of the life of the mind. His wide influence on learning and education in America is reminiscent of the impact two of his heroes had earlier in England and Germany. A portrait of Adolf von Harnack (1851–1930) gazes down from, and an image of the coat-of-arms of John Henry Newman (1801–1890) graces, the wall of Pelikan's study, just as their names stand at the head of each volume of *The Christian Tradition*. Along with his prodigious scholarly output, Harnack served as Director of the Prussian National Library and as President of the Kaiser Wilhelm Gesellschaft for furthering learning and science. It would be hard to name a book that has shaped higher education more profoundly than Newman's *The Idea of a University* (1852). *Publisher's Weekly* said of Pelikan's 1992 book, *The Idea of the University: A Reexamination*, that it "should be required reading for shapers of the university." Pelikan draws upon his work as a professor, scholar, and university administrator to delve into a careful examination of what a university ought to be and why the institution is so important for society. He also boldly champions what Newman called the "embalming of dead genius," in eloquent defenses of university museums and libraries and their central role in the educational process as preservers of knowledge.

Pelikan, however, is not a traditionalist by any means. He is more open to new ideas and new technologies than many younger scholars. Recently, when faced with a technical challenge involving the presentation of numerous original language texts in both Roman and non-Roman fonts, Pelikan realized that he might not really know what all

the options were or might be in the near future, so he quickly convened a meeting of the minds, with scholars and techies and scholarly
techies, to probe the possibilities. He is respectful of the past but he
is also supremely open-minded about what the present may require
and what the future may bring. In an interview in *U.S. News & World
Report* (July 26, 1989), he said: "Tradition is the living faith of the dead;
traditionalism is the dead faith of the living. Tradition lives in conversation with the past, while remembering where we are and when we
are and that it is we who have to decide. Traditionalism supposes that
nothing should ever be done for the first time, so all that is needed to
solve any problem is to arrive at the supposedly unanimous testimony
of this homogenized tradition."

Pelikan's communication skills are extraordinary, honed in a career
in which teaching has played a large part. He has insisted, and demonstrated, that the academy does not live by research alone or teaching
alone, but only when both flourish. He can hold an after-dinner general
audience spellbound with a description of the nominalism of Abelard,
a dry topic indeed in a lesser speaker's hands. His ability to make a connection and to maintain an intense link with everyone in a lecture hall
is an amazing thing to experience. His skills in one-on-one encounters
are equally impressive; he works a crowd like a master politician, giving
each person just the right amount of attention and making everyone
feel special. He delights in occasional name-dropping and can certainly
appear the grand man, but his simple humanity is always ready to shine
forth. At a concert where Pelikan was delivering an introductory lecture, a young man, still a student, who would be playing the organ for
the piece, shyly approached Pelikan with a book in his hand. He introduced himself and asked for an autograph. Pelikan took the book and
asked the student about his interests and studies. After a few minutes
and additional encouragement from Pelikan, the student not only
poured forth his life's plans for study but also brought out five or six
more books from his knapsack for Pelikan to sign.

Jaroslav Pelikan is not just an historian. As a university administrator, educational policy maker, and author of important commentaries

on universities, he has shaped the way that issues in higher education are addressed. He could have been a university president (indeed the position has been offered on more than one occasion), but he chose to devote himself to teaching in the humanities. As a consultant to major libraries, publishing houses, and museums, he has promoted both the preservation of knowledge and innovations that might help disseminate that knowledge to new generations. In his work, he has been an active advocate for the humanities and he has earned the respect of people and institutions throughout America and beyond. The broader implications of his historical work have influenced a variety of disciplines, and his many endeavors outside the field of church history make Pelikan a prominent and powerful spokesperson for the humanities in general. His work with the U.S. President's Committee on the Arts and Humanities and his most recent responsibilities with the Annenberg Public Policy Center "Institutions of Democracy Project" move beyond the academy into the realm of public affairs.

Through all of his activities at the forefront of academic and cultural life, Jaroslav Pelikan has remained a person of the church. He not only interprets the tradition; he loves it. He has identified Saint John's Abbey and University in Collegeville, Minnesota, as one of his spiritual homes, and the Benedictine monks there have testified to their regard for him with their highest honor, the Pax Christi Award. The great Methodist ecumenist, Albert Outler, said of *The Christian Tradition* that it "is more than a major landmark in the history of doctrine. . . . From this sort of understanding of the Christian past, in both its constants and its changing contexts, Christians may gain a more adequately informed vision of their future as members with one another in the body of Christ." And Pelikan's close friendship with Rabbi Abraham Joshua Heschel is an outward and visible sign of his profound understanding of the continuity between Judaism and Christianity.

Pelikan's reception into the Orthodox Church in 1998 was no surprise to his friends, who realized it was not a "conversion" but rather a homecoming. Orthodoxy, as lived by some of its exemplars, is broad and deep, capacious enough for Pelikan's spirit. It was said of Dostoevsky that he had room in himself for all the Karamazovs.

When it came time to celebrate Jaroslav Pelikan's eightieth birthday, it seemed to us, two of his students a quarter-century apart, that the best way would be to do something national that would contribute to the understanding of Orthodoxy and Western Culture. We came up with the idea of a peripatetic lecture series, with distinguished scholar-friends offering lectures in various locations throughout country that had been significant in Pelikan's career: The University of Chicago; Saint John's in Collegeville; St Vladimir's Seminary; Annunciation Cathedral of San Francisco; Bridwell Library in Dallas, Texas; The Library of Congress; and, of course, Yale University. Jaroslav Pelikan and his wife Sylvia were present for all the lectures (especially, of course, for the last one, which he himself delivered!). Indeed, at the Yale homecoming of the lecture series, his entire family, sons Martin and Michael, daughter Miriam, daughters-in-law Martha and A.T., son-in-law Laurence, and grandchildren Matthew, Stephan, and Nikolai were all present, along with many of his Doktorkinder und Doktor-Enkelkinder.

Subsequent to our celebration, Pelikan was given an extraordinary award. Earlier, in 1983, he had received the Jefferson Award of the National Endowment for the Humanities, then the highest recognition conferred by the federal government on a scholar in the humanities. In December 2004, Jaroslav Pelikan, along with his former University of Chicago colleague Paul Ricoeur, was recipient of the John W. Kluge Prize for Lifetime Achievement in the Human Sciences, the "Nobel" for fields in which there is no Nobel. The citation recognizes his importance as scholar, teacher, and as an intellectual force in American life:

> Over the past 50 years, Jaroslav Pelikan has made unrivaled contributions to intellectual, cultural and religious history. . . . He has [also] illuminated many aspects of both political and religious life through the visual arts, music, literature, textual interpretations

and the role of the university. . . . As a teacher, Pelikan had a larger-than-life reputation, relating well both to specialized academic and general audiences. His mastery of so much primary literature enabled him to synthesize and interpret lengthy periods of intellectual history. As one of his former students said: "He teaches in a way that makes the listener feel intelligent; one feels that one is fully understanding (or perhaps discovering for oneself) the intricacies of the argument."

One of us (Henry) edited a volume commemorating Pelikan's 60th birthday, *Schools of Thought in the Christian Tradition*; both of us participated in a gathering on his 70th that resulted in another publication, *The Unbounded Community: Papers in Christian Ecumenism in Honor of Jaroslav Pelikan*; and the other (Hotchkiss) collaborated with him on the immense task of *Creeds and Confessions of Faith in the Christian Tradition*. It is a signal blessing of our lives that our teacher is also our friend. One Pelikan tradition that is perhaps not widely known but means the world to his students is the conclusion to the letter he sends when he gives the final okay to the dissertation. Up to this point he has always been "Professor Pelikan." The letter is signed "Jary," and then there's this P.S. "Please note the signature. As Captain Queeg used to say, 'rank has its privileges.'" So, we exercise that privilege now at the end of this introduction: Happy Birthday, Jary, thanks and Godspeed.

*—Valerie Hotchkiss and Patrick Henry**

---

*Two of Dr Pelikan's Yale students have edited this collection: Valerie Hotchkiss (1990) is head of the Rare Book and Special Collections Library at the University of Illinois at Urbana-Champaign; Patrick Henry (1967) recently retired as Executive Director of the Institute for Ecumenical and Cultural Research, Collegeville, Minnesota.

Notes

[1] Lawrence S. Cunningham, John A. O'Brien Professor of Theology, University of Notre Dame, in a review of *Creeds and Confessions of Faith in the Christian Tradition* (Yale University Press, 2003).

An Introduction to the Essays

VALERIE HOTCHKISS AND PATRICK HENRY

*T*HE ESSAYS IN THIS BOOK are based on lectures that were given in places associated with Jaroslav Pelikan's career. They took place during a year-long celebration of his 80th birthday, culminating in December 2003 at Yale University, where Pelikan himself gave the final lecture. The general theme of the series was the impact of Orthodoxy on Western Culture, a theme that lends itself to the broad range of geographic, chronological, philological, cultural, theological, and philosophical approaches taken by the contributors. To this collection of lectures we have asked Jaroslav Pelikan to add a personal memoir of his life as a scholar. His eloquent essay says more about what it means to devote oneself to scholarship and the life of the mind than the bibliography of his works at the end of this volume, however impressive that bibliography may be in sheer size and number.

The first contributor, Andrew Louth, explores a paradox: a scholar who was chrismated and received relatively late in life into the Orthodox Church is best known for a magnum opus subtitled *A History of the Development of Doctrine*—while Orthodox theologians are characteristically suspicious of the very idea of development. The paradox begins to dissolve when we take account of the difference between historical development as a demonstrable fact (which Orthodox can acknowledge more than they usually do) and the theological *category* of development.

In a wide-ranging and subtle analysis of the many meanings of development in Catholic and Protestant thought—especially of the many meanings within the writings of the single most important theoretician of development, John Henry Cardinal Newman—Louth reaches a middle ground in which Orthodox wariness is maintained but is situated not in a static metaphysics but in a profound gratitude to the apostles and Fathers. "We regard them as living now in the life of the Resurrection, more alive than we are, as they are closer to the source of Life."

Louth redirects the search for development from the history of ideas to the context of Christian worship, where "the first thing to emerge would be a much greater sense of continuity, or stability, in what is called development." And the function of the history of doctrine, like the function of the sacraments itself, is *memory*, which no one in our lifetime, as Louth says, has done more to keep alive both temporally and geographically than Jaroslav Pelikan.

Co-knowing, co-awareness, *so-znanie* in Russian, the attribute of Orthodoxy that grounds the thought of Soviet martyr Pavel Florensky, is the life's work of Jaroslav Pelikan, according to Anthony Ugolnik. "The Orthodox tradition, its sacred labor as it takes root here in the secularized West, will respond to God's mission if it concentrates not on its particularities but on the 'co-knowing' it shares not only with Christians but also with all People of the Book." And this includes not only Jews and Muslims, but also "those who come from a tradition but who for some reason, embedded in their rationality or our secular culture, can no longer say they believe."

Ugolnik is alert to the limits of language and its depths, to the limits of human perception and its great reach. He also reflects on the significant difference between the Western experience of the Bible as a single book and the Orthodox maintenance of separate volumes. "We place *Evangelions* (Gospels) on the altar; *Apostolarions* (Epistles) are a different book, given ritually to a reader; Psalters and Prophets and Wisdom texts are all separate volumes on a spinning lectern."

Orthodoxy, in short, keeps dialogue going. "We should invest less time in attacking each other's answers and more time in recovering each other's questions." And Orthodoxy points us to the arts. "We look for inspiration to those who declare and state and affirm things.

It might be more productive to look to those who imagine, and image-forth, and suggest things."

According to John Anthony McGuckin, a major obstacle to an accurate understanding of Orthodoxy and Western Culture is the fact that the latter has usurped the right to define the former, and the challenge is to "claim our true place by making and describing our own identity instead of taking it from the mouths of others," to send to oblivion "some putative Orient of our imagination."

It is true, he notes, that a colonial mentality—linguistically encoded in "We of the East"—is hard to shake, and that "we are still in economic and emotional recovery from centuries of reversals." But specifically intellectual agendas forced on the Orthodox by the "extraordinarily long run of prejudice" initiated by Gibbon must be dismantled, as Jaroslav Pelikan does in Volume 2 of *The Christian Tradition*, entitled *The Spirit of Eastern Christendom (600–1700)*. The day may come, McGuckin speculates, "when the absence of 1100 years of Christian political and religious culture from the standard curricula of Western theological history" will seem an oversight.

McGuckin calls for nothing less than a reframing of the question of Christian tradition: "Greek Christian civilization is the very foundation of Europe, not an exotic spin-off from it." Moreover, Orthodoxy pervades individual and communal life. "Our theology is not reducible to dogma—as we all know when we reflect on the reality of our real Orthodox experience rather than on the perception of Orthodox identity which others wish to impress upon us apologetically while dismissing us as reactionary conservatives."

Prima facie, the relationship of the Patriarchate of Constantinople to the state appears specialized and remote, but Speros Vryonis, Jr., argues that there are some resonances with current American debates about church and state. The story he tells covers many centuries and tells of the Patriarchate's dealings with Byzantine rulers, Ottoman sultans, and, finally, the secular Turkish state inaugurated by Atatürk—concluding with the sobering statistic that for 400 years following

Constantinople's becoming Istanbul, "the average length of patriarchal appointment was less than three years."

In a particularly fateful reversal, Emperor Justinian in the sixth
century "described disobedience to the imperial law as sacrilege,
while, conversely, the religious offense of heresy was treated politically." This blurring of lines is reflected over and over again in the
story of interaction between patriarchs and political authorities,
especially "in periods of particular stress and strain." And the blurring was not only administrative. Often, "imperial political interests
demanded particular theologies, and it was these theologies that
predominated."

Emperors were supposed to choose one of three patriarchal candidates proposed by the synod, but on occasion peremptorily discarded
the slate. Patriarchs were supposed to crown the emperor, thus acknowl-
edging the church's consent, but when patriarchs refused, the most
they could do was stall; they eventually lost their jobs. The balance
tipped very far one direction, especially in the musical chairs game of
the Iconoclastic Controversy: "Emperors and empresses made and
unmade patriarchs, they controlled synods, and they set the program
of theological choices."

James Billington will catch you off-guard. Reading his first two sentences, you think you know where you are, but by the end of the paragraph you realize you are actually thousands of miles away from there.
And you will begin to see how the story Billington tells contributes to
an aspect of the life's work of Jaroslav Pelikan, integrating "the rich
history of Eastern Orthodoxy into the broader understanding of
Christianity."

How, Billington asks, did Orthodox Christianity make it from the
scorching Egyptian desert to polar Alaska? The map of this vast historical landscape can be plotted as the interplay between empire and
desert, transferred into Russia from the Greek Church, "where it
existed between Constantinople, the imperial city the Russians referred to as Tsargrad, and Athos in the Aegean Sea, the isolated, purely
monastic peninsula." The monks went out to preserve prayer, not to

escape civilization, and people gathered around them, creating a frontier culture somewhat independent of state control.

Journeying is central to Russian spirituality, and in four dimensions: this world to the next; in daily life, where crosses and icons at crucial crossroads serve as guides into time, where the year is defined by feasts and reinforced by the décor of churches; and through space, especially by pilgrimage to three holy places (Constantinople, Athos, Jerusalem). And the journey sometimes ends in martyrdom—"something like 70 percent of all Christian martyrs were created in the twentieth century, and the largest number of these were in Russia."

While Vartan Gregorian's essay is not directly about Orthodoxy and Western Culture, it resonates with other contributions to this volume because the reintegration of knowledge, the reassertion of the ancient ideal of learning as the mental adaptability to comprehend a complex and ever-changing world, is something that the Orthodox tradition—as taught and exemplified by Jaroslav Pelikan—offers to the West. The connection becomes explicit in Dostoevsky's lament about scholars who "have only analyzed the parts and overlooked the whole and, indeed, their blindness is marvelous!"

The story of American higher education, one of the most astonishing chapters in world history, has a number of turning points, including an explosive increase in accessibility and an assignment of research responsibilities to universities that occurred about the time Pelikan was beginning his half-century of scholarly activity. Gregorian's prescription for higher education—a reassertion of the centrality of the liberal arts, including the natural sciences—is one that Pelikan makes to his students and colleagues, to policy makers and benefactors.

Reform is hard, takes time, and meets resistance, but Gregorian is unflinching in his declaration of what is required: "experts who coordinate and synthesize information from the very beginning, not as a final step." That is, integration of knowledge is not an operation you perform when all the pieces have been assembled; it is the way you assemble them in the first place. The challenge is daunting, but

Gregorian believes it will finally be met, because "humanity has a craving for wholeness."

Much of what other chapters in this book have identified as marks of Orthodoxy's impact on Western culture is reinforced and exemplified in Jaroslav Pelikan's own contribution to the celebration of his 80th birthday, "The Will to Believe and the Need for Creed." With prodigious learning and wry wit, he makes the case that a characteristically Orthodox sense of creed, allowing for toleration that is "the direct implication not of unfaith, but of what each community of faith 'believes, teaches, and confesses,'" is the most urgent of contemporary religious imperatives.

Demonstrating chorographical dexterity that those who have studied with him instantly recognize, Pelikan takes an insight from a previous scholar, William James, puts it in a broader context, and shows that it is more profound than its propounder knew. When James, who famously thought religion was something for "individual men in their solitude," said that "our faith is faith in some one else's faith"—not intending to compliment "our faith"—he provided an opening for a radically different understanding of religion as communal in both space and time. As Pelikan says, "we are not thrown on our own individual and feeble resources of believing or speculating or explaining (or even 'experiencing'), such as they may be."

Restoration of the first-person plural in recitation of the creed ("*We* believe"), recognition that "creed is not in the first instance the business of the professional and learned theological elite; *it is meant to be prayed*," and insistence that creed "presupposes the commandment of love," are hallmarks of Orthodoxy and of the ecumenical breakthroughs to which Pelikan is both contributor and witness.

All the essays underscore in particular ways the general contemporary imperative noted by Pelikan himself—toleration that is "the direct implication of faith," not its antithesis. The thematic motifs— paradox (Louth), dialogue (Ugolnik), identity (McGuckin), blurring of lines (Vryonis), journeying (Billington), reintegration (Gregorian), and religion as communal in both space and time (Pelikan)—weave together in a conversation that began long before we were born and will continue long after we are gone. Orthodoxy and Western Culture have had more to do with each other than is usually supposed, even by learned academics, but there is much to be gained on all sides by more communication, and it is fitting that Jaroslav Pelikan's eightieth birthday be an occasion for such interplay.

A Personal Memoir: Fragments of a Scholar's Autobiography

JAROSLAV PELIKAN

R EPEATEDLY IN RECENT YEARS, members of my family as well as my friends, colleagues, and former students have been urging me to write a full-length autobiography. I have resisted these suggestions, objecting that I am much more interested in the phenomenon that John Henry Newman in 1845 called "the development of Christian doctrine" through the centuries than in the phenomenon that he went on in 1864 to call "the history of my [own] religious opinions." At least in part, I tried nonetheless to address this proposal when I accepted the invitation of the Harvard University Press to write, as editor Aida Donald called it, a "middle-sized book" that "could amount to a kind of autobiography in small bites"; it appeared under the title *The Melody of Theology: A Philosophical Dictionary* in 1988. But that was the better part of two decades ago—for me extremely eventful decades, including as they did my Gifford Lectures at the University of Aberdeen in 1992/1993, published as *Christianity and Classical Culture*; my retirement in 1996 after exactly fifty years as a faculty member (although I have been holding one full-time academic appointment or another ever since); my reception into the fellowship of the Orthodox Church in 1998; the publication of the four volumes of *Creeds and Confessions of Faith in the Christian Tradition* with *Credo* in 2003; and several additional monographs, including two for 2005, one of them being my commentary on the Acts of the Apostles. These events, and particularly the third of them, do seem to call for some explanation and comment, even for something approaching an *apologia pro vita sua* (to borrow yet again from Cardinal Newman).

Short of such an *apologia*, this "personal memoir" may in some respects be read as a series of glosses on *The Melody of Theology* (to which, at the risk of perpetrating a self-advertising blurb for my own book, I shall be referring continually even when I do not mention it explicitly). Such entries in that book as "Development of Doctrine," "Harnack, Adolf von," "Languages," and "Newman, John Henry" underlie, and are presupposed by, much of what I am saying here. More than that book was, however, this is intended as a *"personal* memoir." I have been persuaded (though still somewhat reluctantly) by my beloved friends, the editors and the publisher of the present volume, to "feel free" to lay aside much of my usual embarrassment about a public display of my feelings and to speak more personally than is my wont, and to do so quite spontaneously and without hiding behind footnotes or any of the other usual scholarly apparatus. At the same time, my innate and incurable resistance to such display (a legacy, no doubt, from my mother) seems to imply that I should continue to observe a basic distinction between "personal" and "private." This is, then, definitely not my version of Augustine's *Confessions*; and therefore I am afraid, for example, that I must disappoint the currently fashionable curiosity (which, to me, is sometimes difficult to distinguish from voyeurism) about such private matters as my relations to my siblings, my marriage, and my relations to my children. Even about my own childhood I am mentioning only a few details that seem (to me at any rate) personally relevant to my having grown up to be a scholar of this kind rather than something else.

The subtitle of this essay, "fragments of a scholar's autobiography," is (as is, for that matter, more than a little of what I say and write) a quotation from Goethe, who once described his writings as all "fragments of one great confession." That remark has sent generations of his readers scurrying through *The Sorrows of Young Werther*, *Wilhelm*

Meister, Elective Affinities, the lyric poems, and other works, and above all through the twelve-thousand lines of *Faust*, to get at "the real Goethe" lurking behind the various characters. Just to frustrate any oversimplified one-for-one conversion, Goethe entitled his own autobiography *Dichtung und Wahrheit* (Fiction [or Poetry] and Truth), in a tantalizing mixture. And he did say "fragments," which is also the most that I am in a position to promise here.

1

I like to say that I was born into a family that was rich in everything except money—good food in abundance, music, books, languages, and above all tradition and faith. My parents both came from Slovak families and were born in Slavic Europe—my father in what was to become Czechoslovakia (and now Slovakia), my mother in Vojvodina, which eventually became (and still is, at least as of this writing) a province of Yugoslavia, polyglot but chiefly Serbian-speaking. The genetic distribution of labor that Goethe described in his autobiographical verses,

> Vom Vater hab' ich die Statur
> Des Lebens ernstes Führen,
> Von Mütterchen die Frohnatur
> Und Lust zu fabulieren
> [From my father I inherited my stature
> And my seriousness about the conduct of life,
> From my dear mother my happy disposition
> And a delight in telling stories],

worked out rather differently in my case. Not only am I a couple of inches shorter than my father was; but my "seriousness about the conduct of life" acquired some of its special qualities from my mother, with her iron sense of duty and her loving determination that I must not, as she often put it to me, "get by on brains and glibness." The "happy disposition and delight in telling stories" that I have had since childhood and still (thank God) possess, on the other hand, is a reflection of the magical and positive view of the world for which my father was widely known throughout his life. It included a deep and all-but-pantheistic sense of affinity with Nature, which I inherited from him, together with a high energy level and a capacity for sustained effort for long stretches of time, followed by the ability to fall asleep instantly—which has proven to be just the right combination for a scholar.

As his father had been before him, from 1895 to 1930, my father was a Lutheran pastor, from 1919 to 1963, and a preacher of great eloquence and power, both in his native Slovak and in his adopted English. He and my mother, who was a parochial school teacher before their marriage, were therefore my first teachers of theology, which took the form of Luther's *Small Catechism*, of the Lutheran chorales in the Czech translations of Jiří Tranovský, and of many tomes in my father's library that I read or skimmed long before I was ready for them. (My late friend, the Benedictine Godfrey Diekmann, in introducing me for a lecture at Saint John's Abbey, claimed to have discovered that when, as a little boy, I could not reach the dining room table, my parents had me sit on volumes of the *Patrologia*, with the result that I absorbed the church fathers *a posteriori*.) For whatever reason, their teaching stuck, so that I have had to admit, sometimes with a bit of chagrin, that I was quite out of step with many in my generation, especially among theological scholars at universities, in never having had fundamental doubts about the essential rightness of the Christian faith, but having retained a continuing, if often quite unsophisticated, Slavic piety. The kind of orthodox confessional Lutheranism I imbibed from that source may have been slightly tinged with pietism, but it tended to sit rather loosely to ecclesiastical institutions and structures. Having emigrated to the United States with their parents in the opening years of the twentieth century, both of my parents attended German-speaking Lutheran schools: my mother, the first and only member of her family to go to college, Doctor Martin Luther College in New Ulm, Minnesota (1920); my father, Concordia [Junior] College in Fort

Wayne, Indiana (1916) and Concordia Theological Seminary in Saint
Louis (1919). After they married in 1921, my father was drafted by his
father to serve as a pastor in the (unsuccessful) experiment at a
Lutheran church independent of the state in the new Czechoslovakia.
During their two years there, a son who had my name (or, rather, I was
given his name) was born to them and died after a few days; I have long
had the deep sense that I grew up carrying responsibility for Jaroslav
Ivan as well as for myself, which could be seen as an unfair burden to
lay on a young child, but which may well have helped to provide some
of the extra motivating force that a scholar needs.

2

In 1936, at the age of twelve, I followed my father to Concordia Fort
Wayne. This was a transplanted version of the classical German *Gym-
nasium*, equivalent in American terms to the six years of high school
plus junior college. It was, I have often quipped, the best eighteenth-
century education available in twentieth-century America for a hundred dollars a year including board and room, very light on laboratory
science and social science but correspondingly heavy on the Bible and
the catechism and on languages, especially German, Latin, and Greek
(Hebrew having been transferred to the seminary shortly before I
would have taken it). Particularly in Latin and in German—less so, to
my regret, in Greek, which I came to love best but in which eventually
I had to do, and did do, some catching up—I was blessed with patient
and demanding teachers at Fort Wayne. My grasp of Latin took off
very early, and I even won national standing in a competition based on
the poetry of Vergil. Being, as a Slovak, a member of an ethnic minor-
ity there (and in the late 1930s at that), I was determined to master
German better than my classmates, who often knew just enough German from home to have corrupted their English ("Pass me the pitcher
of milk over" or "My hair are wet"). Memorizing the long narrative
poems of Schiller and beginning on my own the annual reading of

Goethe's *Faust*, which I have continued ever since, I even contemplated the possibility of going to graduate school in German language and literature. Combined as it was with my own bilingual background in Slovak and English (plus a fair amount of Czech and of Serbian, which then led easily to Russian by way of the Cyrillic alphabet), this saturation exposure to the Classical languages and to German became, and remains, something of an obsession for me. It was followed by Hebrew when I entered Concordia Seminary at age eighteen, so that well before I left my teens I was at the point that I would automatically read any text in the original (and, as only an eighteen-year-old can, tended to look down on anyone who could not).

Going on to the seminary was a natural step in 1942, even though it was generally recognized, especially by my parents, that my vocation lay in scholarship and teaching rather than in the pastoral ministry. Two of my seminary professors, Paul M. Bretscher and Richard R. Caemmerer, immediately became close friends and mentors (and remained so until their deaths), defending me to their colleagues and encouraging me to carry on my independent study in the well-stocked library above and beyond the rather minimal requirements of the seminary curriculum. There was in the ethos of Concordia Seminary a deep ambivalence: a respect for high level theological scholarship that would lead, for example, to the almost unique phenomenon of a church subsidy for the translation into English of Walter Bauer's *Greek-English Lexicon of the New Testament and Other Early Christian Literature* (published by the University of Chicago Press); but alongside this respect, though not from the same people, dire and constant warnings about the dangers of historical-critical study. (That ambivalence was to erupt into a full-scale schism several decades later.) For me personally, it meant that I was encouraged to pursue advanced studies, but under something of a cloud of suspicion. Many, though not all, of my fellow students manifested some of the same ambivalence, which probably tended to make me even more of a loner than I already was. I had never belonged to an athletic team or a singing group or an orchestra or any other ensemble. In later years I discovered, and began to quote, the aphorism of Harnack that "anyone who is a scholar is part monk, . . . and someone who wants to amount to something in scholarship must get off to a very early start." However, I had believed and practiced that all along.

Above all, my student years at Concordia Seminary gave me what confessional Lutheranism could have been expected to give, a detailed knowledge and technical grasp of church doctrine, especially the dogmas of the Trinity (only in its Western configuration, to be sure) and of the two natures in Christ (which, because of its controversies with Calvinism over the doctrine of the real presence in the Eucharist, sixteenth- and seventeenth-century Lutheranism had elaborated largely on the basis of the Greek church fathers and later councils). The central defining element in Christian faith was seen as doctrine, not practice, and neither church polity nor liturgy nor piety; "consentire de doctrina evangelii [consensus on the doctrine of the gospel]" was, according to *The Augsburg Confession* of 1530, necessary for the unity of the Church, together with the proper administration of the sacraments. Despite occasional twinges of an inclination toward systematic theology or dogmatics, however, I knew that it was the history of Christian doctrine, more usually called (from its German origins and career as *Dogmengeschichte*) "the history of dogma," that I wanted to study and for which this combination of preparatory studies had in a special way been equipping me.

3

But I really hit my stride only in the autumn of 1944, when I entered the Ph.D. program of the Divinity School of the University of Chicago.

> Bliss was it in that dawn to be alive,
> But to be young was very heaven.

I was twenty years old, fully conscious (probably more than fully conscious) of my powers, and in the heady atmosphere of a place where at last it was never necessary to explain—much less to apologize for—a passion for the scholarly life.

What had drawn me to the University of Chicago, in addition to its overall academic eminence under the leadership of President Robert Maynard Hutchins (and, of course, its being in my home city, so that I could stay with my parents), was its faculty in the history of Christianity, specifically two professors, Matthew Spinka and Wilhelm Pauck. Czech-born Professor Spinka was at the time the leading university-based historian of Slavic Christianity in North America—he later wrote what is still in many ways the standard work in English on the church history of the Balkans—and he had already been encouraging me in my earlier explorations of that subject. Wilhelm Pauck, pupil of Karl Holl and Adolf Harnack, was a justly celebrated teacher of the history of Christian thought and a specialist on the Reformation. It had been my plan to work with these two scholars together, concentrating in "historical theology" with a dissertation somewhere in the Slavic East. But by the time I arrived at Chicago, Professor Spinka had departed for Hartford Theological Seminary, and there was no Ph.D. program any more in the Greek and Slavic East. Thus I specialized in the Reformation, writing my dissertation in 1946 on the *Czech Confession* of 1535 and Luther's preface to it. It included the first English translation of that text (which, incidentally, was not published until it was included in the second volume of our *Creeds and Confessions of Faith* fifty-seven years later). A number of my courses I took in other parts of the University, including a memorable seminar on historical method with Louis Gottschalk, historian of the French Revolution and specialist on Lafayette. When I had completed my course work and examinations for the Ph.D. in December 1945, with much of the dissertation completed, I still had three semesters to go at Concordia; by some juggling of credits, this was reduced to one semester. Thereby the seminary did not have to face the problem of a Ph.D. taking its undergraduate courses, and neither did I. I received both the B.D. from Concordia and the Ph.D. from Chicago in 1946.

My first academic appointment was in a department of history (as would my final appointment be). At Valparaiso University from 1946 to 1949 I taught a variety of courses in European history, with a concentration on intellectual history, including philosophy, but I did not have the opportunity to teach the history of Christian thought as such until after those three years I was brought to Concordia Seminary as a junior faculty member. There I took over the existing course in "History of Dogma," which concluded with the Reformation, and added a course on the history of theology since the Reformation. For this sequence I prepared in 1952 a syllabus of 51 single-spaced pages, from which I taught the courses and on the basis of which I hoped to write my book, which did not in fact begin to appear until nearly twenty years later (and with occasional phrases and sentences lifted from that syllabus). Both the burden of my heavy teaching responsibilities at the seminary and the theological climate within the Missouri Synod were making it increasingly clear to me that my pious hopes of being a scholar in the direct employ of the Church were not to be fulfilled; and in 1953, after a total of seven years of that balancing act at Valparaiso and Concordia, I accepted the invitation of the University of Chicago to succeed my mentor Wilhelm Pauck, who had meanwhile accepted the Briggs Chair of Church History at Union Theological Seminary in New York.

For the next nine years at Chicago I gave a year-long lecture course "The History of Christian Thought," usually with an accompanying seminar each quarter on specific topics from across all the periods of the history: for example, Tertullian, Athanasius's *The Incarnation of the Word* juxtaposed with Anselm's *Cur deus homo*, Augustine, Thomas Aquinas, Luther, Schleiermacher, the nineteenth century. I was only half-joking when I explained that I was carrying on my private education in public, filling in gaps from my previous study and deepening my grasp of the larger history. When I moved to Yale in 1962, it was to succeed Roland H. Bainton in the Titus Street Professorship of Ecclesiastical History in the Yale Divinity School, but with the understanding that I would take over Robert Lowry Calhoun's sequence on "The History of Christian Doctrine." My subsequent transfer to the Faculty of

Arts and Sciences, and then my designation as Sterling Professor in 1972, did not alter that concentration. But my appointment as Acting Dean, then Dean, of the Yale Graduate School of Arts and Sciences from 1973 to 1978 took me out of the classroom (though not out of the library or my study), and when I rejoined the faculty, it was as Sterling Professor of History, which I remained until my retirement in 1996. An important component of my portfolio was the graduate program in Medieval Studies, which I also chaired for several years. My signature course in Yale College was a two-semester sequence on "The Intellectual History of the Middle Ages East and West," from the Cappadocians and Augustine to the Renaissance and the fall of Constantinople.

4

In one way or another, therefore, most of my teaching over the years flowed into the project that already in my early student days I had begun to identify as a special vocation: to write for my generation a successor to Adolf Harnack's three-volume *Lehrbuch der Dogmengeschichte*. I would eventually take an almost mystical pleasure in the unintended coincidence that its fifth and final volume was published in 1989, exactly a century after the publication of Harnack's first volume. That sense of vocation, including the emulation of Harnack, brought together a number of both scholarly and personal elements. My grandfather, Ján Pelikán, after studies in Slovakia, completed his theological preparation at the University of Erlangen, where Harnack's father Theodosius, a strict confessionalist Lutheran (as was my grandfather), had earlier been professor. The post-World War I generation of Adolf Harnack's students in Germany had, with some exceptions, been prevented by the vicissitudes of those decades from undertaking a new telling of the history of dogma. In the United States, the two scholars best prepared to write such a history were Robert Calhoun, who also brought to the subject an unrivalled mastery of the history of philosophy, and Wilhelm Pauck, who had studied under the greats in Germany in the 1920s and who spanned the two worlds with a dazzling virtuosity; but for a variety of reasons, some of them no doubt quite personal, neither of these scholars brought it off. Therefore the preparation of a comprehensive history of Christian doctrine had in effect skipped a generation on both sides of the Atlantic.

Intellectual and scholarly trends in theological scholarship, as in humanistic and historical scholarship generally, were at the same time working against such a history. Increasingly, a historical scholar had to be identified by region and/or period, as I was by the Reformation, especially after becoming editor of the American Edition of *Luther's Works* in 1955. But both in my teaching and in my publishing, I was determined not to succumb to the lure of such specialization in one epoch. By selecting only one aspect of Christian history (though still a massive one)—as I would define it at the opening of my first volume, "what the church of Jesus Christ believes, teaches, and confesses on the basis of the word of God"—I strove to be responsible to the primary texts regardless of period or provenance and to pay attention not only to change but also to continuity. My lifelong love affair with all those languages helped to make this possible. So did the growth of ecumenism, as Christians were discovering that there were believers and churches on the other side of the mountains. I had the opportunity to participate in this process directly during the 1950s and 1960s as a member of the Commission on Tradition and Traditions of the Commission on Faith and Order of the World Council of Churches (WCC), chaired by Albert C. Outler and bringing together into the same room my once and future mentors, Wilhelm Pauck and Georges V. Florovsky (with me in the crossfire between them). I saw it as one of my assignments to introduce the several Christian traditions to each other—and, even more importantly, to their own ancestors. The price I paid for such an assignment was the increasing inability to take a direct part in contemporary theological debate. Students and colleagues used to complain that when I was expounding Augustine they thought I was a card-carrying Augustinian, until I came to John of Damascus or Thomas Aquinas or Luther or

Schleiermacher or Dostoevsky, when I was again stating the position of each of them as though from within. There was, no doubt, a certain amount of a tentative relativism at work here, together with a conscious effort to achieve, at least pedagogically, what Samuel Taylor Coleridge calls "a willing suspension of disbelief." But increasingly I came to believe that every theological system, even a heretical theological system, emphasizes one valid aspect or dimension of orthodoxy defined as "the whole counsel of God" (Acts 20.27), but at the expense of others. Therefore I also found, not in theological liberalism and historical relativism (as so many of my predecessors, teachers, and contemporaries did) but in tradition and orthodoxy, the presupposition from which to interpret any portion or period. At some point, therefore, *The Christian Tradition* became the working title of "the big book" (as I usually referred to it unofficially).

Just as various of my books and articles on various periods that appeared before and during the publication of the five volumes of *The Christian Tradition* between 1971 and 1989 were essentially "feeders" providing more detailed documentation for the larger work, so, particularly as I was completing it, I began investigating its implications for several fields of human thought and culture: philosophy already in my first book, *From Luther to Kierkegaard* (1950), and then in others, including *What Has Athens to Do with Jerusalem?* (1997) on Plato's *Timaeus*; music in *Bach Among the Theologians* (1986), on the occasion of the tercentenary of his birth; historiography in *The Excellent Empire* (1987), coming to terms with my boyhood study of Gibbon's *Decline and Fall*; art history in *Imago Dei* (1990); higher education in *The Idea of the University—A Reexamination* (1992); literature in "Russia's Greatest Heretic" on Tolstoy (1989), *Eternal Feminines* (1990) on Dante, and *Faust the Theologian* (1995) on Goethe; rhetoric in *Divine Rhetoric* (2001); and Constitutional hermeneutics in *Interpreting the Bible and the Constitution* (2004). I did not pretend that I had become a scholar in any of these fields, although I did read myself deeply into the scholarly literature and was, on the whole, received hospitably by the inner circles of the specialists. Rather, as a chronicler of one of the most overwhelming explosions in the history of the human mind and spirit, I was looking at its fallout across the cultural landscape. That was also in keeping with my primary location within the academy, which for most of my career has been in the Faculty of Arts and Sciences. I was never dean of a divinity school, much less of a church seminary, but of a graduate school of arts and sciences. I was president of the American Academy of Arts and Sciences from 1994 to 1997, and of the American Academy of Political and Social Science for 2000–2001. The two highest recognitions I have ever received for my scholarship were both humanistic rather than theological or ecclesiastical: the Jefferson Award of the National Endowment for the Humanities in 1983, and the John W. Kluge Prize for Lifetime Achievement in the Human Sciences in 2004. But I have been deeply gratified that my historical scholarship has been of service to the Church, its laity as well as its clergy, and to theological seminaries and church colleges across the denominational spectrum, and increasingly, through many translations (including, now, at long last, even translations into Slavic languages), across the globe.

Both from the observations of my reviewers and from my own "authorial intent" it seems clear that my history of Christian doctrine differs from its predecessors, and specifically from Harnack's, in several important respects. It consciously rejects the arbitrarily narrow definition of the history of *dogma* by which Harnack felt able to ignore not only the individual theologians but also the creeds and confessions of all the post-Reformation churches (which are surely "dogma" even in a technical sense). It takes the relation of Christian doctrine with its Jewish partner not as a problem that the first and second centuries had to overcome, but as a permanent component of the teaching of the Church (as the Epistle to the Romans says it is). By contrast with Harnack, who in the appendix to his first volume could bring himself to say that it was "another instance of the exceptional nature of Christianity [that] for a considerable period it possessed no ritual at all," I interpreted the formulation of church doctrine as the process by which what was already believed in worship was spelled out in creed and confession. And a major component of my narrative was an examination of the key passages of Holy Scripture that the church claimed to be bringing together in articulating its doctrines.

5

There is at least one additional point of differentiation between my history of doctrine and Harnack's (as well as most others): the inclusion of the Christian East. Harnack was born in Dorpat/Tartu, Estonia, in 1851, when it was part of Tsarist Russia, and in school he was required to learn Russian, which in fact he would know better than he did either French or English. Nevertheless he was shockingly tone-deaf to the specific accents of Eastern Orthodoxy such as the devotion to icons. "It was," he said describing the Orthodox liturgy, "to destroy this sort of religion that Jesus Christ suffered himself to be nailed to the cross!" In addition to the heavy reliance on Greek and Syriac patristic materials in my first volume and on Russian and Greek theologians in the fifth volume, I devoted the entire second volume (1974) to *The Spirit of Eastern Christendom (600–1700)*, corresponding in time span to volumes 3 and 4 for the West, which were so much longer because they had to encompass scholasticism and the Reformation. In that second volume, moreover, various readers could discern personal accents along with the scholarly ones, and my late friend Father John Meyendorff was gracious enough to call it "the most comprehensive history of ideas in the Christian East, very perceptive and challenging."

This was one in a series of books over several decades by means of which, I may quote myself yet again, "while others were reading their way into Orthodoxy, I wrote my way into Orthodoxy." Already in *The Riddle of Roman Catholicism* (1959), winner of the Abingdon Award and (at least partly because of its timing in relation to the Presidential election of John F. Kennedy in 1960 and to the Second Vatican Council) the first of my books to receive widespread public attention, it was evident from the chapter "How Christianity Became Catholic," which quoted A. S. Khomiakov on its second page, that the book was animated by a vision of the Church more akin to the Eastern than to the Western tradition. The invitation to deliver the Andrew W. Mellon Lectures at the National Gallery of Art, on the twelve-hundredth anniversary of the Second Council of Nicaea in 1987, became the occasion for an analysis in depth of how "a faith which began by attacking the worship of images . . . eventually embraced such worship and turned prohibition into permission—and permission into command." *The Melody of Theology* of 1988, which has been a subtext for this entire memoir, concludes its preface with the words: "The book bears no dedication . . . If there were a dedication, it would have been inscribed to Georges V. Florovsky (1893–1979), who, more than any other person except my late father, taught me to sing 'the melody of theology' this way." When Clifton Fadiman invited me to prepare *The World Treasury of Modern Religious Thought*, which came out in 1990, I chose as the two bookends for this interfaith collection Dostoevsky's "The Grand Inquisitor" and Aleksandr Solzhenitsyn's Nobel Lecture, "Beauty Will Save the World." And when I was honored by the University of Aberdeen to give the Gifford Lectures on Natural Theology in 1992/93, I defined their scope by "triangulation" from two of my predecessors in the lectureship there, Etienne Gilson (*The Spirit of Medieval Philosophy*, 1930/32) and Karl Barth (*The Knowledge of God and the Service of God according to the Teaching of the Reformation*, 1937/38): "The Metamorphosis of Natural Theology in the Christian Encounter with Hellenism," as this was manifested in "the Three Cappadocians," Saint Gregory of Nazianzus, Saint Basil of Caesarea, and Saint Gregory of Nyssa, together with the sister of the latter two, Saint Macrina the Younger, whom I dubbed "the Fourth Cappadocian"; thus I examined the systems of thought which, taken together, do for the Christian East much of what the theology and philosophy of Saint Augustine of Hippo do for the Latin West.

After all these hundreds of published pages it may have been something of a shock, but I cannot believe that it came to anyone as a surprise, when, on the Feast Day of the Annunciation to the Theotokos

(25 March) in 1998, I was received by chrismation into the sacramental fellowship of the Orthodox Church in America. As I said to my
friend and father in Christ, His Beatitude Metropolitan Theodosius,
who chrismated me, "any airplane that circled the airport for that long
before landing would have run out of gas." Quoting more broadly than
its original meaning the commandment "Every one should remain in
the state in which he was called" (1 Cor. 7.20), I had long been resisting
the ecclesiastical conclusion to which the force of my ideas and beliefs
was increasingly pressing me. Meanwhile, the Lutheran Church in
America, in a series of moves that I had begun to limn, however dimly,
in an essay that was published in *The Christian Century* in 1963, was
becoming, to use the terminology of that essay, less and less of a "confession" and more and more of a "denomination." Thus we were, as
Yogi Berra might have put it, "headed on a collision course by moving
in opposite directions."

I shall happily leave to some future psychobiography (if any) the
task of sorting out the "real reasons" and deeper motivations of my
move. In response to literally hundreds of inquiries, most of them
quite friendly but some rather hostile, I usually ended up using one of
two quotations: from Molière's M. Jourdain, who exclaimed, "For
more than forty years I have been speaking prose without knowing it";
or from Robert Frost, who defined home as "the place where, when
you have to go there, they have to take you in." Scholars of autobiography, as well as its more self-critical practitioners, have long warned
both against the danger of confusing memory with legend and against
the Whiggish tendency to look at an entire lifetime through the prism
of its outcome and therefore to suppose that it could not have come
out any other way than it in fact did. I hope I may nevertheless be permitted, with sincere gratitude to God, to find a certain continuity
between the direction of the drive and the direction of the putt.

Is Development of Doctrine a Valid Category for Orthodox Theology?

Andrew Louth*

EBATE OVER THE QUESTION of development of doctrine has been conducted largely in terms of Catholic-Protestant dialogue—or polemic. In the last century it was often seen as the most fundamental issue in the division of Western Christendom. It was very much in this spirit that John Henry Newman himself approached the concept of development, claiming that the writing of his famous *Essay on the Development of Christian Doctrine* was the decisive intellectual step towards his decision in 1845 to leave the Church of England to become a Roman Catholic. The now classic discussion of the notion of development, by Jaroslav Pelikan in lectures that appeared in 1969 as *Development of Christian Doctrine: Some Historical Prolegomena*,[1] also conceived the issue in primarily Catholic–Protestant terms and, implicitly, urged Protestants to recognize development as a category they could no longer ignore. But at the beginning of the twenty-first century, any adequate discussion of such a central matter for the understanding of the study of Christian doctrine needs to take account of the perspective of those who embrace the Orthodox tradition, including me and the one we are honoring.

*Andrew Louth teaches early Christian doctrine, patristic spirituality, the history and theology of the churches in the Byzantine and Medieval eras, and Orthodox theology at the University of Durham. His lecture was delivered on May 2, 2003, in the Swift Lecture Hall at the University of Chicago Divinity School.

The first time I became aware of any Orthodox attitude to the notion of development was when, many years ago, I found myself at dinner sitting next to Archbishop Athenagoras, then, and until his death, the Greek Orthodox Archbishop of Thyateira and Great Britain, the leader of the Greek Orthodox community in the U.K. He began a conversation with me, then a young Anglican priest, by asserting that he was sure we were at one in rejecting the notion of development. It is this, he said, that divides us most fundamentally from Rome. I can't remember much of the discussion, but I do remember that I was quite surprised. To me, a young Anglo-Catholic priest who counted Newman a hero, it seemed that development was almost obvious. It was clear that such doctrines as the Trinity and Christology were affirmed only in a very inchoate way in the pre-Nicene Church compared with the Church of the fourth and fifth centuries, so a notion of development was needed if one was to maintain that these fundamental doctrines were an essential part of Christian confession.

Now, years later, if asked about development, I would be a little unsure as to how, as an Orthodox theologian, to respond. It is not a topic much discussed in Orthodox theology, save by some of the more traditionalist theologians of Greece and Russia who would wholeheartedly agree with the late Archbishop Athenagoras. Something like the notion of development is occasionally used explicitly, but in the cases I can think of it is not Newman's idea but rather the classically Protestant understanding which sees any development as negative—not growth but distortion. One might think, for instance, of Fr Georges Florovsky's use of the biological category, borrowed from Oswald Spengler, of pseudo-morphosis in relation to the history of Russian theology. Conversely, Orthodox theology has tended over the last half-century or so to be presented in a basically historical guise—as well as Fr Florovsky, others too are or were more of an historical than a philosophical bent— Vladimir Lossky, Fr John Meyendorff, Fr Alexander Schmemann, Bishop Kallistos Ware—and this historical approach has meant that Christian doctrine is presented as an historical development even though the category of development is not generally invoked explicitly.

On occasions when, one might have thought, it would be of value to employ such a notion, it is striking that Orthodox theologians do not do so. A couple of examples spring to mind—the doctrine of icons and the distinction between essence and energies in the Godhead. It would seem obvious to an historian that neither the eighth-century doctrine of the necessity of making and venerating icons nor the fourteenth-century Palamite distinction between essence and energies can really be found in the fourth-century Fathers—especially, in both cases, St Basil the Great—to whom appeal is generally made, yet I know of no Orthodox theologian who calls on the category of authentic development to justify the later doctrine. Development does not seem to be perceived as an available category for Orthodox theology.

So I feel myself venturing on to virgin territory as an Orthodox theologian choosing to discuss this topic. Yet it seems a quite pertinent subject to raise when honoring Professor Pelikan, whose great five-volume work has the general title, *The Christian Tradition: A History of the Development of Doctrine,*[2] and who, a few years ago, was chrismated and received into the Orthodox Church.

"Development" in Western historical disciplines

We begin with the fundamental question: What is development of doctrine? What do we mean by "development" in this context? It has a general and some more specific senses or connotations or entailments.

The general sense of development is easy to characterize and seems almost obvious to anyone trained in Western historical disciplines. In this sense, development is something acknowledged as one acquires a sense of history, including the sense that ideas are not floating eternal truths but thoughts entertained and pursued by human beings living in human societies that develop through time. It is difficult to overestimate the importance of this sense of historical development—the growth of such a sense marks a kind of caesura in the history of Western thought. It is a product of both the Enlightenment and the

Romantic reaction against the Enlightenment, of the power of reason to analyze the structures of human society and at the same time of the rejection of the Enlightenment's attempt to escape the constraints of history in some universally valid society, a rejection which came to value the societies of the past—Classical Greece or the Western Middle Ages—as societies very different from ours but perhaps exemplifying values that were slipping from the grasp of modern Western people. This produced both a sense of the distance of the past and nostalgia for some aspects of those earlier societies, especially their sense of community.

This sense of historical epochs is an important element in Hegel, for whom a grasp of philosophy is gained through understanding its historical development and our place at the culmination of this centuries-long progress of the human spirit. Newman, too, has a sense, very differently articulated, of historical sequence. In his *Essay* in particular he is concerned to demonstrate that we can intelligently affirm that Christian doctrine asserts the same faith in different historical circumstances only by appeal to a notion of development that allows for real differences in the ways Christians express their beliefs in different eras. I suspect that anyone educated in Western historical disciplines finds it very difficult to imagine how else one might think about intellectual history and therefore the history of Christian doctrine. Ideas are expressed in terms of a developing human society, and even if they correspond to eternal realities, they do this in ways that are historically conditioned and consequently subject to change.

One reason such a notion is less accessible to Orthodox theology is readily apparent. If development is a concept traceable to the Enlightenment and Romanticism, then it belongs to movements bypassed on "the historical road of Eastern Orthodoxy," to evoke the title of Fr Schmemann's famous book. But many Orthodox theologians in what we call the "diaspora" have actually been educated in Western historical disciplines. That ideas are historically conditioned is not in the least foreign to them, though this notion tends to be used in a one-sided way. The idea that the West, from Charlemagne onwards, developed in a historically conditioned way is part of the thesis of Fr John Romanides in *Franks, Romans, Feudalism and Doctrine*,[3] but Fr Romanides did not seem to see that this is presumably true of the Byzantines just as much as the Carolingians. He utilizes the notion of development, in relation to the West, but in a negative way—a phenomenon we have already noticed.

Newman's understanding of development

However, the notion of development as Newman expounded it is more than this general sense of historical development. It involves at least three specific senses, or connotations or entailments.

First, development—or rather authentic development—does not just mean change; it also means *progress*. Development of doctrine does not just mean that the expression of doctrine is historically conditioned and therefore subject to change; it means some sort of advance in doctrine, growth, or accumulation—in Newman's own words, it involves "the germination, growth and perfection of some living, that is, influential truth, or apparent truth, in the minds of men during a sufficient period" (p. 99).[4] Newman draws on a whole range of images or metaphors of growth or advance. Take this famous passage:

> It is indeed sometime said that the stream is clearest near the spring. Whatever use may fairly be made of this image, it does not apply to the history of a philosophy or a sect, which, on the contrary, is more equable, and purer, and stronger, when its bed has become deep, and broad, and full. It necessarily rises out of an existing state of things, and, for a time, savours of the soil. Its vital element needs disengaging from what is foreign and temporary, and is employed in efforts after freedom, more vigorous and hopeful as its years increase. Its beginnings are no measure of its capabilities, nor of its scope. At first, no one knows what it is, or what it is worth. It remains perhaps for a time quiescent: it tries, as it

were, its limbs, and proves the ground under it, and feels its way.
From time to time, it makes essays that fail, and are in consequence
abandoned. It seems in suspense which way to go; it wavers, and at
length strikes out in one definite direction. In time it enters upon
strange territory; points of controversy alter their bearing; parties
rise and fall about it; dangers and hopes appear in new relations,
and old principles reappear under new forms; it changes with them
in order to remain the same. In a higher world it is otherwise; but
here below to live is to change, and to be perfect is to have changed
often. (p. 100).

There are at least three images being used here. There is the image
of the stream, growing from a trickle at the source to a great river carrying all before it, passing through different regions, remaining the
same but constantly changing, and only revealing its real nature and
power in the course of its mighty flow—think of the contrast between
the trickle that emerges from the fountain at Donaueschingen and the
great river Danube that flows through Vienna or Budapest. There is
the image of a plant or an animal (sometimes Newman's language suggests an amoeba-like being), growing and developing. Finally there is
the image of a people or a community, moving on to new territory and
developing new forms of life in a new setting—not without struggle
and conflict.

These three images are rather different, though in the context of
Newman's rhetoric the differences are made to seem complementary.
The central one, controlling the impression created by the other two,
is the organic metaphor—in this case there is unequivocal growth or
progress of something that remains the same organism. This is what
we would expect from the earlier quotation of Newman, in which
development is characterized in primarily organic terms. But neither
rivers nor human communities are organisms, though in the latter case
we often use organic imagery of the development of human societies.

The use of organic metaphors for a community is, however,
not without attendant dangers, despite—or perhaps because of—its

popularity. When we talk of societies learning or being a repository of memory, we are using these terms in a sense much less clear than when we talk of a child learning or of memory constituting a major part of an individual's sense of identity. What a society forgets, for instance, does not remain latent in that society in the way what is forgotten remains latent in an individual (at least in some cases). The organic metaphor draws our attention to the positive aspect of change and development in a way that may not be altogether appropriate in the case of human communities, even the community that is the Church. This is something we shall develop later.

Second, and rather strangely, Newman's idea of development appears to anticipate Darwin's notion of evolution in the way that it envisages what to an historian might appear to be unpredictable jumps in the development of Christian doctrine. Newman's careful distinction of his idea of development from others that had already found a place in earlier Catholic theology is explored with characteristic lucidity by Owen Chadwick in *From Bossuet to Newman*.[5] Newman explicitly goes beyond logical or mathematical development, which is simply drawing logical conclusions from initial premises. Again this is seen to be a characteristic of life, which is broader and deeper (as Newman might have said) than what can be discerned by human reason.

Third, Newman's idea of development entails an infallible teaching office to adjudicate. Here Newman abandons his reliance on the organic model. For him, there needs to be some definite way of distinguishing authentic development from corruption. Newman is no longer prepared to stick to his organic metaphor, and makes it clear that recognition of authentic development ultimately needs an unquestioned and unquestionable authority, such as developed in the teaching office of the see of St Peter (though there is a certain circularity in the argument here, as the development of the teaching office of the pope is an example of development).

These three specific points are linked. The organic idea opens up the notion of development, taking it beyond mere logical development; this is emphasized in the second point, which makes a great deal (particularly in the examples Newman gives from church history) of the way in which these developments could hardly have been predicted; which opens the way for Newman's final point, that an infallible teaching authority is necessary to distinguish authentic development from corruption. It is important to realize that this final point is essential for Newman. Discussions of development, often forgetting that this was where his argument was leading, simply recount the various tests he gave for distinguishing authentic development from corruption—Preservation of Type or Idea, Continuity of Principles, Power of Assimilation, Early Anticipation, Logical Sequence, Preservative Additions, and Chronic Continuance (to use the terminology of the first edition of the *Essay*). But these tests need to be applied, and Newman was not prepared to leave their application to scholars and theologians.

Romanticism and development

Now, clearly, Orthodox are in agreement with Protestants in resisting Newman's final step to an infallible authority. The other two specific points are more amenable to assimilation. This might seem odd, as it could well be argued that the first two points are expressions of a fundamentally *Romantic* attitude to faith. They emphasize the organic and look for authenticity in evidence of life. For Newman, this is rooted in the second of the two proverbs that had guided him from his earliest days: "Holiness rather than peace," and "Growth the only evidence of life." But this only shows how much a man of his times Newman was, for it was a characteristic of Romanticism to see authenticity in life and feelings rather than in rationally ascertained truths. One only need glance through Coleridge's *Aids to Reflection* to see ample evidence for this in the religious sphere, something summed up in his exclamation, "*Evidences* of Christianity! I am weary of the word. Make a man feel the *want* of it; rouse him, if you can, to the self-knowledge of his *need* for it; and you may safely trust it to its own Evidence. . . ."[6]

There is much of the same feel in Newman's *Essay*, which is concerned with evoking a sense of the living organic development of Christianity as a movement to which one wants to belong, outside which there is simply torpor and corruption.

But despite—or because of—the Romantic roots of the idea of a developing organism, it is an idea that is very congenial to at least some Orthodox theologians, especially Russians. Such an organic conception of the Church is central to Alexei Khomiakov, whom we find declaring, "Wherefore it must be understood that creeds and prayers and works are nothing of themselves, but are only an external manifestation of the inward spirit"[7]—the Church is an organism and to belong to the Church is primarily manifest in living its life. Khomiakov's idea of *sobornost* as characterizing the Church seems to me an entailment of his profound sense of the organic nature of the Church—the Church is a living organism, and the members of the Church are characterized by sharing in that life; *sobornost*, togetherness, characterizes the life of Christians in the Church.

This sense of togetherness is so emphasized that the Orthodox Christian has no sense of identity over against the Church, nor does he or she feel the need for anything to define the nature and extent of the Church. Within the Church there is unity and freedom—both signs of authentic life. In contrast, the Western Church has lost this sense of *sobornost* and either protects unity by authority at the expense of freedom—the Catholic way, not noticeably diminished since Vatican II—or affirms freedom to the point of destroying unity—the Protestant way. I suspect that here too we can see the influence of Romanticism, a Romanticism imbibed from German sources to which the Slavophils, like Khomiakov, had turned with enthusiasm. Andrei Walicky calls the Slavophils in general, and Khomiakov in particular, "conservative romantics,"[8] a term that might well be applied to Coleridge. A comparative study of Khomiakov and Coleridge would reveal interesting convergences.

Probing the Orthodox reluctance

Despite the way the idea of *sobornost* expresses an organic notion of the
Church and therefore, one might suppose, could render Orthodox
theologians open to the first two specific points evoked by Newman—
those expressing his sense of development as organic—it is nevertheless the case that Orthodox theologians are not at all happy with the
idea of development. As I mentioned earlier, even in cases where the
notion of development might seem very helpful—the theology of
icons and the Palamite distinction between essence and energies—we
do not find Orthodox theologians availing themselves of this idea. I
want to probe this reluctance.

I begin by confessing that, to some extent at least, the reluctance
reveals what seems to be a weakness in Orthodox theology. There is a
tendency in Orthodox theology to represent the teaching of the various Fathers of the Church in a rather flat way, as if they had all lived at
the same time, so historical considerations are scarcely necessary. In
this respect, such Orthodox theology recalls older ways of presenting
the history of doctrine in the West. It has been remarked of several of
the older histories of dogma (I won't single any one out) that so far as
any sense of historical, political, and/or social context is concerned,
the whole story of Christian doctrine might well have taken place on
the moon. The same failing is to be found in what Karl Rahner called
"Denzinger theology," where extracts drawn from Denzinger's
Enchiridion Symbolorum were simply laid side by side without any
attention to context and therefore to meaning. The overcoming of
this kind of theology in the West has been one of the more serious contributions to the possibility of ecumenical theology, as Professor
Pelikan long ago remarked in the lectures already referred to.[9]

Simply understanding our history has helped towards the realization that in many cases what appear to be examples of dogmatic opposition are really examples of much the same thing being asserted
in strikingly different historical contexts. Nevertheless, there is still
a tendency in Orthodox theology to give an account of historical

doctrine that tends to be unhistorical or ahistorical. This is a weakness we Orthodox need to overcome. A sense of critical distance in expounding the thoughts of those of different ages does not necessarily entail any lack of commitment to the truths the Fathers were expressing. We need that sense of critical distance if we are not to gloss one Father with another and so lose a sense of their individuality and historical context. For instance, we shall, I am sure, understand the Cappadocian Fathers better if we know something about the social and political circumstances of fourth-century Cappadocia.

However, there is a reason for Orthodox reluctance to make very much of the sense of historical development. One way of putting it is to recall the language we habitually use in speaking of Christian teachers from the past centuries. We Orthodox call them the "Holy Fathers"—we do not approach them as dead teachers from the past, as we might Plato or one of the Classical philosophers. We regard them as living now in the life of the Resurrection, more alive than we are, as they are closer to the Source of Life. This goes beyond the fact that great thinkers, poets, and artists of the past are not in any normal way superseded by their successors (and in the case of Plato, there are even traditions, such as one preserved among the writings of St Anastasios of Sinai, that see him coming to faith in the Resurrection).[10]

We do not hope to surpass the Fathers in our grasp of the mystery of Christ; rather, we look to them to help us to a deeper understanding. We do not stand over against the Fathers; we come to them to learn from them. This entails that if development means that there is an historical advance in Christian doctrine, making our understanding of the faith deeper or more profound than that of the Fathers, at least in principle, then such a notion of development cannot be accepted as a category of Orthodox theology. We shall not advance beyond the faith of the Fathers, nor shall we advance beyond the faith of the apostles. As we sing at Pentecost, in the troparion for the feast, "Blessed are you, Christ our God, who revealed the fishermen to be most wise by sending down to them the Holy Spirit, and so through them catching the whole world in a net. Lover of humankind, glory to You!"

.

This sense of the witness of the Holy Fathers is something not found at all vividly in Western scholarship. Scholarship inspired by the idea of development can produce a kind of hubris; as if we know more than they did and can sit in judgment on them, whereas real scholarship is aware that, in fact, we know very much less than the Fathers did both about extant Christian tradition (for instance, the Cappadocian Fathers probably knew more of Origen than we ever shall, just as Origen himself knew more about Hellenistic philosophy than we can hope to with the sources that have come down to us, not to mention the multitude of second-century Christian traditions) and about the circumstances of their time, where we rely on sources, often late and fragmentary, that happen to have survived. Awareness of this should induce a sense, if not of humility, at least of caution in our judgments. As a young Romanian Orthodox former student and friend of mine remarks in a recent article, "The conviction that we know more than the actors in the events of the fourth century makes possible the presentation of the 'development of Christian doctrine' in terms of intellectual emancipation. It is quite perplexing to see the confidence of so many contemporary scholars who depict the fourth-century controversies as a mere fruit of mutual misunderstanding."[11] We might recall what T. S. Eliot remarked in an early essay: "Someone said: 'The dead writers are remote from us because we *know* so much more than they did.' Precisely, and they are that which we know."[12]

Learning from a genuinely critical intelligence

This does not mean retracting what I said earlier about how much Orthodox theology has to learn from cultivating a genuinely critical intelligence. On the contrary, the way in which historical scholarship can place the Fathers more securely in their historical context should make them more alive, not less. Yes, we may discover things that we might like to forget (and which certainly the hagiographers have passed over)—Athanasius and Cyril were prepared to resort to violence, Basil had a rather grim way of treating his friends, and so on. But averting our gaze from the less admirable features of those we admire is no way of honouring them. Saints—we call them the *Holy* Fathers—are not unreal ideals but genuine human beings, with all their faults, beginning to respond to the transfiguring power of the Holy Spirit.

However, historical scholarship may raise more fundamental questions: Who are the Fathers? Why honor Athanasius rather than Arius, Gregory of Nyssa rather than his fellow Cappadocian Eunomius, or (a more difficult one) Leontius of Byzantium (though he is not honored as a saint) rather than Severus of Antioch, dubbed by the Orthodox a "monophysite"? I think from within Orthodoxy all we can say is that the Fathers are *our* Fathers, because we are their children. Behind this assertion lies faith in the Holy Spirit's guiding of the Church through the tradition of the Fathers and the Councils. A Western theologian might well feel this inadequate, and want either, with Newman, an infallible teaching authority, or with my friend and mentor, Professor Maurice Wiles, the freedom to revise the tradition and make a Father of Arius—though it seems to me that he does not make the final step very convincingly.

To recall what we said earlier about Khomiakov and the notion of *sobornost*: it has never been very clear how Khomiakov found authority and freedom united in *sobornost*, but nevertheless the idea of *sobornost* seems to have meant something, even outside the bounds of Orthodoxy, to judge from the way it has been taken up in twentieth-century Western ecclesiology.

Theological ideas in the context of worship

Hence, though I would welcome a greater historical sense in Orthodox theology (and there is plenty of evidence that this is becoming more common), it seems to me that this would not entail that the idea of development itself is a valid category for Orthodox theology.

In discussion of development, attention is sometimes drawn to what J. N. D. Kelly called "a highly original theory of doctrinal development" put forward by St Gregory Nazianzen.[13] In the last of his *Theological Orations* Gregory says,

> Here, growth towards perfection comes through additions. In this way, the old covenant made clear proclamation of the Father, a less definite one of the Son. The new covenant made the Son manifest and gave us a glimpse of the Spirit's Godhead. At the present time, the Spirit resides among us, giving us a clearer manifestation of himself than before.[14]

Though Kelly calls it a "theory of doctrinal development," Gregory's idea is very different from Newman's, for Gregory is not suggesting that the fourth century had a deeper grasp of the Holy Spirit than the first. The rest of the paragraph makes clear that the manifestation of the Spirit reaches its fullness among those in whom he resides after Pentecost—the fishermen made "most wise" by the coming of the Holy Spirit.

It is becoming customary in modern patristic scholarship to emphasize the difference between Basil the Great, with his reserve about affirming clearly the Spirit's divinity, and Gregory of Nazianzus, with his explicit affirmation of the Spirit as God and indeed *homoousios*. But they shared a great deal in their approach to theology, and this we can see here. The Holy Spirit is manifest through his residing with us—it is in the community of the Church, in the sacramental community, that the Spirit is revealed. Basil had argued similarly in his work *On the Holy Spirit*. The doctrine of the Spirit belongs to the *dogmata*, as he calls them, those doctrines preserved within the bosom of the Church by unwritten traditions. All the examples Basil gives of these unwritten traditions are liturgical—the use of the sign of the cross, facing east for prayer, the epiclesis in the Eucharist, blessings of water for baptism and oil for unction; the Trinitarian doxology is the explicit occasion of his work *On the Holy Spirit*.[15] This means that, again, emphasis is put on the experience of being part of the sacramental community of the Church.

Some modern Western theologians have sought to promote the idea that it is in the context of *worship* that theological ideas emerge and are tested.[16] This seems to me a thoroughly Orthodox insight. It would indeed be interesting to look at the notion of development in the context of Christian worship. The first thing to emerge would be a much greater sense of continuity, or stability, in what is called development. The doctrine of Christ's divinity and lordship is immediately apparent in the Church's tradition of prayer and worship; the same can be said for the doctrine of the Trinity. Christian doctrine would then be seen as the attempt to articulate what is involved in the Church's sacramental worship.

Seen like this—to digress briefly—we can see how close to the central tradition of the Church is that mysterious theologian who called himself Dionysios the Areopagite, for he sees theology as an attempt to elucidate the terms we use, the names we use, when we praise God—*hymnein* is the Greek word. Such a theology may be demanding in intellectual terms—such is certainly the case with Dionysios—but it can scarcely become merely intellectual, for it is grounded in the sacramental life of the Church and our participation in it through prayer.

Theology, in the sense the word has nowadays, means, then, seeking to give expression to the truth glimpsed in prayer and worship. The history of doctrine is not properly characterized as a "search for doctrine," as Richard Hanson put it.[17] It is rather a search for truth, an attempt to give expression to the truth experienced in communion with God through the sacramental communion of the Church. It is a search for truth, because we are seeking to find ways of expressing that truth, using the historically conditioned categories available to us. These expressions of truth we may expect to change over time, and there may well be cumulative change, because the "dead writers" are that which we know, but to speak of this as "development of doctrine" is perhaps to mistake our categories. To quote again from my young Romanian friend, Mihail Neamțu:

Like Christ's apostles and their immediate heirs, martyred in the
first three centuries, the Christian theologians of the fourth century were not in search of a doctrine, but *in search of truth.* To spread
the gospel to the Gentiles meant for St Paul to present the image
of Christ in different cultural idioms, which despite their peculiar-
ity were meant to preserve the universality of a unique proclamation. This explains why the elements of the Christian doctrine of
God stemmed from the earliest times of the Church and could
acquire new connotations even one thousand years after Nicæa. . . .
The profound dogmatic elaborations of the fourth century, on the
side of the orthodox theologians, did not bring the apostolic faith
somewhere further, on to a deeper level of understanding. Given
their relative flexibility regarding the language, the champions
of orthodoxy in the fourth century only provided new means
of conceptualization of what is essentially encapsulated in the
proclamation of Christ's lordship and divinity. . . . "Development
of doctrine," within and beyond the fourth century, represents not
the evolution from a primitive stage (of the primitive Church)
towards more recent and more intelligent levels of understanding,
but the spontaneous process of unfolding of what is already given
in the apostolic and unsurpassable confession of Christ as "God
and Lord."[18]

These wise words seem to me to represent an authentic Orthodox
understanding of the limitations of the idea of doctrinal development.

Refreshing the memory of the Church

We can, perhaps, take this a step further.[19] I have suggested that we
cannot expect to surpass the Fathers because it is as *Fathers* in the faith
that we reverence them. This might lead to a deeper reflection, if we
consider what they thought theology to be. The word *theologos* in the
Greek Christian tradition does not mean what the word customarily

means nowadays—that is, someone able to present a religious view of things, or who expounds the religious teaching of the Church (when, indeed, it is not used pejoratively).[20] It is, rather, a word with a very restricted connotation—primarily the inspired authors of sacred Scripture, both the Old and New Testaments, with a tendency to regard John the Evangelist as the pre-eminent theologian. Only rarely is it used with any wider connotation, and it still carries the charge of its original meaning. St Gregory Nazianzen comes to be given the title, ranking his exposition of the doctrine of the Trinity alongside the teaching of the Fourth Evangelist. Evagrios' oft-cited assertion—"If you are a theologian, you will pray truly; if you pray truly, you will be a theologian"[21]—in reality exalts the one who has acquired true prayer to the level of the scriptural writers.[22] The central theological task, as the Fathers see it, is to interpret the writings of the *theologoi*, that is, the Scriptures, in the light of the mystery of Christ. It is a task that cannot be surpassed; it remains for us all the touchstone of any authentic "theology" in our sense. There is no development beyond seeking, again and again, to deepen our understanding of the Scriptures in the light of the mystery of Christ.

So I would conclude that, though the notion of development is bound up with ways of historical understanding from which we Orthodox have plenty to learn, the idea of development itself is not an acceptable category in Orthodox theology. This might seem a dispiriting conclusion, especially as we honor a scholar and theologian who has devoted his life to historical theology. But that would be to misunderstand the nature of my conclusion.

Historical methods, I repeat, have much to offer theology, especially perhaps Orthodox theology. What such methods implement, however, is not the tracing of some upward curve of development but rather the preserving of access in the present to the great theologians of the past. Historical theology is, if you like, a way of refreshing, or revitalizing, the *memory* of the Church. It prevents our paying too much attention to the clamoring voices of our contemporaries, and enables us to hear the voices of the great witnesses of the past, those to whom we owe our faith, our Fathers in the faith. And no one perhaps, in our lifetime, has so helped keep Christian memory alive—over the whole Christian tradition, both temporally and geographically—as Professor Jaroslav Pelikan, whom we honor today.

Notes

[1]Pelikan, *Development of Christian Doctrine: Some Historical Prolegomena* (New Haven and London: Yale University Press, 1969).

[2]Pelikan, *The Christian Tradition: A History of the Development of Doctrine.* 5 vols. (Chicago and London: University of Chicago Press, 1971–89).

[3]John Romanides, *Franks, Romans, Feudalism and Doctrine* (Brookline, MA: Holy Cross Orthodox Press, 1982).

[4]Citations from the *Essay* are referenced by the page number in parentheses, according to the edition prepared by J. M. Cameron from the first (1845) edition for Pelican Classics (Harmondsworth: Penguin Books, 1974).

[5]Owen Chadwick, *From Bossuet to Newman* (Cambridge: Cambridge University Press, 1957).

[6]Samuel Taylor Coleridge, *Aids to Reflection*, 1904 edition (London: George Bell and Sons), 272.

[7]From Khomiakov's essay on the Church, in W. J. Birkbeck, *Russia and the English Church* (London: Rivington, Percival and Co., 1895), 1: 201.

[8]Andrzej Walicki, *A History of Russian Thought from the Enlightenment to Marxism* (Oxford: Clarendon Press, 1980), 107.

[9]Pelikan, *Development of Christian Doctrine*, 51–62.

[10]Preserved as *Quaestio* 111 in Anastasios, *Quaestiones et responsiones* (PG 89.764C). A learned man, accustomed to curse Plato daily, has a dream in which Plato appears to him and says, "Man, stop cursing me; for you are merely harming yourself. I do not deny that I was a sinner; but, when Christ descended into hell, no one believed in Him sooner than I did."

[11]Mihail Neamțu, "The Unfolding of Truth: Eunomius of Cyzicus and Gregory of Nyssa in debate over Orthodoxy (360–381)," *Archæus* VI (2002), fasc. 1–2:113. English somewhat modified.

[12]T. S. Eliot, *Selected Essays*, 3rd enlarged edition (London: Faber and Faber, 1951), 16. From the essay, "Tradition and the Individual Talent," 1919.

[13]J. N. D. Kelly, *Early Christian Doctrines* (London: A. & C. Black, 2nd ed., 1960), 261.

[14]Gregory Nazianzen, *Oratio* 31.26, Wickham's translation in *On God and Christ. St Gregory of Nazianzus: The Five Theological Orations and Two Letters to Cledonius* (Crestwood, NY: St Vladimir's Seminary Press, 2002), 137. A not dissimilar idea of progressive disclosure of the persons of the Godhead can be found in Origen, *De Principiis* I.3.1.

¹⁵See Basil, *De Spiritu Sancto* 27.66 (for unwritten traditions), 2.4 (for the Trinitarian doxology).

¹⁶See, e.g., Geoffrey Wainwright, *Doxology: The Praise of God in Worship, Doctrine and Life* (London: Epworth, 1980).

¹⁷As in the title of his book, *The Search for the Christian Doctrine of God. The Arian Controversy 318–381* (Edinburgh: T. & T. Clark, 1988).

¹⁸Neamțu 2002, 119–20. English again somewhat modified.

¹⁹I owe this insight to discussions with Fr John Behr, though it is not perhaps expressed quite in the way he would.

²⁰See *A Supplement to the Oxford English Dictionary* (Oxford: Clarendon Press, 1986), 4:802, *s.v.* theology, 1.d.

²¹Evagrios, *On Prayer* 61.

²²See my " '. . . And if you pray truly, you are a theologian': Some Reflections on Early Christian Spirituality," in my *Wisdom of the Byzantine Church: Evagrios and Maximos the Confessor* (Columbia, Missouri: Department of Religious Studies, University of Missouri, 1998), esp. 7f.

Jacob's Ladder:
Jaroslav Pelikan and the
People of the Book

ANTHONY UGOLNIK*

*T*O BE ASKED TO HELP celebrate the career of Jaroslav Pelikan is a great honor. His coming to Orthodoxy is the primary connection between us. When I first encountered his name on books others directed me to, I felt an immediate kinship because of his name. If a "Jaroslav" wasn't Orthodox, I thought, it was only an accident of history. And history has corrected the disjunction.

Edmund Wilson, reviewing Carl Sandburg's then celebrated biography of Lincoln, said it was the worst thing that had happened to Lincoln since he'd been shot by John Wilkes Booth. Now if academic careers were similar to political ones, to dare to call oneself "Orthodox" in these times is surely equivalent to assassination. Professor Pelikan has had a stellar career and met the concerns of our era in the process. But of all the career choices he has made in his life, becoming Orthodox was surely the worst. Being an Orthodox Christian may be a wondrous, fulfilling thing, but it has a certain inconsistency with fame or eminence. After all, the whole point of tradition is that one becomes utterly replaceable. If I should drop dead at the altar—which

*Anthony Ugolnik is Professor of English at Franklin and Marshall College in Lancaster, Pennsylvania, and a Ukrainian Orthodox priest. His lecture was delivered on May 4, 2003, in Collegeville, Minnesota, under the auspices of the Institute for Ecumenical and Cultural Research and Saint John's University.

I probably will, and probably on Holy Thursday because that service can seem to last more than a lifetime—somebody else will take up the service at exactly the point where I leave off. By claiming his communion with the rest of us, no matter how wonderful the career we celebrate today, Professor Pelikan has trumpeted throughout the world his complete dispensability.

Jaroslav Pelikan has the eminence, and certainly, the intellectual capacity, to have an entire theological system named after him. Like a parade of academics through history, he could have aimed for the Pelikan Christology, the Pelikan Ecclesiology, and if not a Pelikan Brief, then surely that highest of academic ambitions, a Pelikan Systematics. But by turning his back on those possibilities, he has acted in concert with his life's progression and simply asserted the Great Tradition of which he was always a part. I am a part of that tradition. It's a great tradition, a venerable tradition, a beautiful tradition. And though the majority of Christians are not precisely of the same expression of Orthodox continuity, it is this Orthodox continuity that makes me claim what I see as our greatest possible achievement in the coming century.

Co-knowing

In the West we've come to know primarily those Orthodox thinkers who breathed the bitter air of exile, and whose estrangement from East Europe during revolution and war gave them access to the rest of us. But there are other thinkers who stayed and who suffered on their own soil, some of them martyrs. Pavel Florensky based his religious thought not on the particularities of Orthodoxy but on its universals. And the most universal attribute of all he saw as consciousness, *so-znanie* in Russian. *So-znanie* is, he said, not merely awareness or knowing; it is a "co-knowing," a "co-awareness," together, of that which is most precious and valuable to us all.

Jaroslav Pelikan has devoted his life to this "co-knowing," the Christian consciousness, if you will. The Orthodox Tradition, its sacred labor as it takes root here in the secularized West, will respond to God's mission if it concentrates not on its particularities but on its *so-znanie*, the "co-knowing" it shares not only with Christians but also with all People of the Book. Orthodox thought, in focusing on what has always been declared in the Christian tradition, will also focus on our interrelationship with each other in the great, arching web of humanity, spread over the world and glistening in the dew distilled from the breath of God.

We are called to an interrelationship among three traditions—Christian, Jewish, Islamic—and I add to these a fourth and very important constituency originating from all three—those who come from a tradition but who for some reason, embedded in their rationality or our secular culture, can no longer say they believe. These secular children are born of all three of us. Separate as we are, stained as we are by the blood we have shed in offense and hatred against each other, we share an increasingly fragile and shrinking world. And as a constituent of that world, even as the lens through which we see it, we share even more—stories, a web of tales, common reverence for Abraham, Isaac, and Jacob. We have been called, in fact, the People of the Book.

Jacob's dream

In Genesis 28:10–17 there is a brief but profound image that has called forth responses in all three traditions in various ways and times. Jacob had a dream of a ladder, upon which "the angels were ascending and descending" in communion with their God. When many in the secular world look upon faith and its dynamics, they see only the occasion for conflict and division. But in this dream of Jacob we see a common aspiration. In all three traditions the ladder calls forth two fundamental facts about communication with the Divine and with each other.

First, it is incremental—step by step we ascend, and if by design we descend, we do so also step by step lest we fall. If we *do* fall, in one sense we end up where we started—the only trouble is, we end up there in considerably worse shape. Climbing is perilous, and must be done with great care.

Second, the ladder with its perils hosts a great divine communion worthy of those angels who engage in it. In seeking to commune with God, we inevitably communicate with each other, for in all our traditions the angels are dialogic beings. They are messengers of God's Word to us, but not only messengers. They also sing forth praise, that eternal attribution of the holiness that is God's by God's nature. If we want to participate in that nature, we must also sing the song, not alone but as they do, the angels — in chorus. In chorus our voices are attuned harmonically, which means we must ever be aware of each other, adjusting and modulating what we sing to the tone of all others who sing it. I have a dear friend, a physician, not a believer at all, whose favorite activity is sacred song because, he says, in that harmonic attunement he feels he can enter some divine space in his own experience, a space his mind can never bring itself to find. Thus even our secularized progeny can sing.

"The hats"

A distinction of our own culture, one not shared by any culture that Orthodoxy has heretofore embraced, is its multicultural nature, most vividly its separation of church and state. Something in us Orthodox, even those of us who are thoroughly American in birth and fealties, has been uneasy with this system. Fr Thomas Hopko, recently retired Dean of St Vladimir's Orthodox Theological Seminary, sees in our system a dangerous tendency toward civil religion, toward both "desacralizing" human experience on the one hand and "re-sacralizing" the political particularities of America and its culture on the other.

The condition of multiculturalism, with the widespread choice of no religious culture whatsoever, has placed my tradition on this soil at odds with itself. Certainly in our long history we have not been strangers to a pluralist option. In the Ottoman and the Austro-Hungarian

Empires, for example, we co-existed with other traditions, but in a system that gave the church not less but more political presence. When Orthodox monarchs were no more, then Orthodox hierarchs became in effect the political expression of their people. And tragically, this is still the condition in which we have placed ourselves, and from which we must break free in order to play any real role in the culture of which we are now a part.

Ottoman rulers gave the Ecumenical Patriarch a subordinate, but still a powerful, political presence—in many ways they made him even more of a despot in the modern sense. Austro-Hungarian emperors gave Orthodox hierarchs a place at the table. It is this paradigm that still gives our "photo ops"—the visits of various Orthodox hierarchs to the White House—resonance with the past. The hierarchs are most often invited not as representatives of a viable theology, of which most presidents are no doubt utterly clueless, but as representatives of ethnicities and hence constituencies. When George, the epically self-centered friend of Seinfeld in the TV series of the same name, chose to convert to Orthodoxy, a comically puzzled ethnic priest asked him, "Why?" George said, "It's the hats! I love the hats." As far as our image to the world is concerned, we haven't changed all that much. It's the hats—the Greek, Russian, Serbian, Ukrainian hats, quaint and exotic and yet so very politically useful in their symbolism—that still make us visible. And since these are the terms on which we are publicly engaged, and through which we raise funds, it's the hats we are still unwilling to surrender.

Pluralism in a pluralist world challenges the very relationship between the secular and the sacred. Some of the greatest diplomatic errors of our history have rested on the assumption that the separation between church and state we have declared as a civic principle extends to every other society, or to the human mind's ability to dissect itself from its own motivations. Acting on occasion as a (very) minor consultant to government officials on issues relating to church and state in East Europe, I have been amazed at the extent to which those who make public policy can misconstrue the popular mind of the people their policies seek to affect. The fact is that our faith traditions, even here in this pluralist society, are of vital importance to us as we strive to respect and relate to each other. A Christian can be no less a Christian—rather more a Christian—as he or she comes to understand a Jewish or Islamic concept.

Yet we subsist, and are happy to do so, in a society that demands of us a certain tolerance for those whose traditions are just as important to them as ours are to us. What does fidelity, what does Orthodoxy, what does tradition itself mean in such a world? The same question may be asked in an utterly secular context. What do the concepts of national identity and patriotism mean in a multinational world? In the wake of what we call a victory in Iraq, and in the flush of the vision of a *Pax Americana* reigning in the shadow of our power, we might ask that question all the more urgently.

Ambiguities of patriotism and faith

In a *Washington Post* column on a recent Fourth of July, E. J. Dionne, Jr, addressed the problem aptly. "What does patriotism mean," he asks, "in a world where the international financial system daily shift[s] money around the globe at the speed of light?" He points out the inconsistency with which people invoke patriotism for their purposes. People on the right speak with "patriotic urgency" on behalf of new defense spending but recoil at even a hint of trade protection. People on the left can be more hospitable to economic nationalism while renouncing the military on behalf of international concord. Dionne rightly condemns neither for hypocrisy. This is not a question of patriotism as the last refuge of scoundrels, but a commentary on patriotism's ambiguities.

The same can be said of our various orthodoxies, even of my own Orthodoxy, which assigns itself a capital "O." There is an ambiguity to our own absolutes, for while we seek an avenue to God, a communion with our fellow beings, a ladder of Jacob which any, indeed all of us, must climb, each of us makes claims in the process that cut us off from at least a part of those with whom our God has called us to commune. Take ecumenism, a movement born in hope and now too often become the province of a very small, maligned, and frustrated community of religious professionals. Those opposed to ecumenism, swollen like the python with their own sense of truth swallowed whole, condemn the movement as a threat to identity and a bow to compromise. Those committed to ecumenism see in their own embattlement a new schism even deeper than those that divide us into separate communities. This is not a question of religion as the last refuge of scoundrels, but a commentary on faith's ambiguities.

The lungs with which the human mind breathes

To seek out the source of ambiguities, we have to look where most of us embed our certainties: to our reverence for the text. For we are all People of the Book. We revere the Book, and we revere it in the form of the text it contains. All of us raised in these various traditions know how it is in fact revered. In my tradition the Gospel text is clad in gold and borne in procession. People come forth and kiss it. When I read it, proclaim it before the people, I touch my lips to the text. I have seen in Jewish communities the same reverence for the Torah borne in procession, and joy manifest throughout the congregation. In an Armenian church in Glendale, California, the similarity to the synagogue procession was marked—people came forth to touch the hem of the garment of the bearer of the Book. In Islam, the text of the Holy Qur'an is an emblem and a paradigm for form itself. One of my favorite modern sculptures is the entrance gate at King Saud University in Riyadh, Saudi Arabia. The design consists of two books representing knowledge and faith, the lungs with which the human mind breathes. They have been so placed that their pages interlock, and verses from the Qur'an, shaped in that reverence for calligraphy that is a hallmark of the Islamic visual arts, mark the cover of each.

Practical Baptists and Lutherans may be feeling that this is all very exotic. But visit the local Christian book store. You can get your Bibles in leather or denim, Bibles with little packets so that they can fold up like a raincoat. You get your scripture verses for your pocket, verses on plastic for your wallet, verses on magnets to stick on the refrigerator. That's to say nothing of the misty, water-colored landscapes and sunsets with scripture verses integrated or imposed beneath. Evangelical Christian crypto-iconography has begotten an industry that rivals the rosary sellers of Rome and the icon shops of Athens. The Bible that is Word has been transmuted as well into an emblem, each little piece of which in some mysterious way implies the whole. It is not too far a stretch to say that the little scripture magnets for the refrigerator, or the micro-engraved Lord's Prayer on a pocket coin, are analogues to the Jewish *tefillin* strapped to the arms for prayer, the amulets at the threshold, or the elaborate calligraphic engravings of passages from the Qur'an.

Many books

This wholeness, or "object-endowment" we attribute to the sacred text, undoes one aspect of its reality. The Bible or Torah or Qur'an is in reality many books in many genres, with different historical dimensions to each. My own tradition respects this differentiation—in Orthodox ritual there is no single bound Bible with that thumping solidity found on a Protestant pulpit. We place *Evangelions* (Gospels) on the altar; *Apostolarions* (Epistles) are a different book, given ritually to a reader. Psalters and Prophets and Wisdom texts are all separate volumes on a spinning lectern. If you wanted to use a single Bible in the context of our Orthodox ritual, you would have to rip it into pieces. Why? Because many books were bound into one in the last great print revolution, and that one Book has become an icon of its own.

Ritual contains collective memory, and many have discovered that we dispense with it at our peril. Ritual practice and reading in Judaism and Islam also, in many and various ways, respects the differentiation among the texts that make up the Book. For so many of us, when the sacred text becomes one thing, a bound object, even constructed in such a way that it embodies a certain solidity and unarguable solidarity, it can take on the quality of the idol which the Book in its genesis condemned. The new incarnation into a bound solidity neglects the nuance, the variation, even the internal tensions contained for us within the bestowal of the Word. Jacob's ladder reaches one divine destination but it is made up of many distinct rungs.

Consistency, solidity, indisputability are features we sometimes look to the Book to provide. We tend to think we need them, in this world of rapid change and fluctuation, as reinforcements of God's Law. Yet all our traditions suggest that while this Word is enshrined in the text, it is in some way distinct from it. For insight, let us look to Islam, which among us all has perhaps the greatest reverence for the written Word of the Prophet. When the Prophet Muhammad died in 632, the Qur'anic revelation stopped. The content of the Holy Qur'an was passed from lip to lip by *huffaz*—those who memorized and recited the contents of the Qur'an by heart. Many of the *huffaz*, however, were killed in the battles that followed the death of the Prophet. Omar Ibn al-Khattab, one of the disciples of the Prophet, urged the Caliph Abu Bakr to put the Holy Qur'an into writing, and Ibn Thabit, who served as scribe to the Prophet, was assigned to compile and collate the revelations into the texts that make up the Book. The Book pre-existed, in this sense, its own calligraphy or written form. The Book *existed* before it was compiled.

In Christian terms, Luke is very explicit about the derivative nature of the Gospel books from oral testimony. The Epistles are by definition letters to an audience. Jewish tradition, in its distinctions between Torah, Mishnah, and Talmud, recognizes and respects their differences. Many texts are in fact records of words in utterance, and to this day in Hassidic and some Orthodox traditions the words of the teacher are revered and repeated, even as they emerge from the mouth.

The mouth and the pen

The mouth and the pen are images with tensions and harmonies. That
the words emerge from the mouth of the prophet are the hallmark of
their validity. In Isaiah the prophet's words are seared into his lips by
the image of a burning coal. "Amen amen I say unto you" is a formulaic
utterance of Jesus as he instructs. "In the beginning was the Word and
the Word was God and the Word was with God" begins John in his
Mystical Gospel. Yet the transition of that Word into its encrypted,
written form is also part of the process of revelation. The instruction
given in the very first Qur'anic revelation received by the Prophet
Muhammad was this: "Recite in the name of thy Lord . . . Who has
taught by means of the writing of the pen" (Surah 96, al-A-laq 1–4).

Writing, however, exists in a sometimes uneasy relationship to the
written word. In our secular lives we spin through evanescent forms of
writing as we comprehend with great rapidity. These words as I first
composed them took shape in the cyberspace of Microsoft Word.
Many of us consume words, or even vomit them out, in total silence.
That is not the sense of the "written word" that guides the People of the
Book, for even in the act of reading there is a re-enactment of its genesis in utterance. In my tradition, we chant virtually everything. Even the
"silent prayers to be uttered at the altar" while the people are themselves chanting are to be shaped by the lips. The five times daily purifi-
cation of human action in prayer mandated in Islam is announced by
chanted prayer, and is enacted by the utterance of sacred discourse.
And Jewish children learning sacred texts in Hebrew under the guidance of a strict rabbi make a lot of noise—East European Jewish folk
tales tell often of cacophony in the classroom. The venerable (and influential) Augustine once received a famous call from a group of children
playing a game in the courtyard below: *Tolle lege, tolle lege*, they
chanted—"Take up and read." Augustine, living quite a wild life as you
can read in his *Confessions*, commenced his career as a theologian and
laid aside his sex life for himself—and subsequent generations. He
"took up and read," and the context makes clear that he did so aloud.

Awakening to language

We have no such sense of the uttered written word any longer. At least so they say. But I have found it among writers and poets, who can awaken us to language as it means and as it sounds. Reading Gerard Manley Hopkins—"I caught this morning morning's minion, kingdom of daylight's dauphin, dapple dawn drawn Falcon"—I not only see that windhover hawk, but his swooping and boldness of flight are re-enacted in my utterance. Emily Dickinson needs to be read aloud to recover the startling, chilling abruptness of "I heard a fly buzz when I died." And on the radio I heard a poet whose name I did not hear but the power of whose verse has been with me since. He described the desire of his lover, dying of AIDS, to touch and stroke a dog as he endures his advancing paralysis. The poet wraps himself and his hearers around the words: "Why do men, when they die, grasp to form attachments?"

Whether or not the poets believe as we construct belief is not of the slightest importance. They can stir us up from our torpor over the written word and reconnect it once more to sound. The problem, the conundrum, is the sacred languages themselves. My own tradition respects the vernacular in which we speak, yet it preserves a certain position of respect for the original Greek in which our Greek congregations still pray or the Slavonic in which the Slavs first received the Word. For the Jewish and Islamic traditions, there is no question of the pre-eminence of the language of revelation. Hebrew and Arabic are the bearers of meaning. To delve seriously into those traditions, one must wrap one's tongue around a new language, and the experience will in some way drench one in the sacred.

The distance between meaning and text, for one who does not know the language that has this special relationship to sacred meaning, can be daunting. In the days when Catholics prayed primarily in Latin, the main objection to Latin was that nobody spoke it any longer. The resonance of the sacred remains, and for more than Catholic people—witness the popularity of Gregorian chant, often in "New Age" bookshops. Yet this insistence upon a privileging of the tongue in which the significant text appeared acknowledges an important truth. Text has context. That is, you cannot completely grasp the content of the meaning until you recover in some sense its linguistic incarnation. If one could grasp in totality all the nuances of meaning, there would be no insistence upon the language of origin.

This insistence, however, also implies a kind of profound humility. Text has a context. That is, every word we utter belongs in some sense to the moment and the dialogic relationship of that moment. My words today belong to us, together, here today at Collegeville; they exist in a Saint John's context, as it were, and as they take written form later (in this Festschrift) they lose something of that context. Absolutists insist upon literal truth—but if all truth were in that sense literal, we would have to recover the language of the moment and its context. We painstakingly learn the original texts—not only scholars, but also all those who are serious about entering the space of the texts. I know converts to Judaism or Islam or Orthodoxy who have paid for their new traditions with a lot of study. Jaroslav Pelikan embodies this re-creation of context, for text, for image, for understanding.

Limits of perception

The mark of Professor Pelikan's excellence, and of his Orthodoxy, is the humility to understand the limits of our own human perception. Our common consciousness, our *so-znanie*, is an expansion of what any single mind, any single culture or age, can comprehend about the Divine—hence the significance of Pelikan's tracing the changing face of Jesus through the centuries, of his updating, after more than a century, the collection of the creeds of Christendom. Like the modern deconstructionists and relativists, the studious Orthodox mind knows the limitations of our ability in any age or culture to utter the Truth in totality of comprehension. Unlike the postmodernists, however, this Orthodox awareness in no way invalidates a belief in the existence of

Truth. Truth resides in the *Mysterion*, in what none of us in any age or time or culture can comprehend in totality, but which we can catch glimpses of, perhaps, in the age and time and culture of others with whom we are bound in communion. Truth is ineluctable, always uttered in the best form available but always complemented, always expanded by another utterance.

Orthodoxy, then, is in a position both to engage the postmodern sensibility and to challenge the often paralyzing anxiety with which Christians are tempted to respond to those who test the edges of truth's formulations. Let us take the issue of scripture and literal truth—or, if not precisely literal, then as close to the literal as we can get. The text is "true," but its truth (if we construct it absolutely) is available only to those who recover its context completely. And no one, in any literalist tradition, goes quite that far. For some Christian proponents of literal biblical truth, the most ancient reliance upon literalism rests in the brilliant but poetic and often un-literal translators of the King James Version. We Orthodox retain a reverence for the text, and yet we celebrate it ritually in many linguistic forms. One of our revered theologians, Georges Florovsky, said in his own biblical commentary, "Scripture is not truth in itself. Scripture is the icon of truth."

This humility about literalism is necessary for any meaningful communion among people who seek to climb the ladder of Jacob. The distance between believer and unbeliever, orthodox and heterodox, absolutist and heretic, often rests in the presumption of understanding. It is my contention that the most conservative among all traditions respect, if truly they respect the text, its context as well. They realize that the text "comes to mean" in its declared—that is, its uttered—form. They realize that the uttered form demands a discipline for recovering, insofar as possible, its original linguistic and cultural context. A "modern Jew" cannot be a Jew without in some sense recovering or recapitulating a lived Jewish history and culture. Islamic believers, growing rapidly in number among us, face their greatest challenge in helping us to understand this about them.

Carrying the bones of the ancestors

Professor Pelikan's great talent has been his ability to reclaim the various contexts of Christian belief—and not only to reclaim and explain them, but to place them in juxtaposition and allow us to see the dialogue within. He has, in effect, entered most deeply the *so-znanie* that Pavel Florensky and Dostoevsky both saw as the core of our communality in love. None of us certainly can claim any tradition if we abandon its cultural context. Christians sometimes forget this fact about themselves, for they often stop retracing their history at the genesis of their own tradition or even their own local community. Our dogma teaches us, after all, that even God "is begotten" of God. And we, in pale imitation of that internal dialogue of the Trinity, are begotten of each other. Some Christians express this realization with great courage and poignancy. The Greek author Nikos Kazantzakis, in *The Greek Passion*, vividly describes a ragtag collection of refugees from the ethnic cleansing in Asia Minor who literally "carry the bones of the ancestors upon their backs." We all carry those bones. And in our attempts to recover the text, we give those bones flesh in our *own* day, our *own* time, our *own* context. Without the bones we would be lost.

We each make claims in our own context, depending upon our understanding of those who came before. What happens when these claims conflict? For many who long ago rejected the option of belief, the answer is all too clear. We kill and maim and destroy, to carve out our own historical domain. A recent biography of Constantine and his bishops revealed to me, in excruciating detail, a horrific fact about those bishops who shaped the context of Orthodoxy as I know it. The number of Christian martyrs was greater after Christianity was legalized, or became a "state dogma," than before. The reason? Christians killed each other for heresy and heterodoxy with greater efficiency than the emperors had ever killed them.

The skeptics who reject faith and "organized religion" should not grow too smug, however. Our communality in love has its parallel in our communality in hatred and rejection. Skeptics and rationalists too have been known to organize, and when they do the results can be devastating. In the century just past, the unbelievers and rationalists have racked up their own kind of orthodoxy and their own list of victims numbering in the millions, as the Chinese are doing at this very moment in Tibet. We kill each other over our claims.

Recovering each other's questions

It is not my place as an Orthodox Christian to claim for my tradition immunity from this horrible sin. Indeed, in East Europe I have seen with my own eyes our hospitality to the exclusivity of claims and its compatibility with bloodshed. The answer to this crucial problem cannot be, as cliché sometimes suggests, the abandonment of faith traditions. Rather, the answer lies in their recovery as posers of the problem. Each of our traditions is in origin the response to a question, a question our sacred texts raise among us again and again. We should invest less time in attacking each other's answers and more time in recovering each other's questions.

The mission implicit in our Judaism or our Islam or our Christianity lies in a vision, a vision of a world at concord and in peace. All of us see the angels ascending and descending the ladder, inviting us to join them. The activity in which we engage has a certain harmony. If we appreciate, each of us, what the other is doing and how they are doing it, we will discover a sympathy that is the antithesis of hatred. And if hatred rears itself as a pretext for violence and dehumanization, it will be exposed within our various, interlacing texts as unacceptable, as sin, as anathema in and of itself.

My experience in the former Soviet society, and, even more poignantly, in Albania where the effort to eliminate the God issue was more systematic, proved to me that empirical rationalism will not eliminate what we call religion. But I have another body of experience — experience as a teaching professor with many students for whom the object of the quest is vague if not invisible. They are hard-wired for some kind of search. They have unmistakably what I'd call a spirituality, just as did my dear friends in Russia who were not educated to believe and who felt they never could. One of the warmest, most forgiving people I know gets a hard edge on his voice when he speaks of religion. He's a hardworking, taxpaying, very loving guy. He's also a gay male raised in a very anti-gay religious tradition. Why is it that all these people—the rationalist professor, the agnostic longing for but estranged from belief, the person estranged by reason of life choice or sexuality—are drawn to engagement with an Orthodoxy, if only Orthodoxy will address them?

The arts effect communion

If the bald and essentially rhetorical terms of dogma cannot reach or appeal to a significant segment of our human family, then the experience conveyed through celebration in the arts most certainly can. No one need be excluded, indeed *can* be excluded from art's embrace. Maybe my buddy the doctor can never say to me with good conscience, "I believe in God," but when he reaches down into his gut and pulls up a baritone *Credo in Unum Deum* from a Cherubini Mass, he *feels* what he says, *experiences* what he says, *celebrates* what he says in union with his symphony chorus. In that moment of consciousness, *soznanie,* in which he participates in the performance, he becomes as it were a believer. It is that place—that precious place in the consciousness of all of us—that Orthodoxy is beautifully equipped to address in this new century. And as more people find their voice in connection with the larger human condition, rather than in the particularities of our Byzantine or Slavic or Middle Eastern cultural incarnations, we will take up the Orthodox mission in this new century. Orthodoxy is an embodied tradition—embodied in culture, in the senses engaged in worship, in ritual, and above all in the image, in the arts. We see in the arts an accessibility to each other, not only to other People of the Book, but also and just as crucially to those deriving from us who no longer see themselves as "believers." For unbelievers are begotten of us; in some measure they are begotten of our own failures.

Art is a way of experiencing another person's experience. Those who have seen the Iranian films focused upon children have been dazzled and charmed by the gems of insight they provide into a rich and complex society we had, most of us, stereotyped and simplified. Judaism, through literature and through comic impresarios, has so entered the fabric of American humor that at one point or another all of us laugh not only with Jews, or at some dimensions of the Jewish experience, but in some real sense as Jewish at least in our laughter. Christ, one of my dearest Jewish friends has told me, was one of the most complex problems of his own growing up. "He's so attractive and compelling in his manifestation on the one hand. Yet his followers are so obnoxious and even dangerous on the other. Go figure." And with the non-believers, the skeptics and agnostics and rationalists who make up so much of the intellectual and arts-producing world around us, we can embrace the abandonment of certainty. This can be a salve, a wondrous gift. For in order to take on, in the space of a novel or a painting or a musical composition, the perspective of another, we must lay aside at least for that moment our own models of certitude. True faith subsists not in certainty, but in mystery.

Orthodoxy envisioned by others is often seen in terms of its own particularities. Our fascination is, like George in *Seinfeld* observed, "in the hats." But when you get past those hats, often (as the joke goes) worn so tightly that they stifle the ideas in the brains beneath them, we see some stirring possibilities for our thought in the century to come. Professor Pelikan has already engaged many of those possibilities in his own work, long before he became openly affiliated with us. And in that phenomenon—a theologian who was Orthodox in his thought before he became Orthodox in his affiliation—we see the precise point of dialogue. Time does not exist in God, and often in the phenomenon of our own lives it collapses as well.

Often what we don't know saves us

I see the core of our dialogic insight in our lending of a context to the
phenomenon of text. This is the meaning of tradition, and we can envi-
sion a broader Tradition within the human longing for God, our collective *so-znanie*. But this gives birth to other possibilities. We
Orthodox are a people of the image. We are a people of Mystery, and
if we view Mystery as "the Art of Unknowing," we can see how it is
often what we don't know, and know we cannot know, that saves us.
Orthodoxy and the artistic minds it generates can also express a harmony between the so-called "believing" and "non-believing" artists
and the souls they express. We are a people of dogma, and most of us
see in dogma the uncompromising declaration. Yet dogma is a product
of dialogue—the things of which we feel so certain are in fact the product of our mutual uncertainties. We need each other in order to know
who we are, and if we eliminate our differences we will in fact eliminate our identities as well.

As a scholar of culture and the arts, here is what I see as the greatest possibility for our tradition, if only it can break free from its isola-
tionism in North America. Theology has been the prisoner of rhetoric
in the West; it is enmeshed in declaration. We should empower our
artists as well as, or perhaps even more than, our rhetoricians. We look
for inspiration to those who declare and state and affirm things. It
might be more productive to look to those who imagine, and image-
forth, and suggest things. This is the most subversive of Orthodoxy's
possibilities. Theologians talk a good game when it comes to the arts,
but they regard them as profoundly dangerous. They won't go so far as
to kill an artist outright, but all our traditions do a very good job of
starving them slowly instead—it's much more effective.

Rediscovering the art of being perplexed

I conclude with what may seem like paradoxical contributions of an
Orthodox consciousness in the next century. God in none of our

traditions lends us certainty. Text is set in context. The rich tradition of commentary upon a text—and from that point to commentary upon the commentary—begets the very essence of what constitutes the rabbi in Jewish tradition. The rabbi and the rabbinate in dialogue continually mine the text to dispute and discuss its conundrums, its puzzles. It is the nature of the Book not only to instruct us, but also to perplex us. Commentaries upon the Qur'an show the same respect for the posed problem. To be perplexed is part of what it means to be instructed.

To rediscover the art of being perplexed, and even of praying in the midst of perplexity, is a part of unlocking the Word to the growing audience of those who call themselves agnostics, unbelievers, doubters, and searchers. Faced by the challenges of the Enlightenment and evolution, the apologetics and preaching of recent centuries were declarations of certainty; the texts ceased to be a tissue of testimonies in dialogic harmony, but instead became a single certainty embodied in the object, a Book. But such an apologetics of certainty conflicts with our own era, our hermeneutics of suspicion. In the twentieth century, we faced so many assurances of certainty, embodied in so many ideologies that proved devastating and destructive. So many people today reject, and quite rightly, any assurances of certainty. Many no longer need the right answers. In fact, too many among us believers are too certain—in a kind of arrogance challenging the very nature of God—that we possess the right answers. What we need now are the right questions.

The scholarly life we celebrate is a testimony to that need. Professor Pelikan does not, in his work, impose upon us a formulation or answer. He gives us a symphony of answers. Even more important, he asks the right questions. We need to be perplexed together. We need to rediscover the humility to be puzzled, the courage to engage the ambiguities and conundrums in our texts and look to each other to find the flashes and refractions of answers in places we least expect them. Orthodoxy, with its respect for culturally embodied expressions of the Truth, and its willingness to extend that embodiment to any culture, has the potential to quench the hunger not for the right answers, but for the Mystery, the *Mysterion* that will ever, and forever, engage us all.

Orthodoxy and Western Christianity: The Original European Culture War?

John Anthony McGuckin*

*I*T IS A GREAT JOY to honor Jaroslav Pelikan, one of the world's leading interpreters of Christian history, and one who is without peer if one requires of a writer historical accuracy and theological sensitivity combined—a consummately artful balance that is the heart of the matter but far from a common thing in the lists of basic books in our field.

Balance, or the lack of it, will be the focus of much in this essay.[1] Like the French composer Eric Satie, who used to give structural indications of his works with manuscript annotations such as "In the shape of a pear" or dynamic markings such as "Light as a soufflé," I shall try to give a balanced and ordered presentation. It is in the modality of an extended harangue, and comes, like Caesar's Gaul, in three parts: 1) the lamentable state of things; 2) how we got this way; and 3) what *you* should do about it. It is not so much *au forme du poire* as in the shape of the Michelin Man of the tire advertisements, pretty stacked at the top but dwindling down at the lower legs. I have a clear sense of how we got to be parodied as an exotic, dim, and reactionary

*John Anthony McGuckin is Professor of Early Church History at Union Theological Seminary in New York and Professor of Byzantine Christianity at Columbia University. His lecture was delivered on September 14, 2003, at St Vladimir's Orthodox Theological Seminary in Crestwood, New York.

church, but I have only aspirations how we might get out of this trap
and claim our true place by making and describing our own identity
instead of taking it from the mouths of others.

The colonial mentality

"We of the East . . ." is a phrase often associated with spokespersons of
the Orthodox Christian Church in our age, one of such vastly increased
intellectual mobility and ease of informational transmission that the
theologians of the past (not excepting many in the present) would have
been rendered dumb in the face of it (if such a thing is conceivable for
a theologian). Compared to the era when one of the students of Eva-
grius would have meditated for a week on a couplet from the *Sententiae*,
we now have the capacity in that same time to read, or at least peruse,
books, journals, and ephemera; to see visual iconic forms flashed at us
that collectively amount to more literature and far more symbols than
an educated ancient might ever have processed in a lifetime.

In the bewildering intellectual welter so grandly shored up by the
gimcrack nomenclature of "postmodernism," the phrase "We of the
East" floats reassuringly across the mental horizon, proceeds in
stately fashion like a duchess crossing the carpet. It usually precedes
an attempt to explain something of our religious identity as Orthodox, in reference to, or more usually in contradistinction from, the
more common matrices of Western European Catholicism or Protestant experience. It has a fine cachet, though one that loses much of
its shine when the "East" in question turns out to be the East End of
London, East Pennsylvania, or the East Village of New York, places
where one is today more likely to encounter Orthodox who are
engaged in ecumenical dialogue with "the West" than in some putative Orient of our imagination.

The phrase reveals much about the mindset of Orthodoxy in a dialogue with Western Europe that is still coming of age—for it is, is it
not, a recidivist aspect of *orientalisme*, pretended exoticism, as Edward

Said and others have demonstrated for us, that often masks unappetizing colonial ideologies behind it, either those of the dominant agency or those of the submissive recipient. Nothing so marks the colonial mentality as a desire to adopt the language and value scheme of the dominant culture. Said's later book, *Covering Islam*, wistfully notes how the European and American media's coverage of Islamic life and civilization bears next to no relation to the actuality of the lived experience of millions of real-time human beings, though paradoxically the coverage forces some within the camp to live up to the chimerical expectation imposed upon them as "the dangerous other." "Covering" or "coverage" in this sense, Said remarks, is always presented as if it were an honest "covering the ground" while it is, in fact, more a "covering over." Those who have studied the various appearances not of Islam but of Orthodoxy in the contemporary media could write a book on this subject themselves.

Although "We of the East" looks like a bravely contradistinctional phrase, a rabbinical utterance in the style of "You have heard it said but I say to you, . . ." in fact it is far from this. It is a path to self-identity that tries to fit itself into the agenda of the dominant discourse. Maybe this is why Orthodoxy in the West so often uses the drag linguistic conventions of this pretended orientalism. Our brothers and sisters in Eastern Europe and farther afield regard us Orthodox in the West as the rich Church. However, even here we are poor and ragged, at least in the intellectual assembly. I do not mean to suggest we have nothing of merit to say; rather, we are still in economic and emotional recovery from centuries of reversals.

Two of my greatest laments (I deliberately pass over in silence centuries of personal sufferings of a countless host of Orthodox witnesses) are, first, the loss of a strong and unbroken presence of an Orthodox aristocracy, which in Byzantium, and even more in its counterpart in late medieval West-European culture, fuelled the intellectual life and ecclesiastical vigor of the Church by its patronage and by its bloc influence, and second, the destruction and impoverishment of Orthodox institutes of higher learning—the libraries, universities, and colleges, that for Protestantism and Catholicism became the bright points of a nexus of cultural development. We are still generations away from the rehabilitation of the second. The first is a loss that may never be repaired in any recognizable form, and leaves us with Church structures in which the clerical and monastic voices have coherence of sorts but the position of the laity, once led and given articulation by the Byzantine aristocracy, is like that of a great giant, somnolent and confused, currently without voice.

In such a condition, aware of the tradition of our great glories of liturgy and sacramental practice, of spiritual and evangelical fidelity, we find comfort in the recourse to self-parody associated with "We of the East . . ." even when in more rational mood we might wonder what sense it now makes to continue to talk about Orthodoxy as an eastern phenomenon. How long is it appropriate to be *Millet*, the captive and subjugated race? For that matter, how long shall we be immigrant? How long is it appropriate to be identified as an Orthodox "convert"?

Things have changed. There are many times more Greeks living in America and Australia than there are on the Greek mainland. Christianity in its ancient heartlands of Egypt, Palestine, Anatolia, and Syria is demographically all but asphyxiated, as William Dalrymple's moving but depressing book, *From the Holy Mountain*, shows us. These communities' powerful contributions to our global Christian consciousness and identity—Arab Orthodox, Copts, Ethiopians, Syrians, and Armenians of Jerusalem, for example—continue to be almost "smuggled out" obliquely to the rest of the world through "intermittent" channels such as the diaspora communities in America or the World Council of Churches and its various committees. The truth is that since the rise of Islam and its powerful westward expansion, the central point of Christian geography has been inexorably moving geographically west until its political and geographic axis point currently stands somewhere in America and by 2050 will be south of the border.

In any case, do we nowadays really think that Russians are oriental? Many years ago that perspicacious critic, Fr Alexander Schmemann, put his finger on it exactly when he said:

Only in free encounter with the world could Russia become herself, grow to her full height, and find her true calling, which was to overcome the terrible gulf between East and West, which had been the chief sin of the Christian world since the Middle Ages. There was much dispute about East and West in Russia, but Russia herself revealed a truth that had dropped out of sight in Europe long before: that this contrast was in itself false, and even sinful, for it was a falsehood against the original unity of the Christian world, whose spiritual history goes back to the miracle of Pentecost. All the best that Russia has created is the result of the inward reconciliation of "Eastern" and "Western," of all that was true and immortal that sprouted from Byzantine seed, but could grow only by identifying itself once more with the general history of Christian humanity.[2]

It is only pseudo-orientalism that clings to the notion of Eastern mentality like a mast, forgetting that the Byzantines themselves saw their culture as the Christian expression of *Romaiosyne*: Christian Romanity, neither Latin, Greek, Egyptian, nor Syriac, but rather a fertile synthesis of all and the foundation of a universal Christian polity and consciousness that transcended the pathological fragmentariness of schisms, nationalisms, denominationalisms, and which raised as its masthead the concept of Christian catholicism. Greek Christian civilization is the very foundation of Europe, not an exotic spin off from it. Nevertheless, today even that original Mediterranean-European identity has shifted, and we are better served by the more theologically pure and transethnic identifiers of that catholicity that has made a Christian civilization rise out of the base materials of varied nationalisms.

The long reach of Gibbon

However "Byzantinism" has been a dark veil pulled over our consciousness of our Christian tradition. It used to be a cliché of bad Byzantine writing from Gibbon to the mid-twentieth century that luxurious ceremonial and political intrigue invariably demonstrated the "weakness" of the oriental influences that so sapped the "manly vigor" of the Byzantines, and were transmitted like a contagion to the Russian soul, weakening its claim to membership in the commonwealth of European states. In similar vein, Orthodoxy was not infrequently ascribed, as part of this colonial *orientaliste* agenda, to that dimmer part of the fabled Russian soul that craved for the dark absolutisms of Byzantinism. Can anyone still take this seriously? One is reminded of Irenaeus who, tired of too much reading of Gnostic texts, one day exasperatedly said, "To expound them is sufficient to refute them." Well, the answer is yes. Some people still do take it seriously. One can read Samuel Huntington's *The Clash of Civilizations and the Remaking of the World Order*[3] or Victoria Clark's *Why Angels Fall*[4] to see many of the old faces still there in the gallery winking at us cheekily. In the West, so the refrain goes, it is mainly light and reason and order. Depending on the century in which one wrote, that could be Catholic, Protestant, or liberal secular order, light, and reason. In the East, however, *oh dear, oh dear!*

The view of Byzantium established by Gibbon's highly influential *Decline and Fall of the Roman Empire* has been very hard to shake from West-European and American scholarship, until well into the final quarter of the twentieth century. It was an extraordinarily long run of prejudice, often sustained by scholars who spoke, for this once, in one voice, whether they represented the Mediterranean-Catholic or the North-European-Protestant side of the divide, since disparagement of Byzantium, particularly of its religious aspects, was an affair that served all ideological fronts in early modern European scholarship and buttressed a variety of post-Reformation Catholic and Protestant presuppositions of cultural and religious superiority.

The long narrative of the Western church, with its constant refrain (almost its *idée maitresse*) of the absorption and transcendence of imperial power by the papal monarchy, colluded with the belittling of Byzantine styles of politics. To throw light on the Latin genius for order and clarity and authority, for example, much of East Christian polity was caricatured as chaotic, undisciplined, and devious. The well-known contrasts between Benedictine order and its cenobitic social *gravitas*, on the one hand, and the wild-eyed nomadic monks of Byzantium, on the other, were peddled to the point of becoming religious tropes. That they were a fallacious misrepresentation of the facts mattered little.[5]

For the Protestant world, the notion of a society that sought a profoundly close relation—ideally a harmonious *symphonia*—between church and state, associating the concepts of military power and religious orthodoxy based on the fundamental religious presupposition that the borders of the kingdom of Christians on the earth represented, as in the times of the righteous kings of Israel, the extent of the earthly manifestation of the kingdom of God itself, sent shivers down the spine of those who had but recently emerged from the religious bloodbaths of early modern Europe. The ideas still have the power to shock, particularly in states whose deep-rooted Protestant political principles have more or less been otherwise forgotten. Even today, when so few know anything whatsoever about Byzantine history, the last of that triad of denunciations—chaotic, undisciplined, *devious*—has survived in common speech. "Byzantine" is still synonymous with duplicitous complexity, and often it is raised in sophisticated circles (I myself have heard it used in such ways on several occasions in university committee rooms) by those who have absolutely no consciousness of the offence they would cause to more or less any educated representative of Orthodox Christian culture who heard them.

The word "Byzantine" itself is a neologism, of course, another creation of British scholars imposed imperialistically on a world and a culture that would never have recognized such a description of themselves—and to that extent as implicitly racist as "Eskimo," "Red Indian," or "Gipsy." It was meant to deny the evident truth that there was a continuity of experience between the Romans of "Late Antiquity"[6] and the Romans of the Greek-speaking world of the Levant and Near East, centered round the great capital, the "New Rome," Constantinople. The Byzantines, who simply regarded themselves as

Greek-speaking Christians instinctively referred to themselves as what they were, *Romaioi*, the Christian Romans—not Greeks, one notes, for the word *Hellene* was reserved for pagans, certainly not Byzantines. The identity of the Orthodox was not to be a partial nation but to be the Church on the face of the earth with a global consciousness, an ecumenical scope, and a transcendent destiny.

Gibbon's cause for annoyance was part racist and part imperialist. His thesis, quietly cribbed from Montesquieu,[7] put most simply was that with Byzantium, "the simplicity of Roman manners was inevitably corrupted by the stately affectation of the courts of Asia."[8] This reveals much of Gibbon's character, of course—an eighteenth-century man of the Enlightenment; a hater of absolutism, especially as he saw it in the autocratic exercises of monarchy; and an amused agnostic, deeply hostile to all forms of popular religion that did not conform to his (unconsciously imperialistic) view of the fundamental absorption of the religious impetus into the socio-ethical. In the citation above we have his two themes most eminently expressed—first, that Byzantium is the epitome of decline because it subordinates "classical" Roman *pietas* to the orientalizing decadence of Christianity, most notably its tendency to subservience (the craven acceptance of monarchical absolutism as exercised by either sacred rulers or priests); and second, that it is a shameful model of passivity demonstrated in the seduction from civic virtues to the attractions of mysticism and ascetic seclusion.[9] Both passivities decline from his foundational understanding of virility. Gibbon was obviously a real man, evidently with a "real man's" worries.

Waiting for the ravisher

This, needless to say, *orientalisme* writ large. Gibbon's odalisques are, however, the passive, dreamy-eyed (or slightly hysterical) monastics rather than fleshy maidens reclining in steam baths, as in the orientalism of the more well-known nineteenth-century painters. Returning to Edward Said for a moment, we recall that his own conclusion, in seeing his cultural history as a Palestinian Arab caricatured so negatively in the arts and media, was to express wonderment at the "corrupt scholarship" that produced such twisted views of reality designed for its own self-serving ends.[10] Averil Cameron, one of the leading exponents of Byzantine studies in England today, has explained the connection between this style of *apologia* and the "corrupt"[11] reception of this pejorative "Byzantinism." As she phrases it:

> A corrupt way of seeing can extend to scholarship, literature, and popular imagination, and applies to visual as much as mental images. How we see, just as how we read, stems not least from what we ourselves bring to the supposed object. In this particular corrupt but persistent vision, the Byzantines share the supposed characteristics of the Arabs in orientaliste literature — passivity, factionalism, dishonesty, and corruption. In its peculiarly Byzantine manifestation this vision also typically employs categories such as "rigid" and "uncreative." The entire discourse suggests the idea of Byzantine civilization waiting like some odalisque in an Ottoman harem for the western orientalist to ravish and possess.

As it is with Western European writing on the "Orient" in general, so it is with almost all theological and historical analysis of Orthodoxy in the nineteenth and twentieth centuries. American and European commentators have deliberately infantilized "the East" in the course of subordinating its voice to the competing agendas of Latin Christianity, itself in a noisy state of divorce suit and counter-suit as Protestantism and Roman Catholicism emerged from the dust of the collapsing medieval Church. One of the best examples of this, which means of course a catalogue of the worst types of myopic prejudice one could ever care to read about Orthodoxy, can be found in the writings, a century ago, of British Catholic theologian Adrian Fortescue.[12]

Sadly, and ironically, this vision of waiting for the ravisher is, of course, exactly how the scholars of Eastern Europe, self-styled heirs of the Byzantine intellectual tradition at least in politics and religion, see the historical reality of Latin and Byzantine cultural relations. The pillaging of Constantinople by the Crusaders in the thirteenth century, the rape of nuns by Christian soldiers, and the desecration of churches by *stavrophore* Crusading Knights blind to anything but the possibility of plunder, left no doubt in the minds of those involved, and most Eastern European scholars ever after, that the leering eye of the ravisher-observer was but a prelude to aggressive violations—once Byzantium was sufficiently weakened militarily—designed to bring about the destruction of a venerable but now rival Christian culture whose dissonances served as an unsettling rebuttal of the new totalitarianisms of the West. It is unnerving to hear the same historic episodes recounted every time one discusses the problem of possession of churches—for example, in the current disputes between Byzantine Catholic and Orthodox claimants. Too close to home, all of this, for an Irishman who remembers the bewilderment of bitter fights in childhood England by two otherwise remarkably similar immigrant factions who seemed to be fixated on King Billy and the battle of the Boyne—another episode of colonization which the rest of the world had no knowledge of and little interest in, but which seemed to sum up the pathologies of identity dividing Catholic and Protestant Ireland all too neatly.

Returning to the example of inherent colonialism in the British tradition of Byzantine-Orthodox studies,[13] Cameron cites the example of Costas Carras, a perspicacious Greek educated in England, fed a typical baseline diet of the classics. He complains to his readers about some hilarious nonsense that almost every British child educated in grammar schools up to the 60s of the last century would have accepted as "gospel": "As was repeatedly stated, Greece was unlucky enough to have had no history of consequence between antiquity and the nineteenth century."[14] It needed a Greek in England to speak out what foolery this actually was, so fundamental an axiom had it become.

This attitude is endemic in serious studies of Orthodox history and culture. Nowhere is it more clearly witnessed than in Lecky's *History of European Morals*, published in 1869. Here is an archetypal and powerful nineteenth-century cocktail of racist xenophobia and Protestant cultural imperialism. Lecky dismisses more than a thousand years of East Roman Christian culture in tones of breathtaking pomposity: "Of the Byzantine empire, the universal verdict of history is that it constitutes, with scarcely an exception, the most thoroughly base and despicable form that civilization has yet assumed."[15] Cameron's study points out that many of the leading Byzantine scholars of the British tradition, drawn largely from a university background of classics, themselves found it necessary, for whatever psychological reasons, to deprecate the very specialization in which they most lately discovered themselves to be the lonely protagonists. Romilly Jenkins claimed to espouse a "contempt for the Byzantine tradition"[16] which he professed, and was said by Cyril Mango to have thought of it all as "a gloomy and intolerant despotism" under the "dead hand of orthodoxy."[17] Another important British Byzantinist, J. B. Bury, summed up his personal attitude in words that were, again, almost straight out of Gibbon, claiming that "Constantine inaugurated a millennium in which reason was enchained, thought was enslaved, and knowledge made no progress."[18] In his memoir of the old man, Norman Baynes describes Bury as entertaining "an ideal of scholarship which was almost glacial in its cold restraint."[19]

Cameron puts her finger on it exactly when she notes how the impatience of such cold and "positivistic" reserve can barely restrain its annoyance at the base villains and culprits—religion and romanticism. Was it not true, Bury argued, that Christianity and imaginative empathy (romantic writing) had always impeded the study of Rome?[20] So was this why Byzantium was so distasteful to the Saxon sensibility, since it combined its religion and romance with shameless enthusiasm and that perennial Greek insouciance which made of even the daily street greeting (a world apart from the reserved British "Good morning") the call *Chairete*: "Be happy!"?

A new day in scholarship

If the issue of leaving this dead pile of prejudices behind had been
made so much harder by virtue of the fact that generations of archae-
ologists, schooled in such attitudes, had literally shoveled away much
of the fabric and remains, it was made much easier by the relaxation of
the powerful grip of Western religious orthodoxies over departments
of theology and religion in the latter part of the twentieth century,
thus allowing an interest in multicultural religious thought and experience to emerge, usually in synchronicity with new methodologies
that owed much to postmodernism and postcolonialism. Classics
departments now sometimes welcome the study of Late Antiquity and
Byzantium, even if they are still generally held to have minor status as
tolerated subsets of larger fields. Most of the work being done there
remains focused on military history or socio-political organization—
seriously "secular" subjects, and, as such, properly "virile"—but several
imaginative projects took up the work of looking at monastic asceticism in new ways,[21] and the stimulus given to hagiography in Late
Antiquity proved to be a veritable shot in the arm for the languishing
state of patristics in the latter part of the twentieth century.

By the beginning of the twenty-first century, Byzantine religious
thought in the curriculum of a Western university or graduate school
was still just as rare a bird as the "gilded finches" that once sang to the
drowsy emperor, but it had been given a change of dress. It is now
sometimes called a "hot topic."[22] If it can survive such encomia it may
become a serious element of general curricula. The day may even come
when the absence of eleven hundred years of Christian political and
religious culture from the standard curricula of Western theological
history[23] will be regarded as a slight oversight needing general attention. Who knows? There have been encouraging signs, not least
among them the most fair-minded and careful exposition of Orthodox
theological history that could be wished for, in the second volume of
Jaroslav Pelikan's *Christian Tradition*. On the home front, Orthodox
theologians and historians of St Vladimir's also had an inestimable

impact, with both their teaching and their influential press. Other less weighty attempts are also worthy of note, though they had their curious moments. They were mainly from Catholics interested in ecumenism. The Dominican theologian M.-J. Le Guillou, who knew a good deal about Byzantine history, was invited by Daniel-Rops to compose an irenical volume on Orthodoxy in the *Twentieth Century Encyclopedia of Catholicism*. It was not his fault, I suppose, that the volume was sub-sectioned as Tome 14 in the subdivision entitled "Outside the Church." Le Guillou's general treatment is very appreciative and often enlightening but again, almost despite him, we are transformed into slightly dim odalisques:

> The Western Church has given [its] liturgy a note of sobriety, a very noticeable characteristic of "bareness", even of abstraction, which markedly distinguishes it from the exuberance of Eastern rites. But the emphases proper to East and West respectively do not, in fact, imply such serious and fundamental oppositions as some people make out. We repeat, generalizations are always faulty; and it must be recognized that in practice respect for rational thought is not totally lacking in the East. . . .[24]

A slightly more positive mirage of Orthodoxy and Byzantium had kept our rumor alive among non-Orthodox scholars even in darker times, of course. If not entirely escaping the allure of the exotic, generations of poets and art historians had found much to admire. Those who traveled in the Levant often came back with a lifelong passion, having seen the religious cultures and their ancient Christian art forms enduring bravely under heavy oppressions. Far from the effete decadents they had been led to expect, the first Western visitors to the vestiges of Byzantium in the Levant under Ottoman rule saw for themselves a noble example of how religious culture provided springs of long-term political resistance and nurtured aspirations of freedom even under savage repression. Sometimes the poets were the same as the adventurers—such as Byron, whose legend still has a place in the

hearts of many Greeks despite the manner in which England's politi-
cians actually did more to frustrate the *Megali Idéa*[25] than to assist it
onwards.

The poets and artists, and most recently the historians of music,
kept alive a happier mirage of Byzantium as something akin to
Tolkien's legendary Elf Kingdom in the *Lord of the Rings* trilogy—a twi-
light of lost beauty and grace, captivating in the sad mystique of its
decline. Such an image is at least more empathetic than that of the
Enlightenment *sophistes*, but can be equally misleading. The long slow
decline of Byzantium, as it has aptly been described, is full of pathos
only to those for whom it was not a reality mirrored in increased tax-
ation and the concomitant decay of urban structures and social support systems. The vision of a swansong of heartbreaking pathos is, in
other words, a retrospective threnody, not a useful category for historical analysis. Yeats, as he immured himself increasingly into mysticism and psychic experimentation, found Byzantium an increasing
attraction. He once confessed that if he could travel back to see any
time in world history, it would be to Byzantium he would go :

> I think I could find in some little wine shop some philosophical
> worker in mosaic who could answer all my questions. . . . I think
> that in early Byzantium, as maybe never before or since in recorded
> history, religious, aesthetic, and practical life were one.[26]

Maybe so. A culture that stamped its coins and loaves with the
image of the Christ had a fusion of religion and daily life unlike much
that had been before or was to be seen after in the Christian ages.
However, Yeats's mosaic worker—another mirage of the honest common man, the Fiddler of Dooney dressed in a chiton—may just as well,
in reality, have turned out to appall that effete and hypersensitive man.
Yeats did give us some memorable verses, nonetheless, and his eye for
the religious character of what he saw was uncannily well tutored. You
doubtless know the lines that describe the human condition caught
between mortality and intimations of transfiguration:

> An aged man is but a paltry thing,
> A tattered coat upon a stick, unless
> Soul clap its hands and sing, and louder sing
> For every tatter in its mortal dress,
> Nor is there singing school but studying
> Monuments of its own magnificence;
> And therefore I have sailed the seas and come
> To the holy city of Byzantium.
>
> O sages standing in God's holy fire
> As in the gold mosaic of a wall,
> Come from the holy fire, perne in a gyre,
> And be the singing-masters of my soul.
> Consume my heart away; sick with desire
> And fastened to a dying animal
> It knows not what it is; and gather me
> Into the artifice of eternity.[27]

Therefore, we may be forgiven for dallying a little with that scintillating, and kinder, mirage as expressed in Yeats's great poems on Byzantium.[28]

Yet mirage it still is, and reality calls us back. As the new academic year opens out before us I am dusting off, at Union Theological Seminary, what is to all intents and purposes the first graduate course in Byzantine thought ever offered by that venerable establishment in its 168-year history, and next year will see what I think will be the first-ever course at Columbia University, in 250 years, dedicated precisely to Byzantine religion. These facts alone bear out much of what I mentioned earlier in terms of the blind spots of cultural hegemonies, of all different types. As modern students we can also avail ourselves of the greatly expanded range of critical editions, translated primary sources, and secondary studies of some eminence and weight; resources which finally allow English-speaking readers who are not in command of late Greek and Slavic languages to approach the field with confidence and profit.

Now that we can at last draw near that field and cast our own eyes over it, we would be well advised to be suspicious of the mirage of Byzantium, "Byzantium the exotic or the decadent," and try to look soberly at what we can learn. The field is exciting enough, and certainly strange enough, without the need to rely on such febrile *phantasia* of age-old apologetics. Our engagement with the history of Byzantine and Slavic religious culture is a matter of great importance to the Orthodox, for it illuminates for us the context of our ecclesial tradition, canonical as well as dogmatic; and interpretation of the history within the matrix of the spiritual context is of paramount importance to us today if we are to resist the lapses into antiquarianism or fundamentalism that threaten the vitality of the Church.

A new sense of identity

So, if we take the lesson to heart, and start to recognize—and resist— cultural imperialism foisted upon us by pseudo-Byzantinism, what can this exercise in truth-telling reveal about the more precise aspects of our ecclesial identity? Well, "We of the East" have demonstrated the force of the Slovenian critic Slavoj Zizek's dictum that it is our own complicity in dominant ideologies that enforces them. Let us consider how the apologetic operates. One of the immediate intellectual aspects is that Orthodox theologians who desire to engage in *explicatio*—that form of ecumenical intra-Christian dialogue in books which are generally designed to be read by non-Orthodox but are, in fact, mostly read by Orthodox—tend to approach our self-definition in terms reflecting the major categories of what is presumed to be the main form of Latin Christianity. I take one example from the learned Orthodox historian Fr Demetrios Constantelos:

Western Christendom suffers from a number of dilemmas, such as the opposition of nature to grace, faith to works, the oral word to the sacrament, Scripture to Tradition, the clergy to the laity, and other theological problems. The Orthodox Church has no such dilemmas and confusions.[29]

Ah! If only!

There is much that is similar in numerous analyses by Fr Georges Florovsky too, who delighted in this gnomic style heavy with antinomies. Florovsky had a lifelong interest in ecumenical breakthrough. Part of the dynamism of his understanding of what breakthrough might involve is his resistance to the East-West motif of divided mentality. As he put it in an address to the World Council of Churches in 1960:

> The very problem of Christian reconciliation is not that of a *correlation* of parallel traditions, but precisely that of the *reintegration* of a distorted tradition. The two traditions may seem quite irreconcilable, when they are compared and confronted, as they are at the present. Yet their differences themselves are, to a great extent, simply the results of disintegration: they are, as it were, *distinctions* stiffened into *contradictions*.[30]

A significant insight, although I am not sure that any ecumenical theologian now, fifty years later, could harbor such an optimistic view of reintegration as a way forward, for the above begs the question in what sense West-European Christianity itself is today a coherently unified intellectual tradition and spiritual culture.

Nicolas Zernov ended his own study of *Eastern Christendom* with a similar subscription to the cliché of the boisterous West needing the quiet passivity of the mystical East to help it in a new age. His concluding remarks are as follows:

> One may even say that the type of civilization now regarded as Christian suffers from the defects of its excessively western outlook. . . . Compared to the stormy and invigorating history of the Christian West during the past 500 years, the Christian East seems

to Westerners to have been plunged into moral and intellectual stupor, its development arrested, its creative power exhausted. . . . Today they stand side by side, each with special contributions. The West offers its readiness to experiment, its keenness in the search for truth, and in the defense of individual freedom; the East has its trust in the guidance of the Holy Spirit, its uninterrupted tradition of teaching and worship, and its faithfulness to the corporate wisdom of past generations.[31]

Thus we see that the absorption of the colonial agenda is not simply a facet of populist Orthodox self-imagining but has entered even into the text of some eminent Anglophone Orthodox theorists. I therefore come back, at the end of this essay, to an aspiration that after colonialism can come a new sense of identity that may move us forward. No longer do we, as Orthodox, need to take upon ourselves the false moustaches and exotically weird disguises that European Christian theorists would like us to adopt. We do not aim to be the Church of the East, but know ourselves to be the Church which is the heart and soul of European Christian civilization—a *Romaiosyne* which is as broad as Christian humanity itself. Once again Fr Schmemann has anticipated me in the final words of his study of the historical road of Orthodoxy:

But just as the maintenance of Orthodox externals alone is incapable of concealing the profound crisis in modern Orthodoxy, so modernism is incapable of healing it. The only way out always lies in a return to the truth of the Church itself, and through it to a mastery of the past. In it we find the eternal tradition of the Church, as well as innumerable betrayals of it. The true Orthodox way of thought has always been historical, has always included the past, but has never been enslaved by it. Christ is "Yesterday, and today, and forever the same," and the strength of the Church is not in the past, present or future, but in Christ.[32]

This seems to me to express the essence of our hope—that at the end of generations of oppression by hostile world powers, be they religious or irreligious ones, and after recent centuries of occlusion by the intellectual and religious theorists of Latin Christianity, world Orthodoxy, increasingly with restored institutions of learning and refashioned independence and financial stability, might now begin to leave behind the agendas forced upon us by powerful others and the attitudes of suspicious hostility and sense of inadequacy that made us wish to adopt colonialist images of ourselves as reactionary conservatives.

I can also cite another luminary of St Vladimir's, Fr John Meyendorff, who forty years ago echoed a similar sentiment:

> The social and religious consequences of this migration [of Orthodoxy to Western Europe] are not yet clearly discernible, but we may venture to say that it will certainly be regarded as of great importance in the history of Christianity. The Orthodox Church has now ceased to be an exclusively Eastern Church. . . . By surmounting national differences, by training a clergy that can cope with the new conditions . . . and by their skills in reconciling a faithfulness to tradition with the needs of the modern world, the Western Orthodox can give an entirely new meaning to their witness to the faith.[33]

The truth is, Orthodoxy is simply the Church, not an exotic denomination of it which, if it learns to behave well enough and learns which spoon to use for which plate, will one day be allowed up at the table alongside the more normatively "proper" religious bodies. No, it is simply the Church, attempting simply to live the gospel. Here in this land, in this time, we are not immigrants, we are Orthodox Americans, and just as in all times the Church has dissolved the narrowness of nationalism so that Jew and Greek became something else in Christ. We are no longer poor and uncultured migrants, if we ever were, just as in the Church of Christ there is, or should be, no rich and no poor, only disciples seeking to divest themselves of all that stands in opposition to the call of the poor Lord whose poverty so enriched the world. Our liturgy is no more exotic than the sight of elephants ascending the steps of New York's Cathedral of St John the Divine for the Feast of St Francis—indeed less so; no more exotic than dancers swinging across Presbyterian chapel rafters on purple silk hangings, as I have watched in wonderment—indeed less so in its sober and repetitive rhythms meant to induce the consciousness of prayer.

Our awareness of being the Church is not so fragile and fearful that we need to deny the self-evident truth of the varieties of authentic Christian experience in many lively forms around us. Our theology is not changeless and immobile, as if it were a bottle of dogmas fixed in pickling fluid. We know what our dogmatic tradition is, certainly, and because of its evangelical, patristic, and canonical rootedness it is not vulnerable to the ebb and flow of every strand of theory that passes us by. Nevertheless, our theology is not reducible to dogma—as we all know when we reflect on the reality of our real Orthodox experience rather than on the perception of Orthodox identity that others wish to impress upon us apologetically while dismissing us as reactionary conservatives.

Our true theology is to witness, by the ever-present grace of God, an irrefragable bond between our understanding of reality and our way of life—the perfect conformity of our heart and our mind to the spirit of Christ as elaborated in the gospel. This is something that is at once intimately personal and radically social. As Archbishop Tutu once said, "When people tell me that religion and politics do not mix, I wonder which Bible they have been reading."[34] This is the existential experience of being the Church. It is the totality of the Orthodox destiny. It is not exotic, but mystically wonderful and simultaneously so practical that it will renew the face of the earth by being able to speak honestly and cogently to its pain. It is a Christian consciousness that will renew the very springs of personal life and renew the image of what a true Christian political culture would look like.

We have much to aspire to, and in that reaching out to be ourselves, much to contribute to our country and our world as Orthodox. We make a good start by throwing off the orientalist costume and disguises that have pleased so many of our partners in dialogues past.

Notes

[1]September 14, 2003, the day on which this lecture was delivered, was the Feast of the Exaltation of the Cross, when we celebrated the raising of the Cross over Europe by Constantine and Helena, and then again by Heraclius, in defiance of those who would have wished to see it thrown down permanently as a symbol of European identity. We were gathered in the beautiful new Metropolitan Philip Auditorium at St Vladimir's Orthodox Theological Seminary, which, together with the new library, is another sign of anabasis, exaltation or "raising up," a material sign of the ongoing vitality of the seminary and of its *prokope* or progress into the future—a powerful symbol of hope for the future of Orthodox life and culture in America.

[2]A. Schmemann, *The Historical Road of Eastern Orthodoxy* (New York: Holt, Rinehart and Winston, 1963), 338.

[3]S. Huntington, *The Clash of Civilizations and the Remaking of World Order* (New York: Simon and Schuster, 1998).

[4]V. Clarke, *Why Angels Fall: A Journey Through Orthodox Europe, from Byzantium to Kosovo* (New York: St Martin's Press, 2000).

[5]See J. A. McGuckin, "Variations on a Theme: Monasticism in the Latin & Byzantine Experience." *Medieval Life* 2 (Spring 1995): 5–8, and ibid., 3 (Autumn 1995): 3–5.

[6]A modern term now being used by scholars of Christian origins to try to gain some respect from classicists who for long years have wished to rule out the study of Christian polity in antiquity, from the core curriculum of "classics" and the "pure" classical period.

[7]Charles de Secondat Montesquieu, *Considerations on the Greatness and Decadence of the Romans* (Paris, 1734).

[8]E. Gibbon, *The Decline and Fall of the Roman Empire*, edited by J. B. Bury. (London: Methuen, 1896), 2:159.

[9]In his day, following on classical prototypes, the ascription of "shameful passivity" was a code word for homosexuality, seen as a deviation from the "manly virile norm," which was (needless to say) all "active." The designations of passive (female, homosexual), as distinct from active (male, virile) virtues was a classical pre-Christian Roman ideology which Gibbon continued undiluted as a "norm" of what was good or bad in his philosophy of history. Warrior leaders were virile, and good. Monkish leaders were passive, and bad. The church (generally a bad thing) was ubiquitously monkish (a really bad thing) and thus a major force of the decline of Rome (generally virile and thus a good thing). The military rulers, who opposed the debilitating influence of the Church, were his heroes. Readers who detect a striking resemblance between this and that caricature

of "history writing" presented by W. C. Sellar and R. J. Yeatman in *1066 And All That. A Memorable History of England* (London: Methuen & Co., 1935) may not be mistaken.

¹⁰See E. Said, *Orientalism* (London: Routledge & Kegan Paul, 1978), 326.

¹¹I would specify it further as involving racist and imperialist attitudes that still continued to dominate British scholarly imagination decades after the Suez fiasco had made it clear (at least to the rest of the world) that the British Empire was certainly over, and even the age of the colonies was fast coming to its nadir. I speak conscious of the fact that the last colony, Northern Ireland, yet remains to be dismissed: a fate that will doubtless soon be afforded it now that it has lost any strategic or economic significance for Britain.

¹²Numerous instances abound in his book, A. Fortescue, *The Orthodox Eastern Church* (London: Catholic Truth Society, 1907), 429–39. His account of how the Orthodox patriarchs in 1894, the time of Leo XIII, rejected the Pope's offer for reunion despite the fact that the papacy had guaranteed to provide for all their "customs" "without narrowness" contrasts the noble and disinterested attitude of the Pope with the ungentlemanly "discourtesy" of the Ecumenical Patriarch who had the temerity to suggest Rome had a misplaced sense of its authority.

¹³Byzantine civilization had long been the preserve of the Slavic scholars, but then moved into western Europe with excellent French and German efforts. This paper looks only to the English scene, later in getting off the ground, and (as was often the case with British scholarship) covering over its slow pace with impenetrable and unassailable self-confidence.

¹⁴C. Carras, *Three Thousand Years of Greek Identity* (Athens: Domus, 1983). Cited in Averil Cameron, *The Use and Abuse of Byzantium: An Essay on Reception*. Inaugural Lecture for the Chair of Late Antique and Byzantine Studies. (Kings College, London: The School of Humanities, 1992).

¹⁵Cited in Romilly Jenkins, *Byzantium: The Imperial Centuries* (London: Weidenfeld and Nicolson, 1966), 1. Lecky was almost cocktail-shaking together all the prejudices of the Enlightenment scholars Gibbon, Voltaire, and Montesquieu. The first described Byzantine culture as: "The triumph of barbarism and Christianity"; the second as: "A worthless collection of oracles and miracles"; and the third as: "A tragic epilogue to the glory of Rome."

¹⁶Romilly Jenkins, "The Hellenistic Origins of Byzantine Literature." *Dumbarton Oaks Papers* 17 (1963): 37–52. Cited in Cameron (1992), 9.

¹⁷See Mango's memoir of Romilly Jenkins in *Dumbarton Oaks Papers* 23–24 (1969–1970): 7–13.

¹⁸See N. H. Baynes, *A Bibliography of J. B. Bury* (Cambridge: Cambridge UP, 1929), 21.

¹⁹Ibid., 48.

²⁰Cameron (1992), 9, citing Baynes (1929), 60.

²¹Notable instances are the Evergetis project under Margaret Mullett's guidance at Queens, Belfast; and the Asceticism conference convened in 1993 at Union Theological Seminary, New York, whose papers are now published as R. Valantasis & V. Wimbush,

eds. *Asceticism* (Oxford: Oxford UP, 1995).

[22]So it was described by external *periti* assessing the curriculum of the "New Union" in the summer of 2002.

[23]For whatever else it is, Byzantium is integral to the history of the West, formative and constitutive for the history of western Europe.

[24]M.-J. Le Guillou, *The Spirit of Eastern Orthodoxy* (New York: Hawthorne Books, 1962), 137.

[25]The concept of a restored Greek-speaking Christian civilization, with Constantinople as its restored capital, reclaiming Europe as a Christian bloc. The "Megali Idéa" fell in the dust of Smyrna in 1922, but still raises its head every now and again—most recently in Cyprus in the mid-seventies, and the Balkans in the nineties—both with disastrous results.

[26]Cited by T. R. Henn, *The Lonely Tower: Studies in the Poetry of W.B. Yeats* (London: Methuen, 1965), 150.

[27]"Sailing to Byzantium," stanzas 2 and part of 3.

[28]"Sailing to Byzantium" from his collection *The Tower,* of 1928, and "Byzantium" from his collection *The Winding Stair,* of 1933.

[29]D. Constantelos, *The Greek Orthodox Church: Faith History and Practice* (New York: Seabury Press, 1967), 108.

[30]G. Florovsky, "The Ethos of the Orthodox Church." In *Orthodox: A Faith and Order Dialogue.* Faith and Order Paper No. 30, 50 (Geneva: WCC, 1960).

[31]N. Zernov, *Eastern Christendom: A Study of the Origin and Development of the Eastern Orthodox Church* (London: Widenfeld and Nicolson, 1961), 300.

[32]A. Schmemann, *The Historical Road of Eastern Orthodoxy* (New York: Holt, Rinehart and Winston, 1963), 341.

[33]J. Meyendorff, *The Orthodox Church* (New York: Pantheon Books, 1962), 231.

[34]In an address in South Africa before the dismantling of Apartheid: an event he looked forward to then merely in hope, but with an anticipation of victory that derived from his deep Christian faith.

The Patriarchate of
Constantinople and the State

SPEROS VRYONIS, JR.*

*T*HE SUBJECT OF THIS ESSAY has been characterized by lively scholarly discussion and often by adversarial animus that has overflowed into the realm of political life. The relations of religion and the secular authority are of great concern today to Americans, in both internal and external politics of the American democracy. The American secular government has formally separated church and state, but is in effect under constant pressure to erase the fine line that separates them. Historically, Christianity, Islam, and Judaism, the three primary monotheistic religions, have been so thoroughly integrated into the functioning of their ancient, medieval, and even their modern societies that in varying degrees they have had a profound influence on both the state and the local cultures.

In the case of the Patriarchate of Constantinople, its relations with the state have had a long, complex, and fascinating history from the time of the conversion of Constantine the Great in the early fourth century down to the present day. My examination of this relationship will operate at a historical level rather than on the levels of faith and theology.

The conversion of Constantine after the battle of the Milvian Bridge resulted, by the end of the fourth century, in the adoption by

*Speros Vryonis, Jr. is the Alexander S. Onassis Professor of Hellenic Civilization and Culture Emeritus at New York University. His lecture was delivered on October 18, 2003, at the Annunciation Cathedral of San Francisco, California.

Theodosius I of Christianity as the official religion of the Byzantine state. Polytheism and, eventually, heresies were forbidden by imperial legislation that prescribed lethal or highly injurious penalties on all those who persevered in their ancient religions. The fact that the Byzantine emperors thus became the custodians of the church attains profound historical significance in the relations of the Patriarchate to the emperor.

The emperor and the imperial cult

In the past, scholars characterized the relations of the Byzantine state and the Patriarchate as constituting "caesaropapism." The entry in the *Oxford Dictionary of Byzantium* under this term states: "The term has been rejected by most scholars as a misleading and inaccurate interpretation of Byzantine political reality. . . . The church insistently defended its ideological independence. . . . In sum, the term caesaropapism altogether exaggerates the degree of actual control of the church by the state."[1]

What then, historically and theoretically, was the position of the patriarchs and the church in the face of the Byzantine emperors and their government? This is only the first phase of the question, for with the destruction of the Byzantine Empire by the Ottoman Turks, the relation of patriarchs and emperors ended, to be replaced by the relation of all subsequent patriarchs to the Ottoman sultans. This, in turn, was terminated when Mustafa Kemal Atatürk put an end to both the Ottoman Sultanate and Caliphate in the first half of the decade of the 1920s. Thereafter, the patriarchs had to deal with the modern Turkish state. Though each successive change of political masters brought many differing consequences, the basic question remained that of the relation of the Patriarchate to the state.

When Constantine converted to Christianity, he began a series of imperial pronouncements on behalf of the church. These suddenly transformed the position of Christianity from one of periodic persecution to that of favored status. He bestowed a substantial tax immunity on the clergy, gave gifts, and eventually subsidized church buildings. By the mid-fifth century this had culminated in a plethora of imperial legislation that led to the severe punishment of all pagans.

The emperor in Roman times had served as the supreme priest of the pagan cult, with the title of *pontifex maximus*. The Byzantine imperial theory was all embracing and made of the emperor the supreme ruler in all matters. This had been buttressed by classical and Hellenistic political theory, as well as by the deification of the emperor. All this was strengthened by the legal opinions of the Roman jurisprudents, and was finally fixed by Justinian's codification of Roman and customary law.[2]

The emperor stood, literally, atop the law and legislation. His authority was absolute and incontestable. In the middle Byzantine Greek version of Justinian's Codex we read the following two statements: "That which is pleasing to the emperor is law;" and "The later rescripts prevail over those that came before them." The *Basilica* note: "The emperor is not subject to the laws." Both the Theodosian and Justinianic Codes state that any dispute concerning an imperial judgment or law is sacrilege, as obviously the laws came to the emperor from God.[3]

Worship of the deified emperor was an aspect of late Roman paganism the earlier Christians had resisted to the point of martyrdom. It is remarkable that the church, in seeking the protection, patronage, and intervention of Constantine the Great, indulged itself in the cult of the emperor. What then was this imperial cult in Byzantine times, and what, if any, was its relation to the cults of deified emperors in Roman and Hellenistic times?

Origen, and after him Eusebius of Caesarea, the important church historian of the fourth century, led the way in making the imperial cult more palatable and acceptable to the Christians of Constantine's domain. In his *Preparatio Evangelica*, Eusebius declared that God had created the Roman Empire in order to do away with political polyarchy and to prepare the way for Christianity and the evolution from polytheism to monotheism. By the time of Constantine the cult of the emperor was associated with the supposed divine nature or character of the imperial office. It was thus that Justinian in his legislation described disobedience to the imperial law as sacrilege. Conversely, the religious offence of heresy was treated politically. The church often called upon the emperor to enforce punishment on heretics as an action proper to the imperial rather than to the patriarchal office.[4]

The cult of the emperor was marked by many of the trappings of divinity as they had developed by the late third and fourth century. In Greek, the official epithet that described the emperor, the parts of his body, his thought, his empress, his palace, his coinage, etc., was *theios, theia, theion*—divine. It is interesting to note that this important word has no entry in the *Oxford Dictionary of Byzantium* nor is it mentioned under the entry "emperor." Yet, the man who succeeded to the throne, once properly enthroned, acclaimed by the senate and the people, and crowned by the patriarch, was, in the eyes of the Greek speakers, *theoprovletos*—ordained or put forward by God—not unlike the classical Chinese theory of the imperial mandate of heaven. The eleventh-century general Katakolon Kekaumenos writes, in a book dedicated to the emperor, "O holy lord, God promoted you to the imperial rule, and by His divine grace . . . he made you a god on earth to do and make what you decide."[5] Theophylact, archbishop of Ohrid, wrote that "every emperor is an image of God." Emperor Romanos IV Diogenes, after his defeat, capture, and release by the Turkish sultan Alp Arslan in 1071, progressed, says the historian Attaleiates, "through the very villages and lands in which formerly he had [progressed] with the imperial bodyguard and [in which] he had been regarded as the equal of God (*isotheos*)."[6] When Nikephoros Botaneiates was declared emperor in Nicaea in 1078, the imperial guards of the palace in Constantinople sent him a message to hasten his arrival "as that of a true god."[7]

In short, the imperial theory included an intimate association of each emperor with God, to the degree that he enjoyed the epithets of divinity. Many of the authors who used this language were themselves bishops, metropolitans, and patriarchs. How far had the church come (or gone) in its stance as to the divinity of the emperor?

Relation of patriarch to emperor

The actual relation of the patriarch to the emperor can be gauged best by the historical unfolding of these relations in periods of particular stress and strain.

The question whether the relations of church and state were characterized by caesaropapism cannot be judged merely on the basis of the documentation that describes these relations in the abstract. Undoubtedly, this theoretical material is important, but it has to be interpreted within the context of historical deeds of rulers and ecclesiastical hierarchs. To the degree that the patriarchs, the ecumenical councils, and the patriarchal synod were intertwined with the political policies and needs of the ruler, the church was in certain respects not purely and merely a religious institution. It was also a political institution that developed an immense administrative structure, parallel to that of the imperial bureaucracy, which operated throughout the great rural and urban extent of the empire. Its economic needs were thus great in order to pay its bureaucracy and to support its institutions and their multifaceted functions. Finally, it had its own legal system and regulations that constituted the body of canon law. Justinian had already given the canons the force of Byzantine law by providing them a status in his legal corpus.

The relation of the patriarch and the emperor was always close. Generally the election of a patriarch operated through both the patriarchal synod and the emperor in a process by which the synod selected the names of three candidates and the emperor chose one from the three. Eventually the emperor announced the election in the imperial palace, just across the street from the church of St Sophia and the palace of the patriarch, and then invested him. Eventually the ceremony of enthronement took place in St Sophia, where the emperor

invested him with the patriarchal insignia and the metropolitan of
Herakleia carried out the consecration. This showed that the role of
the emperor was essential, as the candidate could not attain the patriarchal office without the approval of the emperor. At the same time,
however, the approval of the synod was considered important, and
those who insisted on this could bring schism within the church
should the appointment proceed without synodal approval. Nevertheless, the historical realities were different. The emperor could
ignore the three candidates proposed by the patriarchal synod and
choose his own man, and often the synod approved; in other cases it
became the cause of an ecclesiastical schism. However, even here this
was eventually healed by the exercise of the principle of *oikonomia*.

A few celebrated cases of successful imperial intervention in the
appointment and removal of patriarchs will suffice to underscore the
principle that imperial authority extended beyond that of both patriarchs and synods, and that reasons of state were dominant in the relations of church and state.[8]

Emperors in charge

The seven ecumenical councils acknowledged by the Byzantine
church were all called by the emperors or empresses; all were either
attended by them or by their representatives. For the most part, the
acts of these councils seem to have been signed by the rulers. Their
interests and involvement with the lesser councils and particular
meetings of the patriarchal synods that affected the imperial interests
were also occasions in which imperial authority made its forceful presence a factor.

Much in this pattern was established when the church appealed to
Constantine the Great to heal both the problem occasioned in the
North African Church by the Donatists and the problem of Arius and
Arianism in the eastern half of the church. Thereafter, the official
orthodox position in the Trinitarian and Christological discussions

and divisions was settled similarly, as were the Monothelite and Icon-oclastic controversies. If one takes a historical approach to an understanding of the interplay of imperial authority and patriarchal and synodal theology, the pattern is, for the most part, clear. The imperial choice in such matters was decisive. When Constantius opted for an Arian "Trinity," he forced that doctrine on two large synods. When Theodosius called the Second Ecumenical Council in Constantinople in 381, Arianism was condemned and the see of Constantinople was elevated to a higher standing in the hierarchy of the great churches on the grounds that it was the New Rome.

When Justinian I attempted to bring the Monophysites within the larger camp of the Chalcedonians, he put forth his theological solution of Aphthartodocetism. When the patriarch Eutychios manifested his opposition, the emperor had him removed and sent him into exile in 558. The case of the long theological dispute over religious images exemplifies the importance of imperial positions in religious decisions. In these cases, imperial political interests demanded particular theologies, and it was these theologies that predominated.

By the time of the Council in Trullo (691–692), called by Emperor Justinian II, the practice of embellishing churches and personal worship with painted images had become one of the dominant signs of Christianity in the Byzantine Empire, as it still is among Orthodox Christians today. The Council in Trullo issued a canon requiring Christ to be depicted as a human, not symbolically as a lamb. This was justified on the Christological grounds that Christ was not only divine but also human, so to this degree he could be depicted physically in religious art.

All the while, there were voices from within the Church that, remembering the Mosaic prohibition against the making of images, objected to the widespread popular belief in the power of the images or icons. This came to a political head when Emperor Leo III issued an edict calling for the destruction of icons and religious images. When Patriarch Germanos I refused to sanction the edict, Leo promptly removed him and appointed his own patriarch, Anastasios.

When Leo's son, Constantine V, called the iconoclastic council at Heieria in 754, icons were formally condemned as the synod and the assembled representatives of the patriarchates in Arab lands succumbed to the wishes of the emperor, and obeisant patriarchs succeeded Anastasios in unbroken line.

All of this was temporarily reversed by the accession to the throne of Empress Irene. After appointing the layman Tarasios as patriarch, Irene planned a council, known to history as the Seventh Ecumenical Council (Nicaea 787), which condemned, chapter-by-chapter, the decrees of the council of Heieria, and the icons were restored. It was a difficult process, as Iconoclasm had taken root in many quarters. Thus, when Leo V succeeded to the throne in 813, he was determined to resurrect the council of 754 and the iconoclastic policies. Since Patriarch Nikephoros I refused to comply, the emperor removed and exiled him and appointed a new patriarch, Theodotos, in 815. At a synod in St Sophia the council of 754 was restored and the Council of Nicaea (787) was condemned. Twenty-eight years later Empress Theodora decided to restore the icons and to condemn the iconoclastic council. She removed the recalcitrant iconoclast Patriarch John VII, and the next day elected as his successor Methodios, who was enthroned only one week later. The Council of Nicaea was finally restored and the council of Heieria and Iconoclasm finally condemned. What is of interest here, in the relation of patriarchs and rulers, is the fact that the emperors controlled, made, and unmade patriarchs, with or without synodal approval, in order to promote their policies in theology.

I have examined this sampling of evidence in a historical and not in a theological manner. To speak of Iconoclasm as a heresy is historically justified only at the time of the first or the second imperial and synodal condemnation of the doctrine. It became a heresy only after the fact of its official condemnations by the state and the synod. Though the Studites and other monks steadfastly opposed Iconoclasm, they ultimately depended on the imperial power to settle the issue, as they did not have the power to do so as a religious body or party. As for the power of the state over both patriarchs and synods, the evidence speaks eloquently. Emperors and empresses made and unmade patriarchs, they controlled synods, and they set the program of theological choices.

Succession to the throne

Theology in a political theocracy, such as Byzantium, was a matter that concerned the state. Nevertheless, the control of the Church, at least of the patriarchs and the synods, was a matter of concern for the Byzantine rulers in other areas as well. Dynastic politics and succession to the throne once more brought the patriarchs and synod within imperial control. After the regularization of a coronation ceremony in St Sophia, where the patriarch crowned the emperor, patriarchal consent became an important element in legitimate accession to the throne. Accordingly, a recalcitrant patriarch—recalcitrant for whatever reason—was a problem for the emperor-elect. Emperor Leo VI was singularly unfortunate in that his wives (three) died early, without leaving him a male heir. He then lived with his concubine, Zoe Kabronopsina, who gave him a son, Constantine, but the patriarch Nicholas Mystikos refused to allow a fourth marriage since it was contrary to the canons. In early 907 the emperor deposed the patriarch, replaced him with Euthymios, and the fourth marriage was acknowledged according to the practice of *oikonomia*. The fourth marriage had been a political and dynastic necessity, inasmuch as the Macedonian dynasty would have had no male succession. Eventually, in 912, Nicholas Mystikos was allowed to return to the patriarchal see. This episode is of further interest in that it involves not only the relation of the emperor to the Church, but more specifically it involves the relation, if any, of the emperor to the church canons, for it was the canons that forbade fourth marriages.

The power of the patriarch lay in the ability to withhold coronation or legitimacy of the dynasty, which we see in the violent case of

Michael VIII Palaiologos and the establishment of Byzantium's last imperial dynasty. Michael Palaiologos was a man of inordinate and ruthless ambition and a competent soldier and ruler. He managed to murder the regent of the young emperor, John IV Laskaris, and after having made himself regent, declared himself co-emperor and was successfully crowned in early 1259. After he reconquered Constantinople from the Latins and had been crowned a second time, this time in St Sophia, he had the young emperor John IV blinded, upon which Patriarch Arsenios excommunicated him. Eventually Michael Palaiologos had the patriarchal synod depose Arsenios (1265) and replaced him with Joseph I. The followers of Arsenios, the Arsenites, refused to recognize Joseph and all his successors until the schism was healed in 1310. Until this final healing, the schism had political consequences in Asia Minor, rendering questionable the loyalty of many to the new dynasty. In any case, the emperor found that as the present patriarch was "uncooperative," a new one would do just as well. The synod, and therefore the patriarch, were thus under the control of the emperor.

One last example, that of the politically ambitious patriarch, Michael Keroullarios (1043–58), illustrates clearly that the patriarch was indeed a political as well as a religious figure and leader. Arrested for conspiracy to seize the imperial throne (1041–42), he was eventually forced to don monastic garb, and in 1043 Emperor Constantine IX saw to his appointment as patriarch. He attempted to dictate government policy in the short reigns of Theodora and of Michael VI, and succeeded in acquiring a central position in the government of Isaak I Komnenos. For when Isaak revolted, successfully in the Anatolian provinces, Keroullarios then took control of the city after having roused the citizens to revolution, and transferred government to St Sophia until Isaak Komnenos should enter the city.

His rewards after he crowned the new emperor were considerable—direct administration of the enormous wealth of the St Sophia church was turned over to him, and his two nephews were given important offices in the court. Nevertheless, these felicitous relations with the emperor soon soured, as Keroullarios increasingly admonished and pressured Isaak in governmental policies. He began to wear imperial regalia (the purple boots) and to harangue the emperor that the *sacerdotium* was superior, in power, to the *imperium*. He then threatened to destroy the emperor if the latter did not heed his advice, quoting a folk saying in the vernacular, "I built you, O Oven, and I shall destroy you."

The emperor did not dare to arrest him in the city, as Keroullarios enjoyed great popularity among the Constantinopolitans, so he waited for an occasion when the patriarch would exit from the city walls so he might arrest him outside. This presented itself in November 1058, on the feast of the Archangel, when Keroullarios proceeded to a monastic foundation outside the city. The Varangian Guard arrested him, along with his two nephews, and they ended up on the island of Imbros, there to await their fate. Isaak was aided in his successful efforts to depose the patriarch by members of the court and by metropolitans who were part of the patriarchal synod. The president of the senate, the famous intellectual figure Psellos, was ordered to prepare the indictment which was to be leveled against Keroullarios at the synod. The unfortunate patriarch died, probably as a result of the rough handling that was meted out by the Varangians, so was at least spared the lengthy indictment that Psellos had prepared. There is a hint that Keroullarios was aware of the legend of Constantine the Great and his supposed cure of leprosy by Pope Sylvester, a pious forgery, which began to figure in papal claims to authority in the Middle Ages. According to this fiction, Constantine had given Sylvester, among other things, imperial insignia and other privileges. It is interesting that in the quarrel between Rome and Constantinople, the papal representative, Cardinal Humbert, had given Keroullarios a copy of the Donation of Constantine.

The political nature of the Patriarchate is thoroughly revealed in this fifteen-year career of an aristocratic political adventurist. He became patriarch after a failed political sedition. The solution was the usual method of arrest, deposition, and removal. Isaak promoted his own first minister, Leichoudes, to the patriarchal throne and so was freed of patriarchal threats and political activity.

Latin and Ottoman threats

In the declining centuries of Paleologian rule, and in face first of the threat of a late Latin crusade (that of the Angevins), and then of the far greater threat of the Ottomans, matters of ecclesiastical governance and theological and liturgical content became, once more, of primary importance to both emperors and patriarchal synods. The efforts of Michael VIII Palaiologos to resuscitate the fatally truncated Byzantine Empire relied increasingly on diplomacy. Faced with Latin and Ottoman threats, the emperors attempted to obtain papal and Western support. The only bargaining chip in the hands of the emperors was the offer of the union of the Western and Byzantine churches in return for financial and military help in their uneven struggles with the empire's foes.

The story is well known to scholars and students of Byzantine civilization. It is sufficient for the purpose of further elucidating the nature of the relations between the Patriarchate and the Byzantine state to note that for diplomatic reasons and because of the fast approaching end of the Byzantine Empire, the rulers of the state had to conclude two major agreements as to the union of the churches, first by Michael VIII Palaiologos at the Council of Lyons (1274) and then by John VIII Palaiologos at the Council of Ferrara-Florence (1438–39). When the patriarch did not sign the agreement of 1274, he resigned, and was deposed soon thereafter by the synod. The synod elected in his place the pro-unionist John Bekkos. Though the later patriarch, Joseph II, favored the union at Ferrara-Florence, the last years of the empire's existence were so chaotic and the empire so weak that the consent by this time was of little value. The judge, George Scholarios, had been an active unionist at the council, but on his return to Constantinople he repudiated his consent to the union, became its hardiest opponent, and as a result was finally chosen by the Ottoman sultan, Mehmed II, as the first patriarch in Ottoman Istanbul.[9]

Within the ornate political theory of the Byzantine theocracy, the emperor was a "divine" personage with a special relation to God. He

was, according to the many statements of secular and religious theorists, *theios*, divine, as he was appointed by God. His mere wish or
statement constituted a law that prevailed over all previous law, he was
above the law and not bound by it. The twelfth-century Patriarch of
Antioch and specialist on the ecclesiastical canons, Theodore Balsamon, explained in his comments on the vast body of canons that the
emperor is not bound by the canons as he is greater than, and above,
them.[10] Perhaps the most interesting statement of a churchman on
this matter occurs in the well-known letter of Patriarch Antony IV to
Basil, the grand prince of Moscow, in 1393. The latter had excluded the
commemoration of the Byzantine emperor in the diptychs of the
Russian churches, and the patriarch chides him for this:

> You say that, "We have a church, but neither have we an emperor,
> nor do we reckon one. . . ." For Christians [replied Antony] it is not
> possible to have a church and not to have an emperor, for the
> empire and the church have a great unity and commonality, and it
> is impossible to separate them.[11]

Theophylact, the eleventh-century archbishop of Ohrid, expresses
the matter somewhat more forcibly in his book of admonitions to the
imperial prince Constantine:

> A true king, knowing that his throne should have a firm founda-
> tion, just as the substructure of a house or a church should be firm,
> makes religion his corner stone. He cultivates it so much that he
> does not yield the primacy even to the clergy; for he acts and
> speaks, at all times, as one who surely knows that God sees and
> hears all things. . . . Wherefore God will be all in all to him—father
> and brother; soldier and fellow-fighter.[12]

The continuing issue

As indicated at the beginning of this essay, the question of the relation of the Patriarchate and the state did not come to an end when
Mehmed II successfully besieged Constantinople and destroyed the
last remnants of the Byzantine Empire, putting an end to the imperial dynasty as well, on May 29, 1453. Inasmuch as Islamic political
theory and practice brought with them a place/institution for non-
Muslims in the political, religious, and social structures of the Muslim imperial state, relations between the Patriarchate and the state
continued, but under radically different conditions and circumstances, including the imposition of a diminished status of Christianity and of local Christians.

Resulting relations between the patriarch and the state of the sultans and then the state of modern Turkey had none of the redeeming
features of the regime of the Byzantine emperors. The latter's firm
control of the Church was accompanied by a literary and artistic flour-
ishing, and saw to it that the eleemosynary institutions of the Patriarchate played an essential role in Orthodox society. The Turkish
conquests of Asia Minor, in particular, brought the large-scale
destruction of the Church and the massive Islamic forced conversion
of the former Greek-speaking Christians. The Ottoman conquests in
the Balkans were far less destructive. Nevertheless, within one century most important urban centers in the Ottoman-held Balkans had
become predominantly Muslim, and the majority of the churches and
church properties had been confiscated by the conquerors.[13] The average length of patriarchal appointment for the next four hundred years
was less than three years, and the Patriarchate was increasingly bur-
dened by debt.

Notes

[1]*Oxford Dictionary of Byzantium*, "Caesaropapism," 1:364–365.

[2]For an excellent analysis of these factors, see Milton V. Anastos, "Byzantine Political Theory: Its Classical Precedents and Legal Embodiment," in S. Vryonis, ed., *The 'Past' in Medieval and Modern Greek Culture* (Malibu, 1978), 13–54.

[3]For the Greek texts, S. Vryonis, "Studies in Byzantine Institutions, Society, and Culture." *I: Institutions and Society* (Malibu, 1997), 3–23.

[4]O. Treitinger, *Die oströmische Kaiser-und Reichsidee nach ihrer Gestaltung im höfischen Zeremoniell: Vom oströmischen Staats-und Reichsdedanken* (Darmstadt, 1969).

[5]*Cecaumeni Strategicon et incerti scriptoris de officiis regiis libellus*. B. Wassiliewsky and V. Jernstedt, eds. (St Petersburg, 1896), 93.

[6]Michael Attaleiates, ed., *Historia* (Bonn, 1853), 175.

[7]Attaleiates (1853), 272.

[8]For the examples of this imperial authority over the church, see the references and analyses of Joan Hussey, *The Orthodox Church in the Byzantine Empire* (Oxford, 1986).

[9]*Oxford Dictionary of Byzantium*, "Lyons, Second Council of," vol. 2, 1259. V. Laurent J. Darrouzes, *Dossier grec de l'Union de Lyon, 1273–1777* (Paris, 1976).

[10]*Balsamon*, G. A. Rhalles and M. Potles, *Syntagma tōn theiōn kai ierōn kanonōn*, 6 vols. (Athens, 1852–59), 3:349–50.

[11]John Meyendorff, *Byzantium and the Rise of Russia* (Crestwood, 1981), 11–12. The text is in F. Miklosich and J. Müller, eds., Acta Patriarchatus Constantinopoli, vol. 2, *Acta et diplomata graeca medii aevi sacra et profana*, 6 vols. (Vienna, 1860–90), 188–192.

[12]Theophylaktos as translated in Ernest Barker, *Social and Political Thought in Byzantium* (Oxford, 1957), 147.

[13]Vryonis, *The Decline of Medieval Hellenism in Asia Minor and the Process of Islamization from the Eleventh through the Fifteenth Century* (Berkeley, 1971).

The Orthodox Frontier of Faith

James H. Billington*

*L*ATE ONE AUTUMN NIGHT in 1778 a white Protestant adventurer from Connecticut, Captain John Ledyard, was taken face down in a fragile skin canoe by natives whose language he did not understand toward a large open space crowded with people, where he fully expected to be killed, if not cannibalized. Ledyard was the advance scout for Captain James Cook's third and last voyage of discovery in the Pacific. Many early explorers like him had been killed in such circumstances, but Captain Ledyard was in for what he described in his diary as a joyful surprise. He was being welcomed by hospitable Christian Indians, who immediately took him to celebrate a large meal and then a vespers service not unlike the one this evening for another Connecticut adventurer. Ledyard records in his diaries that

> they said prayers after the manner of the Greek church. I could not
> but observe with what particular satisfaction the Indians performed
> their devoirs to God. And with what pleasure they went through the
> multiple of ceremonies attended on that sort of worship.[1]

He was the first American to land on Alaska, the first contact between a citizen of the new United States and the Orthodox Church. And the mixture of unexpected joy—itself a term used to describe some of the most beautiful icons of Russian Orthodoxy—with a certain amount of

---

*James H. Billington has served as Librarian of Congress since 1987. He is the author of several books on Russian culture. This lecture was delivered on November 20, 2003, at Bridwell Library, Southern Methodist University.

bewilderment about the nature of the service he was watching, has more or less persisted over the years in the Western understanding of Eastern Orthodoxy. We honor now another one-time Protestant from Connecticut who has done so much to integrate the rich history of Eastern Orthodoxy into the broader understanding of Christianity.

I will trace briefly how Orthodox Christianity came to North America. It was a long journey from the eastern Mediterranean to the western Pacific—from the scorching Egyptian desert to polar Alaska. It is largely a Russian story, appropriately recounted in Texas because it is also the story of the opening of a frontier: the great, neglected eastern frontier of European and Christian civilization. On the surface, this frontier was the wild East, no less violent and venal than our Wild West. However, at a deeper level it was a tale of a religious people building a new, multiethnic civilization in an outlying and sparsely populated region.

The story particularly interests me at this time in my capacity as Librarian of Congress because of three projects currently under way at the Library. The first of these is a recording we have recently made at our Cairo office of the yearlong cycle of the Coptic liturgical legacy— the oldest surviving Christian liturgy. The second is the Lewis and Clark Exhibition we have developed for the bicentennial of that great voyage of frontier discovery. We have included in it our newest acquisition, the Waldseemüller Map, the first map of the New World and the first document of any kind that has the word "America" on it. And finally, we have a digital project with the Russians called "Meeting of the Frontiers" that is putting online primary documents from all kinds of Russian institutions to tell the parallel story of how the two frontiers, Russian and American, extended European civilization east and west, met in Alaska, and stretched all the way down to Fort Ross on the Russian River just north of San Francisco. There are many interesting parallels between these two frontiers.

Franz Kafka wrote a haunting letter to the German poet Rainer Maria Rilke saying that the early fathers of the church could go into the desert because they had richness in their hearts, but that with all the riches now in Europe we have brought the desert into our hearts. He was writing on the eve of World War I, the time of the breaking of empires. The one empire that did *not* break up then, but rather recon-solidated itself with a new name and became even stronger after World War II than after World War I was, of course, Russia.

The U.S.S.R. proved more imperial than its predecessors, but with the ultimate desert of atheism built into its heart. That Soviet empire miraculously fell, but not entirely; and the desert was re-fertilized with its Orthodox faith, but not entirely. The ongoing struggle today for the soul and the future of Russia is in many ways a new form of the origi-nal conflict within early Christianity itself, which the late Georges Florovsky described as the contrast between the empire and the desert.[2] He asked if the Christian faith was inextricably tied to impe-rial power when the emperor Constantine converted to Christianity and built a new Rome in Constantinople. Or was Christianity rather rooted exclusively in the sensibility of those totally removed from the powers of earth, such as Saint Anthony who set up the first monastery in the desert (and the place from which we at the Library have now extracted the oral tradition of the Copts)?

Byzantine Christianity came late to the Eastern Slavs, who brought with it this inner conflict. The Eastern Slavs were ardent converts, "laborers of the eleventh hour" as they called themselves, having accepted Orthodox Christianity as a finished product. In the eleventh century they transformed their new capital, Kiev, into a city built around a new cathedral of the Holy Wisdom, the Santa Sophia, imita-tive of the original one in Constantinople. This transformation at the beginning of the second millennium was the work of Jaroslav the Wise, who rooted the culture of high Byzantium at the base of the Russian, Ukrainian, and Belorussian peoples, all of whom saw Kiev and Rus as their place of origin. That Jaroslav, like ours today, can properly be called "wise," a bearer of and witness to an old Christian tradition in a relatively new land for the faith.

In Kiev and Rus, as in the later Russian empire, the classic conflict between empire and desert was technically solved by the central and dominant formative institution of the monasteries. The higher ecclesiastical structure was drawn exclusively from the monastic clergy and was closely attached to the authoritarian imperial government. The rulers of Russia generally sought to be tonsured as monks before they died, symbolizing the way the monasteries bridged these two conflicting worlds. And conversely, the holy men who moved out from the communal core of the monasteries to a lonely hermitage or to a *skit*, a smaller place of refuge or prayer, were actually going out into society, often into virgin territory to found their own settlements, which they called a "desert" (*pustyn*).

The split in Russia between empire and desert was transferred from the Greek Church, where it existed between Constantinople, the imperial city the Russians referred to as Tsargrad, and Athos in the Aegean Sea, the isolated, purely monastic peninsula that was the source of inspiration for the desert tradition. These two poles of the Byzantine Christian world were represented in Kiev respectively by Prince Vladimir, who had preceded Jaroslav as the first prince to impose top-down Christianity on the Eastern Slavs, and by the monk Anthony, who came directly from Mount Athos to found in the caves underneath Kiev the first of the great *lavras*, or mother monasteries, of the Orthodox Eastern Slavs.

Vladimir was the first real ruler of Russia, and his Christian name was later bestowed on Lenin and on Putin. The verbal imperative within it, *Vladi*, is "rule!" and suggests "rule the world." This verbal imperative was imposed on the principal entryway from Russia to the Middle East, *Vladikafkaz*, and on the principal entryway to the Far East, *Vladivostok*—"rule the Caucasus, rule the East."

The rival desert ideal has a very different lineage in Russian history, descending from this hermit founder of the monastery of the caves, the monk Anthony, who took his name from the original desert father Anthony. After the Mongol conquest of Kiev, this lineage moved north through Saint Sergius, who took the desert ideal out from the new capital of Moscow to found, in the nearby forest, the Lavra of the Holy Trinity.

The faith was soon taken still further beyond the reach of any city, out into the virgin forest that stretched northeast all the way to the Pacific, by Saint Cyril of the White Lake. He began his march into the wilderness by escaping from Simona Monastery, the biggest in Moscow and the closest thing to an imperial monastery. He went to his elders rather than to the person who had formal authority for spiritual counsel, and asked, "How can I find silence to protect prayer?" He was not fleeing the country; he was trying to add the desert dimension that one could find only in a "desert" far from worldly distractions. And he had a vision in which, according to his entry in *Life of the Saints*, the Mother of God said to him, "Flee the noise of the city." This is a recurrent theme in Russian culture, as in the great Russian prison lament, *"ne slyshno shumu gorodskogo"* sung by a plaintive tenor. So, Christianity moved from the Black Sea to the White Lake and on to the White Sea in the Arctic north before moving east.[3]

Probably the most important successor to Cyril of the White Lake was Nil Sorsky, leader of the so-called trans-Volga elders who went east beyond the Volga into an unknown frontier. They were opposed to the so-called possessors, who defended the richness and the glory of the monasteries that were closer to the powers in Moscow who were beginning to call themselves Tsars, the Russian version of Caesar. Then the direct conflict between empire and desert came with Philip, a monk who went from the White Lake Monastery of Solovetsk in the White Sea, which became in Soviet times the first gulag. Philip, a great opponent of Ivan the Terrible, met with a tragic fate but was later much revered.

The monks first went to establish a monastery, and then went out to found small *skiti*, which often became monasteries, and it is this that is very much the story of the Russian frontier. The monks moved into the forest with their hermitages. Settlers tended to move in where the monks had once been. Sometimes it was the other way round. But they were out in the desert, as they put it, to preserve prayer, not to escape civilization; and they immediately sought to win converts, not so much by their teaching as by their example of being spiritually purified by the long silence and lonely life of prayer as well as the ordeal of frontier life.

There were two phases to this great frontier expansion. The first, in the fourteenth and fifteenth centuries, took Russians north. The second, in the sixteenth and seventeenth centuries, took Russians east all the way across the great Siberian forest with its broad rivers and swamps and heavy cold. The coldest recorded temperatures in an inhabited place on the planet are in Verkhoiansk, not far from Yakutsk,[4] the jumping-off place for the final move on to the Pacific, the Aleutians, and Alaska.

Russia developed a historical rather than a rational theology, a culture of heroic deeds and images rather than of abstract ideas, a culture that sought beautiful forms of worship rather than analysis of doctrine. Russia developed a frontier culture entirely beyond the borders of the old Russian Empire, whether east or west. As a result, the Russian Church did not inherit the diocesan structures of the old Roman administrative system, and gave much more authority to the monasteries. It was monks who originated the idea that Moscow was the third Rome, while at the same time suggesting that life within the Empire involved passing through a desert to purify oneself for the next world.

Russian Christians believed they were on a journey in four basic ways.

First, life was a metaphysical journey from this world to the next. This suggested a progressive physical shedding of the body. The four great fasts of Orthodox worship programmed believers for this journey. Excessive attention to the physical gratifications of this life had to be shed; this is why the desert fathers went out into the desert. The pain of this journey toward holiness, toward an angelic from a human status, to become *prepodobny*, "very like" the saints, was portrayed in dematerialized figures on two-dimensional icons.

Second, life was a physical journey every day, whatever you did. You were always moving through unclean lands to clean lands. Home was a clean place because there was an icon in the corner. The field you tilled was a clean place because you sanctified it by parading icons around it.

You would have blessed it. There was usually an icon in the field that greeted one after passing a world of temptations, venalities, and distractions. There were crosses and icons at crucial crossroads to guide you on your physical as well as your metaphysical journey,

Third was a journey into time. The community gathered in the cathedral on the great feast days, more numerous in Orthodoxy, and generally taken more seriously, than in most other branches of Christendom. People gathered on those days into a *sobor,* the word for a cathedral that also means the ingathering, to celebrate the feasts by which the year was basically measured. Just as the Revolution in *Doctor Zhivago* is seen as kind of reenactment of Holy Week, so you see in the overthrow of communism the extraordinary fact that it occurred between the Feast of the Transfiguration and the Feast of the Assumption. And it was closed out by the first liturgy ever held for the new Parliament, the first really representative body that the Russians had ever had, in the Cathedral of the Assumption itself.

So there was a sense of journeying through time as defined by these feasts, and the journey through time was illustrated by the very décor within the church. In front of the worshiper was the icon screen that traced time down from the row of kings to that of patriarchs to the *Deisis* or "prayer row" of the company of Jesus to the local saints on the lowest rung. That was the past. On the opposite west wall was a fresco of the Last Judgment (where the Assumption was depicted in Byzantine churches). The Last Judgment was the future, and the congregation in the nave of the church was the present. They stood between this past and this future, and they went out of the church looking at what lay ahead ultimately for them after they lived out their days.

Fourth, the journey went through space. The pilgrimage that defined the identity of *Holy Rus* went through the desert to some kind of land of milk and honey, to a place of redemption. The great space of Russia itself was suggested by going through the forest, over the rivers, to the great monasteries that were across the lake and usually approached by water, to the place where salvation was sought. There were three places of pilgrimage that you wanted to go if you could. And if you could not get there because they were very distant, you would go to their approximation, to a place named after them.

The first place for a kind of secular pilgrimage of empire was Constantinople, known in Old Slavic as "a city of the world's desire." All desires of power and majesty as well as the Orthodox mother cathedral, the Santa Sophia, were to be found there. The second sacred place was Athos, the Holy Mountain, where there was somehow the possibility of greater access to the Holy Spirit (though not for women). If Constantinople was the new Rome, the Holy Mountain was the new Tabor, the mountain on which Christ appeared transfigured to his disciples before his death and Resurrection. His appearance in the uncreated light of divinity and as the future Messiah opened up the possibility that others might get some foretaste of the next world through the type of disciplined prayer developed in the early fourteenth century on Mount Athos by Gregory Palamas, the so-called Hesychast movement (from the Greek word for silence).[5] The key idea was that through controlled breathing, control of one's body, and, at the same time, incessant repetition of the so-called Jesus prayer, a believer could prepare to experience the energies, though not the essence, of God. Out of silence came energies. Storing up spiritual power had enormous physical consequences in Russia. In the second half of the fourteenth century there was an enormous explosion of energies. Monks moved out of the caves in Pskov and Kiev and into the forest. They began taking their energies and light into very dark forests, and later across the steppes. They moved out then not just from the cities to the country, but on to the frontier of taiga and tundra, first to the Arctic, and then on to the Pacific.

This missionary and colonizing movement to the north and west psychologically required a prior pilgrimage to the south even beyond Constantinople and Athos, to the third sacred place, Palestine, the Holy Land, and above all to the Holy Sepulcher, where the great mystery of the Resurrection was enacted. One literally went through the Palestinian desert to get there. Even today in Jerusalem, the Garden of Gethsemane and the Mount of Olives are Russian preserves. At the highest point of the Mount is a great tower with very large bells that were hauled by Russian pilgrims without the aid of wheels or trucks over the desert.

The Russian journey east went first to Perm and along a northern route that recent scholarship has mapped out—making the whole adventure even more amazing. They subsequently followed another route that went from the jumping off place, Kazan, to the city of Irkutsk, and from there they went on to the Pacific.[6] The key figure was the first of two monks named Innocent. The first was supposed to go to Beijing, but the Chinese would not let him in, so he converted the Buriats instead—the first large-scale Asian conversion to Russian Orthodox Christianity. The second Innocent, Innocent of Alaska, who was born in Irkutsk, went to Alaska, was brought back to be Metropolitan of Moscow, and became the principal nineteenth-century primate of the Russian Church. Thus, on the frontier the Church, largely subordinated to state control by the reforms of Peter the Great, began reconstituting itself as an independent force.

Two other great "desert" hermitages closer to Moscow became by the nineteenth-century centers of spiritual renewal.[7] The prophetic monk Seraphim, who had been scheduled to come to America, founded instead a hermitage in Sarov. Those chosen to go to Alaska were eight from Valamo, one of the northern monasteries with the strictest ecclesiastical discipline. It was correctly thought that they would have the strength for the long journey to Optina Pustin, where the great writers all went to try to recover their faith from the elders, the spiritual counselors. The second new establishment of the nineteenth century was Optina Pustin itself, which still exists today. Seraphim's remains have also been returned to Sarov—just opposite a city many recently fear is a site for making weapons of mass destruction. So empire and desert are both still in juxtaposition in Sarov.

Two tragic individuals chronicle the failure of this journey amid the general falling away from faith in the modern world. The first was the great seventeenth-century patriarch Nikon, a towering figure from the north who came to Moscow and tried, in effect, to create a

better-disciplined church if not a theocracy in Russia. He was opposed by traditionalists and banished back north. He had established
the Monastery of the New Jerusalem just outside Moscow, creating
inside the great temple a model of the Holy Sepulcher in old
Jerusalem.

Nikon was exiled to the Ferapont Monastery, which contains
some of the most beautiful Christian art in the world. At the end of
the fifteenth century, expecting the end of the world, and disillu-
sioned with empire, Dionysus and his sons took monastic vows, and
went up in the late summer to decorate the interior of the cathedral
with their vision of the world to come. The Cathedral of the Nativity
of the Virgin suggests the ethereal next world, because the church
calendar in the East had run out in 1492, and it was a time of tumul-
tuous change in Russia. Patriarch Nikon, two centuries later, had this
beauty as his only consolation. He finally ended up creating the defin-
itive "desert" by building in the middle of the lake with his own hands
an island made of stones. He ended up just praying constantly and
finally dying, some say, on that little rock island.[8] He became the ultimate hermit, after having been the ultimate theocratic pretender. His
life can be seen as an example either of imperial overreach on the part
of the church or of heroic effort to resist the creeping secularization
of Russia.

The other tragic pilgrim was the great writer, Nicholas Gogol,
who made his pilgrimage to Jerusalem and sat before the tomb of
the Holy Sepulcher on Easter Sunday, weeping that he could find no
joy in the great feast. He then went back to Moscow and starved
himself to death. His pilgrimage ended in literally getting rid of his
body and burning what would have been the happy part of the divine
comedy that he was trying to write for Russia. His *Dead Souls* never
got out of the Inferno. He left behind the terrible story of a journey
without a destination[9]—his play *The Inspector General* is the tale of a
journey all over Russia, finding nothing good. When the audience
laughed, Gogol said, "What are you laughing at? You're laughing
about yourselves."

I end this account of Russian Orthodoxy's journey through time and space with reflections on the Christian martyrdom suffered in the Soviet period, perhaps the greatest of any single church in modern times. The *Encyclopedia of Christianity* has estimated that something like 70 percent of all Christian martyrs were created in the twentieth century, and the largest number of those was in Russia.[10] Religious persecution was quite ecumenical; all religions suffered. However, since Orthodoxy was the main religion of the U.S.S.R., it suffered specially. The same Russian expanses that saw amazing frontier missionary activity in the early modern period suffered enormous devastation in the twentieth century when millions of people disappeared in the frozen wastes of the North and East. The concentration camps were spread across almost exactly the same places—often using the monasteries for prisons.

Martyrdom means a great deal to Orthodox people. Many of their feasts—major as well as minor ones—celebrate martyrs. Martyrdom can be a reassertion of the central Christian mystery of the redemptive value of innocent suffering, a guidepost on the path to salvation. Eugenia Ginzburg, in *Journey into the Whirlwind*, tells the story of women in one of the camps who wanted to celebrate the Easter liturgy but were told they had to work instead. When they insisted, they were forced to wade out in the water while it froze. When they did just that, the whole place erupted, and it became an important witness to others.[11]

So the breakthrough to "unexpected joy" that Captain Ledyard found may not be the best. The present patriarch of the Russian Church, with whom I have had some conversations over the years, described to me not long ago a trip he made to a new community in Siberia, where he met all kinds of mostly Asian people. They had no church and no money to build one, but they had dug out a hole for a future church. They asked him to bless the hole and conduct a solemn procession around it. "I was blessing this place," he said, "and you know, it was a wonderful thing. I don't even know if they'll ever build that church." What was exciting to me is that there were Asians and different kinds of people. Orthodoxy was a multiethnic faith in

Russia, and the Patriarch was moved as he described this ceremony—looking off into space, and thinking about something very deep, as people of faith occasionally do but rarely share with others.

The concluding vision of Pasternak's *Doctor Zhivago* is a favorite of mine. Zhivago, of course, is Church Slavonic for "living," as in the question posed to the women at the empty tomb: "Why do you seek the living among the dead?" In the poetic last lines at the very end of the novel, Pasternak places all of Russia's suffering and tribulation into the Christian understanding:

> You will see the passing of the years is like a parable
> that along the way could burst into flame.
> In the name of its terrible majesty
> I go, a voluntary sufferer, into my grave.
> I descend into my grave, and on the third day rise again.
> And like little boats scattered across a broad river,
> towards me and judgment, like a caravan of barges,
> the centuries flow forward out of darkness.[12]

Notes

[1] From the "Recollections of John Ledyard, Unalaska 1778," in Nina Nashkina, et al., eds., *The United States and Russia. The Beginnings of Relations, 1765–1845* (n. p., n. d.), 58.

[2] Georges Florovsky, "Empire and Desert: Antinomies of Christian History," *The Greek Catholic Theological Review* (Winter 1957): 133–159.

[3] The connection between the real, scorching deserts of Egypt and the freezing "deserts" of the Russian north was already suggested in the mid-nineteenth century, when the Egyptian term *thebaid* was applied to the "thebaid of the north." See the collection *Severnaia fivaida: Pamiatniki otechestva*, No. 3–4 (1993): 8. The articles in this collection chronicle various aspects of this northern expansion.

[4] An amazing example of a combination church and fortress existed apparently from the mid-seventeenth century at Zashiversk between Verkhoiansk and the future site of the most fearsome death camp of the Soviet gulag system at Kolyma. See A. P. Okladnikov, et al., *Drevnii Zashiversk. Drevnerusskii zapoliarnyi gorod* (Moscow, 1977); and A.G. Chikachev, *Russkie na indigirke* (Moscow, 1990).

[5]See two invaluable studies: by the Athonite monk Basil Krivocheine, "The Ascetic and Theological Teaching of Gregory Palamas," *Eastern Churches Quarterly III* (1938–39): 26–33, 71–84,138–56, 193–214; and by the Jesuit scholar Irénée Hausherr, *Hesychasme et prière* (Rome, 1966).

[6]In recounting this part of the story, I have drawn heavily on the account in Sergei Shirokov, *Valaamskii monastyr' i amerikanskaia pravoslavnaia istoriia i dukhovenye sviazi* (Moscow, 1996).

[7]On "Optyna," see the work of the priest Sergei Chetverikov, *Optina Pustyn'* (Paris, 1926); and of the journalist Alexander Nezhnyi, *Siiala Optina Pustyn'* (Moscow, 1989). On the revival of Sarov and Optyna in more recent times, see *Byl' monastyrskaia: Pamiatniki otechestva* 2–3 (1992): 146–62.

[8]James Billington, *The Icon and the Axe* (New York, 1970), 158.

[9]Gogol contemplated a pilgrimage to Athos as well as Jerusalem, but ended up visiting Optyna three times. He proclaimed that all of Russia is "our monastery" already on the path to realizing Christian brotherhood on earth; that "this path is Russia itself;" and that, as a result, "it is necessary to journey all over Russia." See Gogol, *Dukhovnaia Proza* (Moscow, 1992), 135, 137. The excellent introduction by Vladimir Voropaev ("Monastyr' nash—Rossiia,") describes Gogol's restless desire for pilgrimage and periodic self-deprecation for not becoming a monk.

[10]David Barrett, et al., eds., *World Christian Encyclopedia,* 2nd ed. (Oxford, 2002), I:11, estimates the total number of martyrs for the faith from the first to the twentieth century as 69.4 million: 45.4 million for the twentieth century alone, and 37.4 million Russians. This latter is almost certainly too large; but the detailed martyrology being painstakingly itemized in many parts of post-Soviet Russia deals largely with ordained clergy and religious workers, is meeting many obstacles, and seems unlikely to provide comprehensive statistics for the Russian people as a whole. See recent local inventories and bibliography in James Billington, *Russia in Search of Itself* (Washington, D.C., 2004), 211–12, footnote 12.

[11]Eugenia Ginzburg, *Journey into the Whirlwind* (New York, 1967), 412–414.

[12]Boris Pasternak, *Doctor Zhivago* (London, 1958), 107. I have modified the translation slightly.

Higher Education in an Age of Specialized Knowledge

Vartan Gregorian*

*J*AROSLAV PELIKAN is rightly hailed as the scholar's scholar. One of the leading experts in the world on medieval intellectual history and an authority on the evolution of Christianity, he writes with grace. His lectures are eloquent. He is living proof that great scholarship and great teaching are compatible.

On the occasion of his 80th birthday, what is an appropriate way to pay tribute to this extraordinary man? First I thought I should give a lecture in the form of a commentary on Edward Gibbon's chapter on "The Origin and Doctrine of the Paulicians" in volume 3 of *The History of the Decline and Fall of the Roman Empire*. After all, I had read about the impact of the Paulicians on the Armenian Church and its reaction against them. I was especially intrigued by the fact that the Paulicians of Thrace resisted the storms of persecution, maintained a secret correspondence with their Armenian brethren, and gave aid and comfort to their preachers who solicited, not without success, the infant Christian faith of the Bulgarians. Other options were to comment on the struggle between Unitarians and Trinitarians, or to address the question whether Islam arose as a logical extension of Judaism and Christianity. I could also address the

*Vartan Gregorian is the president of Carnegie Corporation of New York, a grant-making institution founded by Andrew Carnegie in 1911. Prior to his current position, which he assumed in June 1997, Gregorian served for nine years as the sixteenth president of Brown University. His lecture was delivered on September 9, 2003, at the Library of Congress, Washington.

belief of both Unitarians and Muslims that the New Testament is an uncertain guide to the actual events of early Christianity. (Muslims regard the books of the New Testament as mainly the product of the followers of Paul of Tarsus, "who did not know Jesus.")

What I choose, however, is to offer a tribute to Professor Pelikan as educator and administrator by speaking about American higher education. As a former university president, I have a particular angle of vision on this subject and a particular appreciation for what my friend has meant to the traditions of the academy.

For more than two centuries, American colleges and universities have been the mainstay of our nation's progress, helping make it an economic, cultural, scientific, technological, and political power. The American university is, incomparably, the most democratic in the world. It is popular in the best sense of the term, admitting and educating unprecedented numbers of men and women of every race and social class. Students from every imaginable background—here I speak from personal experience—have found a place in this nation's variety of colleges and universities, public or private, large or small, secular or sectarian. Today, there are almost 4,200 colleges and universities in our country, including some 1,700 public and private two-year institutions. Evidence of the growing centrality of higher education to American life can be seen in a few startling statistics: in the twentieth century, total enrollment in institutions of higher education grew from just 4 percent of the college-age population in 1900 to more than 65 percent in the 1990s. And within two years of high school graduation, three out of four students go on for some higher education. Higher education employs more than 2.8 million people, including 590,000 full-time faculty members in what amounts to a $200+ billion enterprise.

The diversity of our higher education system gives it great strength. As Sheldon Rothblatt writes in *The Modern University and Its Discontents*, "What makes the American case so interesting is the strong connection between American colleges and universities and the characteristics of American social life, principally its religious

pluralism and ethnic diversity, its immigrant composition and its pref-
erence for market discipline interspersed with governmental efforts,
many half-hearted or contradictory or unsystematic, to legislate or
regulate."

Traditionally, individual institutions have emphasized different
functions and have complemented each other by meeting different
local, regional, national, and international needs—by providing educational opportunities to a diverse population, by expanding scientific
and technical knowledge, and by providing opportunities for continuing education. Rothblatt also points to this diversification as a
strength, noting, "The history of American higher education is characterized by the growth of multi-purpose institutions which continue
to add functions and responsibilities without disregarding older commitments. New constituencies and new tasks are absorbed compara-
tively readily . . . Market discipline has certainly contributed to the
comparative openness and flexibility of American institutions as a
condition of survival in the public as well as private sector."[1]

Because American higher education has the capacity to be in tune
with and adjust itself to societal needs, it has responded to changing
times, dispensing knowledge, training, and even life skills that have
provided graduates with the tools to, in essence, create the nation's
future. In my opinion, the "secret weapon" behind this flexibility is the
emphasis, in American colleges and universities, on the liberal arts,
which—as we move into an era of complexity, of information overload,
and of workplaces that demand multiple skills and wide-ranging
knowledge for even entry-level positions—provide a depth of experience and understanding that once again is exactly right for the times.
We have moved beyond the age when vocationalism was the watch-
word and one person was trained—and taught—to do one thing. Now,
everyone needs to know something about almost everything, a task
that a liberal arts student is certainly prepared for.

Universities have also educated the technical, managerial, and professional workforce of the United States and helped to develop

generation after generation of national leaders. The unparalleled capacity of higher education institutions to carry out basic research has put the U.S. at the cutting edge of science and scholarship in the humanities and social sciences. Without this vast network of colleges and universities, the nation would never have achieved its current overall preeminence.

As we face higher education's challenges and consider ways to cope with them, we must remember that the university, in the West, is the result of some eight centuries of struggle, oppression, perseverance, and endless refinement. The university is a living institution—and change it must. But as we make changes, we must be careful not to inadvertently undermine its foundations, muddle its architecture, or reduce its priceless value to society. And we must recognize that its success is based in large part on the fact that our nation's institutions of higher education operate in an American tradition of freedom, openness, egalitarianism, and equal access. Nothing must be allowed to diminish these principles.

There are a number of prominent landmarks along the American university's journey to its current place of preeminence; examining them can help us understand both the great ideas and true ideals that have shaped American higher education and continue to be its unbendable backbone. Here are stories of a few examples: Land-Grant colleges, the National Academy of Sciences, the G.I. Bill, and federal investments in university research, international studies, and student assistance.

The first major opportunity for American higher education came in 1862, when Congress enacted the Land-Grant College Act, better known as the Morrill Act. The law was named after Justin Morrill who, before becoming a U.S. Representative and then a U.S. Senator from Vermont, had been a dry goods merchant from a family that had been too poor to send him to college. The law extended the opportunity of higher education to all Americans, including such disenfranchised groups as women and minorities. In effect, the law spread higher education all over the United States. It put universities where the people were. It provided education and specialized training, and it spurred the development of both theoretical knowledge and its practical applications. The Industrial Revolution was in full swing then, and the Morrill Act helped provide the research and educated workforce that were so desperately needed in agriculture and manufacturing. Among other things, the law is credited with making the United States the world leader in agricultural production.

Under the law, states were permitted to sell large tracts of federal land and use the proceeds to endow, in perpetuity, at least one public college in every state. Since their founding, Land-Grant colleges and universities have awarded more than 20 million degrees, annually now at the rate of about 500,000 a year, including a third of the nation's bachelor's and master's degrees and 60 percent of the doctoral degrees.

In 1863, at the height of the Civil War and a year after the passage of the Morrill Act, President Lincoln signed another piece of landmark legislation—a law that created the National Academy of Sciences. The Academy, which was established to advise Congress on "any subject of science or art," has done that job well and expanded to include the National Research Council, the National Academy of Engineering, and the Institute of Medicine. It is extraordinary to consider that even while the nation was engaged in the devastating and heart-wrenching civil conflict that could have destroyed the United States as we know it, the president and Congress were still thinking of the future and of how to expand educational opportunities for Americans.

It was not until after World War II, though, that the federal government began supporting university research in a significant way. Prior to the war, the best research was done in Europe and in corporate laboratories. To strengthen the U.S. role in science, President Franklin D. Roosevelt asked his science adviser, Vannevar Bush, a former professor at the Massachusetts Institute of Technology, to develop a strategy. His landmark report, published in 1945, defined our postwar national policy in science. *Science—The Endless Frontier,* noted that business and industry naturally took the lead in applied research but were deterred by marketplace considerations from conducting much basic research. Bush argued that it was the federal government's responsibility to provide adequate funds for basic research, which pioneers the frontiers of human knowledge to the benefit of society. He also wrote that the nation's universities were, by their very nature, best suited to take the lead in conducting basic research. Public funding, he said, would promote competition between researchers, and projects could be selected on their merit through a peer-review process. Bush suggested that a federal agency should oversee the program, and in 1950 Congress created the National Science Foundation.

Giving universities the lead in basic research turned out to be a brilliant policy. Instead of being centralized in government laboratories—as science tended to be in other parts of the world—scientific research became decentralized in American universities. This policy spurred a tremendous diversity of investments. It also gave graduate students significant research opportunities and helped spread scientific discoveries far and wide to the benefit of industry, medicine, and society as a whole.

At the end of World War II, President Roosevelt signed into law the Servicemen's Readjustment Act of 1944, better known as the "G.I. Bill of Rights." This legislation ranks in stature with the Morrill Act and is widely recognized as one of the most important acts of Congress. The law made an already democratic higher education system open in ways that were inconceivable anywhere in Europe. Among other things, it opened the doors of the best universities to men and women who had never dreamt of going to college. It also created a national fondness for university life that redounded to the advantage of the academic profession—as many who benefited from the law stayed on to teach. In fifty years, the G.I. Bill, and its legislative offspring enacted during the wars in Korea and Vietnam, resulted in the public investment of more than $60 billion in education and training for about 18 million veterans, including 8.5 million in higher education. Currently, the nation offers education benefits as an incentive for people to join the all-volunteer military forces.

In a more recent effort to promote international cooperation and security, Congress enacted the National Security Education Act of 1991, which provides scholarships for undergraduates and graduate students to study many of the less-well-known languages and cultures in key regions of the world, including some in Central Asia and the Middle East.

Another major landmark was the creation of federal loan guarantees and subsidy programs as well as outright grants for college students. In the thirty years since its founding in 1965, the Federal Family Education Loan Program has funded more than 74 million student loans worth more than $180 billion. And in the twenty-five years since the 1973 Pell Grant program—named after Senator Claiborne Pell— was created, grants totaling more than $100 billion have been awarded to an estimated 30 million postsecondary students. It is important to note that Pell grants were originally to have been funneled directly to institutions, but with the passage of the Higher Education Act of 1972—which was influenced by the work of Clark Kerr and the Carnegie Commission on Higher Education—control of the largest share of financial aid dollars was shifted from institutions to individuals, very much in keeping with the American character.

In sum, the Land-Grant colleges, the National Academy of Sciences, the G.I. Bill, and the federal investments in university research, international studies, and student assistance—all of these landmarks helped American higher education flower into the most diverse and creative system in the world. As we enter the twenty-first century, let us also observe that the United States has democratized access to higher education and attempted to nationalize opportunity at a scale unprecedented in world history.

But in this context, we also must consider what it is that has given higher education its authority, credibility, creativity, and its leadership role in our democracy. And I have an answer: it is the strength and boldness that academic freedom has brought to American education.

Academic freedom was not a gift, of course. It emerged slowly with the university in Europe during the Middle Ages. Scholars enjoyed a certain amount of intellectual freedom in those early days, but we all know the cautionary tales of Galileo and others who suffered for sharing their ideas. When knowledge challenged theology or ideology, it was often manipulated or suppressed by church or state. But as religious beliefs diversified, with Protestantism in particular, a right to follow one's own conscience and intellectual freedom gained ground.

Academic freedom has become an accepted democratic value, but it is not always well understood or fully appreciated—and that makes it vulnerable. In his book *The Story of American Freedom,* Eric Foner writes: "Americans have sometimes believed they enjoy the greatest freedom of all—freedom from history . . . But if history teaches anything, it is that the definitions of freedom and of the community entitled to enjoy it are never fixed or final."[2]

Today, as competing ideologies ramp up their attacks on each other and vie for prominence on the world stage, it is critically important that American institutions of higher education continue to provide not only a safe place for dialogue but also a place where debate is welcome and where even warring voices can be heard and acknowledged. A suppressed opinion, I believe, is worse than an offensive one. Academic freedom—the cornerstone of our American universities—is also what nourishes the nation's freedom of speech. As Hubert Humphrey said, "Freedom is hammered out on the anvil of discussion, dissent, and debate." If that's true—and I believe it is—then there is no more powerful hammer in the American arsenal than our diverse, accessible, and robust system of higher education.

That's the good news.

The bad news is that mass higher education is not living up to its promise. One of the starkest measures of this failure is that 60 percent of students in community colleges and 40 percent of students in four-year colleges leave school without completing their degrees.[3] These dropout rates have drawn public attention to a wide variety of related problems, ranging from failures in our K–12 system to the rising cost of higher education.

I want to highlight what I believe to be one other major failure of our higher education. In our rapid expansion of higher education, it has, to a significant degree, come to serve as a job readiness program, and sometimes not a very effective or efficient one at that, as dropout rates and studies suggest. Generally speaking, higher education has lost sight of its primary mission: developing an educated and cultured citizenry to participate in and lead our democracy. This mission includes stirring students' intellectual curiosity, passion, and ambition, as well as providing them with a good sense of ethics, history, science, and culture—in other words, an understanding that there is a difference between making a living and actually living, between means and ends, and between individual rights and collective responsibilities. In this way, higher education must support the idealism and altruism of young people as they continue quests for fulfilling vocations. As Ellen Condliffe Lagemann writes, "The word vocation implies having a calling: knowing who one is, what one believes, what one values, and where one stands in the world . . . Granting, then, that a sense of vocation develops over time, it is still not unreasonable to suggest that one purpose of a college education, and a central purpose of liberal education, should be to nurture an initial sense of vocation."[4]

Anyone who has spent time in a college classroom knows this is what students want from higher education. For most, college is a time for self-discovery, for developing passionate interests and trying to weave them into a meaningful career amid the looming pressures of the job market. Studies bear this out. In 1999 the Mellman Group surveyed college students under 31 years old and found that 80 percent said it is "very important" for them to find work that "will make a difference in people's lives." In 2002 the national survey of 282,000 freshmen done at UCLA found that the top reason for going to college was to "learn more about things that interest me." The next four reasons, offered by between 66 percent and 72 percent of freshmen, dealt with earning a living, starting careers and—please note—gaining "a general education and appreciation of ideas."[5]

Unfortunately, and to the world's loss, there is strong evidence that higher education is not well designed to nurture this idealism. There are a great many reasons for this. To focus on one of the fundamental problems, I cite a recent report on higher education produced by a blue-ribbon panel of educators and business leaders under the auspices of the Association of American Colleges and Universities.[6] The national panel, chaired by Judith Ramaley of the National Science Foundation, called in 2002 for "a dramatic reorganization of undergraduate education."[7] One of the panel's many important findings was that in this age of mass higher education our colleges and universities are falling back on an outdated factory model of education—only in this case the assembly line is more like a chaotic maze where students try to pick up something useful as they search for the exit and the degree needed to find a decent job.

The report, "Greater Expectations," notes that today's students, much like students in the 1950s, fulfill general education requirements, take specialized courses in a major, and fill out their schedule with some electives. Although catalogs euphemistically describe this as a "curriculum," the national panel said it is rarely more than a collection of courses, devoid of planning, context, and coherence. The panel said, moreover, that nothing had changed since 1985, when another association study concluded: "As for what passes as a college curriculum, almost anything goes."[8] This is obviously no way to nurture or guide young people as they struggle with the meaning of life and ponder their role in society.

Underlying the fragmented curriculum is the utter fragmentation of knowledge itself on our campuses, the national panel reported in 2002. Higher education has atomized knowledge by dividing it into disciplines, sub-disciplines, and sub-sub-sub-disciplines — "even though scholarship, learning and life have no such artificial boundaries." This trend, of course, has deep roots in simpler times and smaller colleges. But the trend has accelerated, breaking up our expanding knowledge base into smaller and smaller unconnected fragments of academic specialization even as the world looks to higher education for help in integrating and synthesizing the exponential increase in information. Higher education's structuring of knowledge, which has hardened into an academic bureaucracy, makes it administratively difficult for students to integrate knowledge in a multidisciplinary, interdisciplinary, or transdisciplinary way.

I am concerned that mass higher education is heading toward what I call the Home Depot approach to education, where there is no differentiation between consumption and digestion, between information and learning, and no guidance—or even questioning—about what it means to be an educated and cultured person. I do not believe the nation can afford to let higher education become an academic superstore, a vast collection of courses, stacked up like sinks and lumber for do-it-yourselfers to try to assemble on their own into a meaningful whole.

This trend has serious ramifications for our nation. After all, Thomas Jefferson once described America as an idea—as a "crusade against ignorance." He fervently believed that a nation cannot be ignorant and free. There are those of us today who are still optimists and who believe that societies become more democratic as people become more literate, numerate, and knowledgeable. Our ability to generate, organize, distribute, and use knowledge more effectively is beneficial for our respective societies. Political empowerment and economic opportunity stem from the same root: the spread of knowledge. Understanding the nature of knowledge, its unity, its varieties, its limitations, and its uses and abuses is necessary not only for the success of higher education and sciences but also for the fabric and texture of our democratic societies. This is especially true now when so many questions are being raised about the ascendancy of mass society, technological anonymity, perceived loss of ideals of nature, cultures, personality, and the loss of a sense of place in a world that increasingly lacks human scale.

Reforming higher education is, therefore, critical to our success as a democracy. It is a Herculean task but one that "is long overdue," as the national panel stated. To date, our colleges and universities have largely avoided reform by sidestepping accountability for their students' and graduates' success and by resting on their laurels. I want to honor and respect those laurels while also calling for higher education reforms that are needed to reconstruct the unity of knowledge.

Saying that higher education must promote unity in knowledge may initially sound esoteric, especially to some outside the academy, but it is really just shorthand for saying that the complexity of the world requires us to have a better understanding of the relationships and connections between economics and sociology, law and psychology, business and history, physics and medicine, anthropology and political science—namely, all fields that intersect and overlap.

One way to overcome fragmentation is called general system theory. It was conceived a half-century ago by Ludwig von Bertalanffy, a theoretical biologist who applied system methodology to psychology and the social sciences. What he wrote back then still sounds fresh today: "Our civilization seems to be suffering a second curse of Babel: just as the human race builds a tower of knowledge that reaches to the heavens, we are stricken by a malady in which we find ourselves attempting to communicate with each other in countless tongues of scientific specialization . . . There is this hope, I cannot promise you whether or when it will be realized, that the mechanistic paradigm, with all its implications in science as well as in society and our own private life, will be replaced by an organismic or systems paradigm that will offer new pathways for our presently schizophrenic and self-destructive civilization."[9]

General system theory is based on the idea that complex problems are best addressed as systemic inquiries, engaging many disciplines and many kinds of experts—who coordinate and synthesize information from the very beginning, not as a final step.

As a society, we tend to pay lip service to the complexity of problems—and then continue to gamble on simplistic solutions, such as building prisons to solve the crime and drug problems. But as Bela H. Banathy, a systems theorist, writes: "A technical problem of transportation, such as the building of a freeway, becomes a land-use problem, linked with economic, environmental, conservation, ethical, and political issues. Can we really draw a boundary? When we ask to improve a situation, particularly if it is a public one, we find ourselves facing not a problem, but a cluster of problems . . . It is difficult to pinpoint individual problems and propose individual solutions. Each problem is related to every other problem, each apparent solution to a problem may aggravate or interfere with others; and none of these problems can be tackled using linear or sequential methods."[10]

Why has systemic thinking been slow to catch on, even though the pitfalls of specialization have long been discussed? It was, you may recall, the phenomenon of the modern specialist that prompted Dostoevsky to lament in *The Brothers Karamazov* about the scholars who ". . . have only analyzed the parts and overlooked the whole and, indeed, their blindness is marvelous!" In the same vein, José Ortega y Gasset, in his 1930s *Revolt of the Masses*, decried the "barbarism of specialization." He noted that though there were more scientists, scholars, and professionals, there were fewer "cultivated" men and women who could integrate the achievements of civilization—as in using music to solve a physics problem or vice versa.

One reason for this shortage of multitalented people is that the university, which was to embody the universe of knowledge, has become an intellectual multiversity. Of course, the process of both growth and fragmentation of knowledge has been underway since the seventeenth century, but it has snowballed in the last hundred years. The scope and the intensity of specialization is such that scholars and scientists have great difficulty in keeping up with the important yet overwhelming amount of scholarly literature of their sub-specialties, not to mention their general disciplines. Even the traditional historical humanistic disciplines have become less and less viable as communities of discourse. As Wayne Booth put it wistfully in his 1987 Reyerson Lecture: "Centuries have passed since the fateful moment, was it in the eighteenth century, or the late seventeenth century, when the last of the Leonardo

da Vincis could hope to cover the cognitive map . . . since that fatal
moment . . . everyone has been reduced to knowing only one or two
countries on the intellectual globe . . . [in the universities] we are smit-
ten in our pride . . . when for one reason or another, we discover just
what a pitifully small corner of the cognitive world we live in . . . The
knowledge explosion left us ignorant of vast fields of knowledge that
every educated man or woman ought to have known."

Today, the faculties of our universities are confronted with the difficult choices of balancing analysis and synthesis, methodology and
the relevant value of course content—and thus placing more and more
responsibility on the students to form the synthesis. In our universities, the triumph of the "monograph" or "scientific investigation" over
synthesis has fractured the "commonwealth of learning" and under-
mined our sense of commitment to the grand end of synthesis, general
understanding and integration of knowledge.

In an insightful essay, "Models of the Educated Man," William
Bouwsma wrote, "Specialization, instead of uniting human beings into
a general community of values and discourse, by necessity has divided
them into small and exclusive categories/coteries, narrow in outlook
and interest." This, in turn, tends to isolate and alienate human beings.
"Social relations . . . are reduced to political relations, to the interplay
of competitive and often antagonistic groups. Specialized education
makes our students into instruments to serve the specialized needs of
a society of specialists."[11]

Bouwsma also noted that "the idea of an educated man has been
deeply affected by the 'knowledge revolution' out of which has
emerged the conception of education as preparation for research." He
continued, "As long as knowledge was limited, relatively simple, and
not very technical, education could be fairly eclectic. Although it regularly emphasized the formation of character, it could attempt at the
same time to discipline the mental faculties, provide a common culture and supply a minimum of substantive knowledge. Yet, obviously,
the sheer bulk of the knowledge now deemed necessary for an edu-

cated man has been squeezed out of education, and for the most part, even out of our understanding of it . . . One result has been a broad decline in the idea of a general education, which for all practical purposes has become little more than a nostalgic memory. Indeed the body of requisite knowledge has become so vast that no one can hope to master more than a small segment of it. So in the popular mind, an educated man is now some kind of specialist: and in a sense we no longer have a single conception of the educated man, but as many conceptions as there are learned specialties."[12]

Nowhere is this trend better reflected than in our evolving concept of literacy. It, too, has lost its unity. It, too, has been fragmented. According to the *Oxford Unabridged Dictionary*, "literacy" is the quality or state of being literate, or possessing education, especially the ability to read and write. Today, however, there is a profusion of required literacies—we have proponents of technological literacy, civic literacy, mathematical literacy, geographical literacy, scientific literacy, ethical literacy, artistic literacy, cultural literacy, analytical literacy, and so on. My favorite one is "managerial literacy." According to *The New York Times,* this particular literacy includes 1,200 terms and concepts. We are told that if you are conversant with at least 80 percent of them you can confidently engage in "meaningful conversations with other experienced managers."

Erik Erikson once remarked that human beings are the "teaching species," and the corollary is that we are also the learning species. It is clear from the literacy boom that we have never before had so much to learn. Learning to learn, then, has become one of the most important lifelong skills that education, especially higher education, can give students. And yet, paradoxically, higher education continues to provide an antiquated model for acquiring fragments of knowledge rather than modeling a lifelong process for integrated learning and systemic thinking. On this point, we should recall B.F. Skinner's wise observation that "education is what survives after what has been learnt has been forgotten."

What must survive a student's higher education today is a facility for lifelong learning. Consider how steep the learning curve has become in the professional workplace. Knowledge has become so ephemeral that management experts have tried to get a handle on the educational challenge by using a yardstick they call the "half-life of knowledge." This is the amount of time it takes for half of one's professional knowledge to become obsolete. I've seen estimates that, overall, the half-life of knowledge is somewhere between four and seven years. For technical fields, it is much less; half of what software developers know now, for example, will likely be irrelevant in just eighteen months.[13] As Maryanne Rouse has written, "We used to think of the long run as ten to fifteen years; in many technology-dependent industries the long run may now be six months or less. And while the pace of knowledge-creation is accelerating, the half-life of knowledge becomes shorter each year. What this means for us is that concepts are far more important than facts and the ability to analyze and synthesize has much greater value than the ability to memorize. In short, school may be multiple choice but real life is all essay."[14]

In real life, then, the skills of synthesis and systemic thinking are not just luxuries; they are invaluable. We are, after all, living through an Information Revolution that parallels the Industrial Revolution in its impact and far-reaching consequences. Information—of all varieties, all levels of priority, and all without much context—is bombarding us from all directions all the time.

T. S. Eliot, in a commentary on Dante's *Inferno*, could have been describing aspects of modern life when he wrote that hell is a place where nothing connects with nothing.[15] Elsewhere, he also asked two important questions: "Where is the wisdom we have lost in knowledge? Where is the knowledge we have lost in information?"[16]

To portray the challenge of coping with the info-glut, I must burden you with some more info:

◉ In 2000, the world was annually generating 2 exabytes of data, or two quintillion bytes of information, which was equivalent to about 250 books for every man, woman, and child on earth. Two exabytes is quite a lot of data, especially when you consider that since the beginning of history, humanity has only created six times that amount of information, or a total of 12 exabytes. But the way data was snowballing in 2000, researchers at the University of California at Berkeley estimated that the next 12 exabytes of data would be created in 2.5 years.[17]

◉ Although the total amount of collected information is now doubling every two or three years, we are unable to use 90 to 95 percent of the information that's currently available.[18] Anyone who uses an Internet search engine has a feel for this. In less than one-quarter of a second, for example, Google.com will give you hyperlinks to 2.3 million web sites pertinent to the term "Information Revolution."[19]

In his book *Information Anxiety,* Richard Saul Wurman notes that all this information is tantalizing but very frustrating. He writes: "We are like a thirsty person who has been condemned to use a thimble to drink from a fire hydrant."[20]

Of course, the same information technologies that have been the driving force behind the explosion of information, growth of knowledge, and its fragmentation also present us with profoundly integrative tools for meeting the challenge of that fragmentation. When we are not shuddering at the challenge of coping with the info-glut, we must marvel at the way the world's store of information is increasingly at our fingertips, thanks to such advances as voice recognition software and translation software that automatically translates one language into another. Information scientists—our high-tech librarians—are also making greater uses of artificial intelligence to automate information management tasks, including "data mining," the practice of having a computer continuously monitor and filter information according to set parameters.

Technology is allowing us to radically modify the space-time constraints of the channels linking persons together. Computer communication and electronic communication networks provide new tools and opportunities for the scholarly community to share resources. Thus, the process of assimilating new information technologies can, in the right setting, help us think hard and deeply about the nature of knowledge and even about our mission in higher education. Furthermore, the new technologies and their deployment at the university offer great opportunities for making connections between disciplines.

But progress in using technology to integrate disciplines on campus has been disappointingly slow—and unless we can help students do a better job synthesizing and systematizing information, our society faces many dangers. In *1984*, George Orwell describes a world in which information was denied, true knowledge was denied, and propaganda was substituted for both. In the twenty-first century, citizens can be denied knowledge by inundating them with mountains of raw data. Advances in technology may also deceive us into thinking that whatever is not in the computer or data bank does not exist. But life did not begin with a computer. Colleges and universities must teach not only what we can know, but also what the limitations of our knowledge are and what we do not know. It goes way back to the Socratic notion that true knowledge is to know what you know but also to know what you don't know. So while the computer allows us to access more information, faster and in a more usable form, we must keep in mind Neil Postman's caution: "The computer cannot provide an organizing moral framework. It cannot tell us what questions are worth asking."[21]

I believe higher education must raise such questions and guide students in synthesizing responses, if not answers. Failing to do so is a missed opportunity of staggering dimensions. For history shows that humanity has a craving for wholeness. And when people do not know how to question deeply, to separate fact from fiction, to integrate knowledge, and to give coherence and meaning to life, they can feel a deeply unsettling emptiness in their lives. Sometimes that vacuum is filled by esoteric ideas, cults, and extremist programs—which are very appealing because they provide answers for absolutely everything. Extremists are not wishy-washy people. Sadly, converts to fanaticism are willing to abdicate thousands of years of humanity's quest for harmony.

In the last hundred years we have seen this hunger for wholeness manipulated by radical ideologies and militant theologies. Often they practice hatred and intolerance while proclaiming superiority and exclusivity. Albert Einstein was one who noted the insanity of all this. He said that although "a human being is part of the whole . . . He experiences himself, his thoughts and feelings, as something separated from the rest . . . a kind of optical delusion of his consciousness. This delusion is a kind of prison for us, restricting us to our personal desires and to affection for a few persons nearest us. Our task must be to free ourselves from this prison by widening our circle of compassion to embrace all living creatures and the whole of nature in its beauty. Nobody is able to achieve this completely, but the striving for such achievement is, in itself, a part of the liberation and a foundation for inner security."[22]

I do not underestimate the systemic nature of the challenge of reform, especially in the context of the Information Revolution and the nearly universal access to higher education that puts all kinds of strains on our institutions. Colleges and students already face enormous societal expectations and demands. By graduation, students are expected to be informed about such issues as our nation's history, democratic society, global economy, international relations, computer technology and, for many, to be prepared for graduate study in medicine, law, business, art, architecture, or technical schools.

All this in four years!

Actually, students have much less time, when you consider several complicating factors. Because many high schools don't do their jobs, 53 percent of college students require remedial courses. Colleges, moreover, do not have four years to provide an integrated education because 58 percent of students attend two or more institutions of higher education. At the same time, most students have family or work responsibilities—in 1999, 74 percent of full-time students worked while attending college and nearly half of them worked at least 25 hours a week. Unfortunately, students who have to work their way through college compromise their education, and many of these student workers say that holding a job hurts their grades, and limits class schedules and choice of courses. By one estimate, "college students typically spend less than half the time on their studies than the faculty expects."[23]

Clearly, systemic reforms are needed, especially now that we have a mass higher education system that complements our secondary, elementary, and pre-school programs. We have to reevaluate this entire system of education for what it is: an 18-year learning continuum that prepares citizens for a life of learning. We must address the issues of general education, unnecessary and wasteful duplication, and the coherence and integrity of our curricula.

Reform of higher education, I believe, must focus on a revival of the liberal arts. Paradoxically, liberal education is in decline, just when we need it the most. I am speaking of the growth of technical and pre-professional studies at the expense of humanities and social studies. In 1970, 50 percent of the baccalaureate degrees awarded were in a liberal arts discipline, including the sciences.[24] By 1995, that percentage had shrunk to about 40 percent, and about 60 percent of the degrees were in pre-professional or technical fields. The largest number of BA's granted in the 1990s was in business.[25] Furthermore, I do not believe there is enough communication between people in the technical and pre-professional schools and those in the liberal arts schools; for the most part, they exist in separate worlds on campus, in complete intellectual isolation.

I believe that the decline in liberal arts and in its perceived relevance is largely a result of the way colleges and universities have marginalized liberal arts by fragmenting the curriculum, and worst of all, severing most connections between the arts and sciences. The university's lack of a meaningful liberal arts curriculum understandably sends many anxious students into the safer harbors of study that lead directly to positions in the job market. Writing about the decline of liberal arts and general education in the last three decades, the biologist and Pulitzer-prize winning author Edward O. Wilson observes: "With rare exceptions American universities and colleges have dissolved their curriculum into a slurry of minor disciplines and specialized courses. While the average number of undergraduate courses per institution doubled, the percentage of mandatory courses in general education dropped by more than half. Science was sequestered in the same period; as I wrote, in 1997, only a third of universities and colleges require students to take at least one course in the natural sciences."[26]

We must remind ourselves that the value of a liberal arts education, and education in general, is to enhance men's and women's powers of rational analysis, intellectual precision, and independent judgment. And, in particular, education should encourage a mental adaptability, a characteristic which men and women sorely need, especially now in an era of rapid change.

A proper and balanced education is not a passive act or an end in itself. It is important not only to be able to engage in new ideas, but also to be willing to make public declarations of one's convictions and one's commitments—and then be able to translate them into written words and actions. For education must make us more than well-ordered puppets in the passing show, making gestures with no sense of the significance of the human drama, moved only by the strings that tie to material things.

We must remember that education must make students familiar with the best our culture has taught, said, and done—as well as the dead ends and aberrations that clutter our history. It must help us understand the sweep of our culture, the achievements, the problems, the solutions, and the failures that mark our history. This kind of knowledge is critical to our understanding of who and what we are. A proper education must serve as a tool of enlightenment. It can be an instrument for enhancing individual as well as collective self-determination. It can provide liberation from political, economic, and social ills. It can help us understand the American polity—which is no small task in our pluralistic and multicultural society that allows the unique to participate in the universal without dissolving in it. Finally, this kind of education serves as the vehicle of American democracy as well as its engine, providing a powerful way to tackle our country's unfinished agenda. After all, education promises every sort of advancement to those who, based on their sex or race or age or disability, have not been able to partake in the benefits of our society.

We must also remind ourselves that a liberal education is needed to integrate learning and provide balance—otherwise students will graduate into a world in which dependence on experts of every kind will be even more common than it is today. With that trend comes an even greater temptation to abdicate judgment in favor of expert opinion. Unless we help our students acquire their own identity, they will end up not just dependent on experts but at the mercy of experts—or worse, at the mercy of charlatans posing as experts.

As a people, we need to understand where we were, where we are, and where we are going. Without liberal arts to provide a context for technical training, young people cannot be expected to understand the general nature and structure of our society, the role of the university, academic freedom, or the importance of values—all of this will have no ethical, moral, or societal context.

The challenge for higher education, then, is not the choice between pure research and practical application but, rather, the integrating and resynthesizing of compartmentalized knowledge. On campus, we must create an intellectual climate that encourages the bridging of boundaries between academic specialties. This means encouraging faculty and students to make connections among seemingly disparate disciplines, discoveries, events, and trends, and integrating the knowledge in ways that benefit the commonwealth of learning. The Nobel Prize committee recognized the importance of interdisciplinary scholarship in 1992 when it gave the economics prize to Gary S. Becker at the University of Chicago for "having extended the domain of economic theory to aspects of human behavior which had previously been dealt with—if at all—by other social science disciplines such as sociology, demography, and criminology."[27]

To accommodate this kind of interdisciplinary creativity, the college learning environment must become more open and flexible. After all, some of the most promising areas of research and creativity are interdisciplinary not only in the physical and natural sciences but in the social sciences, the humanities, and the arts, as well. We have to develop creative multi-disciplinary, interdisciplinary, and transdisciplinary approaches in our liberal arts curricula in order to provide intellectual coherence. Colleges and universities must develop strategies for enabling their faculty members, who are steeped in different disciplines, to also have opportunities for this interdisciplinary and multidisciplinary work—as they continue their own lifelong learning.

Team teaching, for example, is one obvious way to provide students with thematic study of interwoven scientific, historical, and literary ideas. Team teaching can also provide multiple and comparative perspectives and expertise. In both instances, students gain knowledge of multiple disciplines as well as their interconnectedness. Within disciplines, of course, teaching should encourage students to draw knowledge together from many sources. Writing on this theme in 1956, Edwin E. Aubrey said: "The student should be educated to think of relations: the relations of an event to its historical background; the relation of a statement to its implications or to its presuppositions, so that it can be logically examined; the relation of facts to each other in the creation of a structure of knowledge, transforming raw data into understanding; the relation of new ideas to established knowledge so as to test them or to modify one's preconceptions. Such relational thinking is a rigorous discipline and needs to be insisted upon if the student is really to become an educated person."[28]

A reform agenda must also include the creation of a balance between specialists and generalists. Although we live in an age of extraordinary specialization and fragmentation of knowledge, it is clear that we cannot abandon specializations or sub-specializations or sub-sub-specializations. After all, the division of labor has greatly advanced the cause of civilization. Specialization is an instrument of progress. Complexity, by necessity, requires specialization.

So we need specialists. But for greater understanding we also need generalists, trained in the humanities, sciences, and social sciences. The challenge is to provide synthesis and systemic perspectives. We need to create a common discourse, a common vocabulary among the various disciplines. Unfortunately, generalists are not held in high regard on campus or in our society unless they are big names, or else because they became generalists after first earning credibility as specialists.

And since our society *respects* specialists and *suspects* generalists, perhaps the way to solve the shortage of generalists is by creating a new specialty in synthesis and systems — much as José Ortega y Gasset proposed in his 1944 book, *The Mission of the University*. He wrote: "The need to create sound synthesis and systemization of knowledge . . . will call out a kind of scientific genius which hitherto has existed only as an aberration: the genius of integration. Of necessity this means specialization, as all creative effort does, but this time, the [person] will be specializing in the construction of the whole."[29]

Today, I've outlined a daunting challenge for higher education, one that calls on institutions of higher education to develop and enunciate a clear philosophy of education. Colleges and universities must address the reunification of knowledge, the process and nature of life-long learning in our fast-paced times, and, most ambitiously, they must join other institutions in addressing the continuities and discontinuities of knowledge within our entire pre-K–16 educational system.

While we must overhaul higher education, we must also treat it with the respect that is due to a national treasure. After all, for more than two centuries American colleges and universities have been the backbone of our nation's progress, helping make it an economic, cultural, scientific, technological, and political power. Not coincidentally, America also became an educational power. The excellence of the American university is reflected in the fact that the largest share of foreign students who choose to study abroad come here.[30] Henry

Rosovsky, the economist and educator, estimates that between two-thirds and three-quarters of the world's best universities are located in the United States—he asks, "What other sector of the economy can make a similar statement? . . . In higher education, 'made in America' is still the finest label." Referring to that label, Rosovsky cautions: "My only advice is to add 'handle with care.' "[31]

Notes

[1]Sheldon Rothblatt, *The Modern University and Its Discontents* (Cambridge University Press, 1997), 27.

[2]Eric Foner, *The Story of American Freedom* (Diane Publishing Company, 2001), 322.

[3]Drop-out rate at four-year institutions comes from Clifford Adelman, *Answers in the Tool Box: Academic Integrity, Attendance Patterns, and Bachelor's Degree Attainment* (Washington, D.C.: U.S. Government Printing Office, 1999), vii. Dropout rate for community colleges comes from ACT; see *http://www.act.org/news/releases/2001/charts4.html*. Statistics as cited by National Panel Report, op. cit., 11.

[4]Ellen Condliffe Lagemann, "The Challenge of Liberal Education: Past, Present, and Future," Keynote Address, Annual Meeting of the Association of American Colleges and Universities, Seattle, Washington, January 23, 2003.

[5]Megan Rooney, "Freshmen Show Rising Political Awareness and Changing Social Views," *The Chronicle of Higher Education*, January 31, 2003: A35–37, *http://chronicle.com/students*.

[6]National Panel Report, op. cit.

[7]Ibid., vii.

[8]American Association of Colleges and Universities, *Integrity in the College Curriculum*, 2, Washington, D.C., 1985 as cited by the National Panel Report, op. cit., 16.

[9]Mark Davidson, *Uncommon Sense, the Life and Thoughts of Ludwig von Bertalanffy* (Boston: Houghton Mifflin, 1983), 184 as quoted by Thomas Mandel, "Is there a General System," International Society for the Systems Sciences, *http://www.isss.org/primer/data.gensystm./htm*.

[10]Bela H. Banathy, "The Evolution of Systems Inquiry, Part 2" International Society for the Systems Sciences, *http://www.isss.org/primer/data/004evsys.htm*.

[11]William J. Bouwsma, "Models of the Educated Man," *The American Scholar* 44 (1975): 195–212.

[12]Bouwsma, "Models of the Educated Man," 207.

[13]Various estimates on the half-life of knowledge. See Karl M. Kapp and Carrie McKeague, "Blended Learning for Compliance Training Success, 2002," 2 at *http://www.eduneering.com/press/articles/kapp_mckeague_white_paper.pdf*. See also speech by

Radm (NS) Teo Chee Hean, Minister for Education, at that NIE Teachers Investiture, July 4, 2001, in Singapore, *http://www1.moe.edu.sg/speeches/2001/sp04072001a.htm*.

[14]Maryanne Rouse, "Teaching Philosophy," College of Business Administration, University of South Florida, *http://www.coba.usf.edu/departments/management/faculty/rouse/teach.htm*.

[15]T. S. Eliot, *Murder in the Cathedral* (London: Faber and Faber Ltd., 1943), 71.

[16]T. S. Eliot, *The Rock: A Pageant Play* (London: Faber and Faber Ltd., 1934), I:7.

[17]Peter Lyman and Hal R. Varian, "How Much Information," 2000 School of Information Management and Systems at the University of California at Berkeley *http://www.sims.berkeley.edu/how-much-info*.

[18]Richard Saul Wurman, *Information Anxiety*, (New York: Doubleday, 1989).

[19]See Google.com, lycos.com, or altavista.com.

[20]Wurman, op. cit., 36.

[21]Neil Postman, "Informing Ourselves to Death," (Speech given at a meeting of the German Informatics Society on October 11, 1990 in Stuttgart).

[22]Albert Einstein, *Ideas and Opinions* (New York: Crown Publishers, 1954) as quoted by Mandel, op. cit., at International Society for the Systems Sciences, *http://www.isss.org/primer/data/gensystm.htm*.

[23]National Panel Report, op. cit., x.

[24]Carol M. Barker, "Liberal Arts Education for a Global Society," *2000 Carnegie Challenge* (New York: Carnegie Corporation of New York, 2000), 4.

[25]Ibid., 4.

[26]Edward O. Wilson, *Consilience: The Unity of Knowledge* (New York: Vintage Books, 1999), 13.

[27]Wilson, ibid., 220.

[28]Edwin E. Aubrey, "Humanistic Teaching and the Place of Ethical and Religious Values in Higher Education," *The Educational Survey of the University of Pennsylvania*, September, 1956.

[29]José Ortega y Gasset: *The Mission of the University* (Princeton: Princeton UP, 1944).

[30]Institute of International Education, *http://www/iie/org/fulbright/posts/guide/intro4.htm#1*. See also National Center for Policy Analysis, "Foreign Students Studying in the U.S.," at *http://www/ncpa.org/pi/edu/pd120798e.html* and also information on the Educational Testing Service Network's web site: *http://www/ets/org/usiarprt.html*.

[31]Henry Rosovsky, "Highest Education," *The New Republic*, July 13–20, 1987: 13–14.

The Will to Believe and the Need for Creed

Jaroslav Pelikan*

*I*F THIS TITLE, "The Will to Believe and the Need for Creed,"[1] were to be properly documented in accordance with *The Chicago Manual of Style*, it would bring together a truly "odd couple" of footnotes. For its first member, "The Will to Believe," was the title of a lecture that was delivered by William James to the Philosophical Club at Yale (which he, being of course a professor at Harvard, called "your good old orthodox College") and that was first published as an article in the journal *New World* in June 1896, and then in 1897 as part of a book that has been reprinted several times since then and to which it gave its title.[2] "The Need for Creed," on the other hand, was the headline of an article about a modern rock group, in the Sunday supplement to *The New Haven Register* (although I had in fact already formulated it on my own well before that article appeared).

---

*Delivered on December 5, 2003, at the Beinecke Rare Book and Manuscript Library in conjunction with a "Concert of Credo Settings in Honor of Jaroslav Pelikan" by the Yale Schola Cantorum, the Yale Russian Chorus, and the Hellenic College Schola Cantorum of Brookline, MA. The event was sponsored by the Yale Institute of Sacred Music and the Beinecke Rare Book and Manuscript Library, Yale University, New Haven, CT.

1

Having had the privilege in 1990, while I was preparing my own Gifford Lectures of 1992/1993, *Christianity and Classical Culture*, of laying a wreath of homage in memory of William James by writing the "Introduction" to the Library of America edition of his Gifford Lectures, *The Varieties of Religious Experience*,[3] I want to use his Yale lecture as a springboard into the one "variety of religious experience" for which (borrowing Adolf von Harnack's pungent metaphor about the theology of his student Karl Barth) William James seems to have "possessed no antenna,"[4] perhaps even (if I may presume to suggest this about such a giant as William James) no real understanding: the no less authentically "religious experience" that I am calling here "the need for creed."[5] To cite only one example: "If . . . we could descend upon our subject from above like Catholic theologians," James opined in *Varieties*, "with our fixed definitions of man and man's perfection and our positive dogmas about God, *we should have an easy time of it.*"[6] Tell that to Saint Augustine, the Catholic theologian who wrote the *Confessions*! Or to my late friend Father Alexander Schmemann, who could write in his recently translated *Journals*:

> I become filled with disgust for the role I have been playing for
> decades . . . I feel that everybody around me knows what to do and
> how and what for, but I only *pretend* to know. In fact, I don't know
> anything; I am not sure of anything; I am deceiving myself and oth-
> ers. Only when I serve the Liturgy am I not deceitful.[7]

But "the need for creed" entails as well the need for dogma, defined as the official public teaching of a community of faith, whose development from the New Testament to the end of the twentieth century I have charted in the five volumes of my history, *The Christian Tradition*;[8] that was why I entitled the comprehensive doctrinal index I prepared for *Creeds and Confessions of Faith* "A Comparative Creedal Syndogmaticon."[9] Appropriately, a study subtitled "The Origins of Unbelief in America" bears the dual title, not only *Without God*, but *Without Creed*.[10] After all these years of research into it and publication about it, I have good reason, of course, to be as keenly aware as anyone could be of how unfashionable it is nowadays even to speak about creed, not to mention dogma: "Any stick to beat a dog," the old proverb says, and therefore "Any stigma to beat a dogma."

In "The Will to Believe" William James took off from Blaise Pascal's celebrated but highly controversial *argument du pari*, "the argument of the wager," in his *Pensées*:[11]

> "Either God is or he is not." But to which view shall we be inclined? Reason cannot decide this question . . . Yes; but you must wager. There is no choice . . . Let us weigh up the gain and the loss involved in calling heads that God exists. Let us assess the two cases: if you win you win everything, if you lose you lose nothing. Do not hesitate then; wager that he does exist.[12]

Defining himself in relation to Pascal, James made his own case for the role of individual human volition in shaping religious belief:[13]

> My own stake is important enough to give me the right to choose my own form of risk. If religion be true and the evidence for it be still insufficient, I do not wish, by putting your extinguisher upon my nature, . . . to forfeit my sole chance in life of getting upon the winning side, — that chance depending, of course, on my willingness to run the risk of acting as if my passional need of taking the world religiously might be prophetic and right.[14]

It was on the basis of such statements as this that Justice Oliver Wendell Holmes, Jr., a fellow member with William James of "the Metaphysical Club" in Cambridge, devised his posthumous *bon mot*, witty but cruel, about William James, "His wishes made him turn down the lights so as to give miracle a chance."[15] At the same time, that quotation from "The Will to Believe" is an example of William James's propensity for focusing his attention on the individual in the here and now, at the cost of both of Tradition and of Church. Indeed, in the Gifford Lectures he went on, famously, to define "religion" as "the feeling, acts, and experiences of *individual men in their solitude,* so far as they apprehend themselves in relation to whatever they may consider the divine."[16] Nevertheless, in at least one passage of "The Will to Believe" he had moved beyond this limitation to acknowledge: "Our faith is faith in some one else's faith, and in the greatest matters this is most the case."[17] That passage, in turn, makes a natural transition from "the will to believe" to "the need for creed" and the need for Tradition.

2

Fundamental to any other consideration of the need for creed and confession of faith is its function as an indispensable key to the living and dynamic reality of the heritage of the faith of Israel in one God, enshrined in the *Shema,* "Hear, O Israel: The LORD our God is one Lord" (Dt 6.4), which I have called "a monument and a fiery pillar, the primal creed and confession of the Christian church."[18] This is the very first text of the more than two hundred that we have included in *Creeds and Confessions of Faith in the Christian Tradition;*[19] and all the thousands of pages of trinitarian creeds that follow may properly be seen as glosses on it, steadfastly affirming the oneness of God as the nonnegotiable presupposition for everything else, including and especially the dogma of the *homoousios* at Nicaea and the dogma of the Trinity at Constantinople I and the dogma of the Incarnation at Ephesus and Chalcedon. The *Shema* is, then, the most ancient of all our creeds—and the most daring, and the most shattering: the affirmation that within and beyond the Tower of Babel of voices in William James's "varieties of religious experience," within and beyond the metaphysical welter of William James's "pluralistic universe," is not the Many but the One; "and underneath are the everlasting arms" (Dt 33.27). It is an affirmation that has never, *pace* James's condescending phrase, had "an easy time of it." In what Dostoevsky called "the whirlwinds of doubt"; after a personal reprise of the hammer blows in chapter after chapter of the Book of Job; perishing for the faith in the Nazi death camps or the Communist gulags; at the senseless death of an infant or in the wake of 9/11 or after the numbing triumph of demonic evil—who could ever, at any period in history, "have an easy time of it" affirming faith or making "God-talk"? But when personal religious faith has exhausted its allotted supply of "the courage to be," when the only Psalm it can remember is not the one that begins "The Lord is my shepherd" (Ps 23.1) but the one immediately preceding it, which begins "My God, my God, why hast Thou forsaken me?" (Ps 22.1), then, precisely then, we are not thrown on our own individual and feeble resources of believing or speculating or explaining (or even "experiencing"), such as they may be. Rather, though perhaps in a sense that he may not have intended, it is then that the admission of William James comes through and rings true: "Our faith is faith in *some one else's faith*, and in the greatest matters this is most the case."[20] For then it is time to confess: However much or however little I may be able to believe on my own, existentially, as of this precise moment, I affirm myself to stand, trembling, in the continuity and heritage of that community which has been confessing without interruption for entire millennia, "Shema Yisroēl, Adōnoi Elōhēnu, Adōnoi Echod; Credo in *unum* Deum."

3

This monotheistic faith and creed has been carefully guarded by (each in its own special way) Judaism, Christianity, and Islam—putting them, for now, in chronological order—the three peoples of the Book, who identify Abraham as, in the words of the New Testament, "the father of *all* who believe" (Rom 4.11) in the one true God. In the history of each of these three peoples of the Book, both within each community and above all in the history of each in its relations to the other two, however, the monotheistic creed has repeatedly become the text—or the pretext—for violence, coercion, and persecution against those who hold to another creed. Words like "crusade," "pogrom" (which as Slavs need to be reminded, is not a Germanic coinage but a Slavic one, from *grom*, the word for thunder),[21] and "jihad" have entered our vocabulary because of the prevalence of such conflict of creeds; and the expectation that the age of such violence had come to an end because of the forces of Enlightenment (whether "Enlightenment" is spelled lowercase or uppercase) has been, quite literally, going up in smoke. For quite understandable reasons, consequently, this clash among creeds has led, in the eighteenth, nineteenth, and twentieth centuries, to what Claude Welch has labeled "the antidogmatic, antienthusiastic temper of an age tired and disgusted with religious controversies."[22] Toleration among the creeds was and is, for many moderns, rooted in that "antidogmatic," anticreedal, and relativistic temper of the age; and in the presence of any unequivocal affirmation of a creed, therefore, the hope for civil peace and religious toleration is based on the wish that if only "those people" (whoever they may be) could give up their creedal beliefs for a nondogmatic faith, everything would be all right. One of the most powerful and persuasive statements of this case is Gotthold Ephraim Lessings's play of 1779, *Nathan the Wise*, with its Legend of the Three Rings.

Yet the outlook for that anticreedal and antidogmatic wish is—to use the title of a book published in 1927 by Sigmund Freud for the exact opposite of his authorial intent—"the future of an illusion." For as one of the most sensitive and provocative of the literary interpreters of Freud, Professor Lionel Trilling of Columbia University, pointed out in 1950, in an essay entitled "Wordsworth and the Rabbis": "It is probably true that when the *dogmatic principle* in religion is slighted, religion goes along for a while on generalized emotion and ethical intention—'morality touched by emotion'—*and then loses the force of its impulse, even the essence of its being.*"[23] From quite another direction but at almost exactly the same time, in a lecture that he gave on 12 December 1951 at the New Jersey College for Women (now part of Rutgers University) and that I heard him deliver at Saint Louis University, Etienne Gilson of Paris and Toronto, who since my days as a graduate student has been my principal scholarly guide to the intellectual history of the Western Middle Ages,²⁴ called for a dogmatic basis for tolerance, a doctrine of religious freedom that would be based not on the rejection of creed, but on the affirmation of creed.²⁵ The catastrophic experience of Europe in the 1930s was, Professor Gilson argued, a cautionary tale about any case for religious toleration that is based on creedal indifference and on the absence of specific belief. For the "will to believe" is so relentless — or, if I may put it this way, so *insidious* — that when it is denied or frustrated and when religious toleration, instead of being "justified by faith" (Rom 3.28), is justified by non-faith, belief will (in Dostoevsky's phrase) go around the locked doors and sneak in through a window, substituting Wotan for the God of Abraham, Isaac, and Jacob, the Father of the Lord Jesus Christ, and replacing the *Shema* and the *Nicene Creed* with the creed of *Blut und Erde*. "Heartily know," said Emerson: "When half-gods go, / The gods arrive."²⁶ But unfortunately the movement can go in the opposite direction, too: with the disappearance of the "the gods" or of the One True God, "the half-gods" may arrive, wearing a hammer and sickle or a swastika and bringing in their train a creed that is even more ready to persecute than any of the historic creeds have been.

Etienne Gilson's call for a dogmatic and creedal foundation for tolerance had been anticipated, albeit with certainly less of dogma than he would have liked, in England and the Netherlands.²⁷ But the most ambitious response to it, and the most creedal, was the "Declaration on Religious Freedom of the Second Vatican Council," *Dignitatis humanae*, officially issued on 7 December 1965. *Dignitatis humanae* freely acknowledges, speaking about various of the Christian traditions not excepting its own, that "at times in the life of the people of God, as it has pursued its pilgrimage through the twists and turns of human history, there have been ways of acting hardly in tune with the spirit of the gospel, indeed contrary to it." But over against these "ways of acting," which include the Roman Catholic Inquisition as well as

Protestant New England and Orthodox Russia and other examples literally too numerous to mention, the Second Vatican Council promulgated this formula as a binding creedal confession: "The human person
has a right to religious freedom. Such freedom consists in this, that all
should have such immunity from coercion by individuals, or by groups,
or by any human power, that no one should be forced to act against his
conscience in religious matters, nor prevented from acting according
to his conscience." The case for this freedom is said to be derived from
"the dignity of the human person as this is known [first] from the
revealed word of God and [second] from reason itself," so that it is not
only a teaching of the Church but a universal human right.[28]

But especially at a time like the present, it is salutary to be
reminded that of the three monotheisms of the Book, as during the
Middle Ages they lived side by side in Spain and in the Levant, the
most advanced scientifically, the most sophisticated philosophically,
and the most tolerant religiously was Islam: the leading systematic
exposition of the Eastern Orthodox Christian creed, *The Orthodox
Faith* of Saint John of Damascus, and its counterpart for the Jewish
creed, *The Guide to the Perplexed* of Rabbi Moses Maimonides ("the
Rambam"), were both published under the protection of Muslim
rulers (and the latter in Arabic, in 1190)—not because these Muslims
were skeptics or relativists about religious faith and creed, but because
they accepted and obeyed the respect for other faiths that their creed
and their Holy Book and their God required. As it is written in Surah
29 of the Qur'ān,

> Do not argue with the people of the Book
> unless in a fair way . . . and say to them:
> "We believe what has been sent down to you.
> Our God and your God is one,
> and to Him we submit." (29.46)

There is no religious imperative more urgent in our own time than the
recovery, by each of the three monotheisms, of the need for a creed

that will find in such toleration the direct implication not of unfaith, but of what (to employ a standard confessional formula) each community of faith "believes, teaches, and confesses" as divinely revealed truth. For if anyone supposes that a minimal religious toleration and civil peace will have to wait for one billion Muslims to exchange their creed for Western Enlightenment skepticism and relativism, then, as I have been quoted as saying, we had better fasten our safety belts!

4

The one overriding impression that Valerie Hotchkiss and I have carried away from all these years of examining, selecting, and then editing and translating creeds and confessions of faith from over a span of so many centuries is their pertinacity as a literary and theological genre. Quite counterintuitively, that pertinacity has manifested itself the most dramatically of all not in the fourth century or the sixteenth (both of which certainly produced a great many creeds and confessions of faith), but during the nineteenth and twentieth centuries, amid what has been called "the discomfort with creed caused by the consciousness of modernity"[29] and often in those very denominations where we might have least expected it to appear. For example, at least partly because of pressure from other groups for evidence that they really were Christian, the Church of Jesus Christ of Latter-day Saints (Mormons) in 1842 and the Church of Christ, Scientist in 1879 both formulated their distinctive tenets in statements of faith that ended up being much more traditional in their confessional form than they were in their doctrinal content.[30] Similarly, the Society of Friends (Quakers) have been more thorough in eliminating sacraments than in dispensing with creeds, producing from the beginning a spate of confessions leading up to *The Richmond Declaration of Faith* of 1887.[31] A particularly intriguing example of such persistence in an unexpected context is the formulary adopted by the Unitarian General Convention in 1935, which concludes, "Neither this nor any other statement shall be imposed as a creedal test," but then continues: "provided that the faith thus indicated be professed," which does sound very much like a creedal test.[32] Like *The Universal Declaration of Human Rights* of 1948,[33] an earlier secular consensus issued in 1776 had found it necessary to speak confessionally: "We hold these truths," it affirmed, not "We cannot know anything for sure."[34] Paraphrasing the warning in a fragment attributed to Aristotle about why it is impossible to escape philosophizing: "You say that one must confess one's faith; then you need to confess your faith. You say that one must *not* confess; to say that, you will need to issue a confession! Either way, creeds and confessions are unavoidable."

One of the most frequently recurring of the modern objection to the need for creed within Christendom is the insistence that there is no need for creed because the authority of church confessions conflicts with the authority of Holy Scripture, and Scripture is enough, *sola Scriptura*. In the challenge of Thomas Campbell, the intellectual founder of the Disciples of Christ, even as he was issuing a set of "propositions" in his *Declaration and Address* of 1809, "Let none imagine that the subjoined propositions are at all intended as an overture towards a new creed, or standard, for the church . . . They are merely designed for opening up the way, that we may come fairly and firmly to original ground upon clear and certain premises and take up things just as the apostles left them. . . . disentangled from the accruing embarrassment of intervening ages."[35] But as the Protestant Reformers of the sixteenth century had already discovered, one of the "accruing embarrassments of the intervening ages" was the question of just what belongs in the Bible in the first place, and therefore of who has the authority to define what belongs in the Bible—in short, the problem of the canon, to which eventually all of the major confessions were obliged to turn.[36] The earliest Protestant confession opens with an attack on "all who say that the gospel is nothing without the approbation of the church";[37] this seems to be an attack on Saint Augustine, who had declared, in a passage that was repeatedly quoted in the Reformation controversies, "For my part, I should not believe the

Gospel except as moved by the authority of the Catholic Church."[38] For *The Scots Confession* of 1560, authority in the church is "neither antiquity, usurped title, lineal succession, appointed place, nor the numbers of men approving an error," but "the true preaching of the word of God."[39] But if it is not "the approbation of the church" from which we have received the canon of Scripture for "the true preaching of the word of God," then where did the canon come from? The *Confessio Gallica* of 1559/1571 answers that question head-on, by frankly invoking an utterly subjective criterion to validate the professedly objective authority of the Bible: "We know these books to be canonical, and the sure rule of our faith, not so much by the common accord and consent of the church, as by the testimony and inward illumination of the Holy Spirit, which enables us to distinguish them from other ecclesiastical books upon which, however useful, we can not base any articles of faith,"[40] making it possible, presumably, to use this filter to tell the difference between the canonical Book of Proverbs or Koheleth and the deuterocanonical Book of Wisdom or Sirach.

To affirm a creed as heritage is, then, to make one's own a tradition that has been handed down and passed on. For not only are the creeds themselves part of Tradition; they come out of Tradition and point back to Tradition. That quality of creeds makes itself palpable in the decrees of the seven ecumenical councils of the Church: I Nicaea 325, I Constantinople 381, Ephesus 431, Chalcedon 451, II Constantinople 553, III Constantinople 680–681, II Nicaea 787. Each one reaches forward by first reaching backward to the authority of the Prophets, to the authority of the New Testament, and to the authority of Tradition, especially as this has been articulated by the previous councils, in the summary formula that concludes the *ekthesis* of the Council of Chalcedon of 451: "just as the [Hebrew] prophets taught from the beginning about him, *and* as [in the Gospels] the Lord Jesus Christ himself instructed us, *and* as the creed of the fathers handed it down [traditioned it, *paradedōke*] to us [at the Councils of Nicaea, Constantinople, and Ephesus]."[41] Even when the preceding council, the Council of Ephesus of 431, promulgated what John Henry Newman acknowledged to have been "an addition, greater perhaps than any before or since, to the letter of the primitive faith"[42] by declaring the Virgin Mary to be the *Theotokos*, "the one who gave birth to God; the Mother of God," the council itself identified this not as an "addition [*prosthēkē*]" of what had not been there before, but as an "amplification [*plērophoria*]" that made explicit what had previously been only implicit.[43]

But because Tradition is *living* Tradition—nothing I have ever written or said, I suppose, has achieved wider circulation than the epigram in the introduction to *The Christian Tradition*, "Tradition is the living faith of the dead; traditionalism is the dead faith of the living"[44]—the obverse side of this orthodox continuity and creedal fidelity is the creative engagement of creed with each new culture into which it comes. When, in the ninth century, Saints Cyril and Methodius of Thessalonica came from Constantinople to my ancestral "Great Moravia," they did not Hellenize the Slavs, but they Slavicized the liturgy and the gospel; this is why the subtitle of a recent book about them reads "The Acculturation of the Slavs."[45] Among all the hundreds of creeds and confessions in our collection, my favorite illustration of such acculturation is *The Masai Creed* from East Africa in the 1960s:

1. We believe in the one High God, who out of love created the beautiful world and everything good in it. He created man and wanted man to be happy in the world. God loves the world and every nation and tribe on the earth. We have known this High God in the darkness, and now we know him in the light. God promised in the book of his word, the Bible, that he would save the world and all the nations and tribes.

2. We believe that God made good his promise by sending his Son, Jesus Christ, a man in the flesh, a Jew by tribe, born poor in a little village, who left his home *and was always on safari*, doing good, curing people by the power of God, teaching about God and man, showing that the meaning of religion is love. He was rejected by his people, tortured and nailed hands and feet to a cross, and died. He lay buried in the grave, *but the hyenas did not*

touch him, and on the third day, he rose from the grave. He
ascended to the skies. He is the Lord.

3. We believe that all our sins are forgiven through him. All who
have faith in him must be sorry for their sins, be baptized in the
Holy Spirit of God, live the rules of love, and share the bread
together in love, to announce the good news to others until
Jesus comes again. We are waiting for him. He is alive. He lives.
This we believe. Amen.[46]

The motto underlying this simple and yet profound *Masai Creed* is:
"We must Africanize Christianity, not Christianize Africa."[47]

From what I have already said it will, I hope, be clear that the locus
of creed and confession is the believing community, and therefore that
an essential component of the need for creed is the need to be situated
within that community. As Martin Luther once put it, characteristically, you must do your own believing as you must do your own dying;
but when you believe, as when you die, you are surrounded by "a cloud
of witnesses" (Heb 12.1). And here a textual and grammatical anomaly
arises in the most universal of all the creeds in the Christian tradition,
the so-called *Nicene Creed* (which scholars, and probably only scholars,
call the *Niceno-Constantinopolitan Creed*). As everyone knows, the English word *credo*—which has even occasionally become the title for a
book—comes from the first person *singular* of the Latin verb *credere*,
"to believe," because, as today's concert has demonstrated in the rich
and glorious variety of many languages, the Creed opens with the
words "Credo in unum Deum, *I* believe in one God"; in Greek, too, it
is *Pisteuō*, and in the Church Slavonic tradition in which Igor Stravin-
sky stood, *Věruju*—both of these also in the first-person singular (or,
as a colleague used to call it, "the first-person perpendicular"). But
what the Second Ecumenical Council promulgated as its creed at
Constantinople in 381—and, for that matter, also what the First Ecumenical Council had already promulgated as its creed at Nicaea in
325—both begin with *pisteuomen*, "*We* believe."[48] In the East, this
change from the plural to the singular seems to have taken place

because of the use of this creed in the rite of baptism, where both the renunciation of the devil and the affirmation of the faith are individual acts, spoken by the candidate or by the godparents in the name of the candidate. In the West, the creed at baptism is the so-called *Apostles' Creed*, whose *original* text already had "*I* believe"; [49] but by the time the West in 589, explaining in so many words that it was following long-standing Eastern liturgical practice,[50] first made the *Niceno-Constantinopolitan Creed* a prescribed part of its celebrations of the Mass (though the liturgical practice did not actually become universal in the Western Church until several centuries later), the first-person singular had already been established. As a consequence of the new emphasis on the doctrine of the Church throughout Christendom during the twentieth century, "*We* believe in one God" has been restored as the wording of the creed in most of the Western denominations that still recite it in their celebrations of the Eucharist. And in view of the well-known sensitivity of Eastern Christendom to any changes in the text of the Creed as the Council originally formulated it, as that sensitivity has expressed itself in the controversies over the addition of "Filioque,"[51] the presence of the plural *pisteuomen* in the original text would appear to have a presumptive claim there, too, at any rate when the Creed is being employed in the Eucharistic liturgy rather than in the baptismal rite. For one of the primary needs for creed is the need to declare the faith together—together with those standing next to us as we worship, together with all those around the world who worship and confess as we do, whatever the language, together with all the generations who have gone before us worshiping and confessing and who, as the faith and the hope of the Church affirm, still go on doing so before the face of God together with the holy angels. To quote again from William James, "Our faith is faith in someone else's faith, and in the greatest matters this is most the case."[52]

The reason for this corporate dimension of the need for creed and confession of faith is rooted in the basic nature of creed as a liturgical act. It was (perhaps surprisingly for some) John Calvin who said that *The Nicene Creed* was meant to be sung rather than spoken—presumably, so long as those who sang it were not encumbered by too many fancy vestments or enveloped in too much incense. And here it is important to be reminded of the historical philology of the word "orthodoxy." It comes, of course, from the Greek adjective *orthos* ("straight, correct," as in "orthodontist," one who straightens and corrects teeth) and the Greek noun *doxa.* Now *doxa* in Classical Greek basically meant "opinion," so that ortho-doxy means "holding to the correct opinion or doctrine." But quite early on, *doxa* acquired the more specific meaning of "*laudatory* opinion" about someone, therefore of "praise." In the Septuagint Greek version of the inaugural vision of the prophet Isaiah, the seraphim sang, "The whole earth is full of his *doxa*" (Is 6.3 LXX); and in the original Greek of the song of the Bethlehem angels (original to Saint Luke's Gospel, that is, whatever the native tongue of those angels may have been), "*Doxa* to God in the highest, and on earth peace" (Lk 2.14). *Doxa Patri,* "Glory be to the Father and to the Son and to the Holy Spirit," is repeated over and over again in the Liturgy; and for a long time, as the so-called Common Doxology in English hymnody also shows, it was the practice in Western churches to chant it as the concluding verse of every Psalm, not only in the Liturgy but in the canonical Hours.

From that meaning of *doxa,* "orthodoxy" was construed to mean "the correct way of giving glory." Because the word for "glory" in all the Slavic languages is "slava," "ortho-doxy" is translated *Pravo-slavie.* The Feast of Orthodoxy, observed as part of the Eastern Orthodox calendar on the first Sunday of Lent, was instituted in 843 to celebrate, not correct doctrine or right theology as such, but the restoration of the images to the church's worship after the iconoclastic controversies — therefore "correct worship," which is ultimately inseparable from "correct doctrine. And that, of course, is precisely the point: creed is not in the first instance the business of the professional and learned theological elite; *it is meant to be prayed,* right alongside the Lord's Prayer, as an act of adoration and worship; and it has been a universal experience, far beyond the borders of Christendom, that the best way to preserve genuine spontaneity in the life of prayer is, paradoxically, to formulate fixed and traditional liturgical texts for recitation, on the basis that the spirit of devotion, individual and corporate, can then go on to improvise. In a real sense, therefore, the task also of the theologian in relation to the creed can be summarized in the Latin mottos of the two Western religious orders: the Jesuit *sentire cum Ecclesia,* "to think along with the Church," by first reciting the Church's creed and then, like Bach or Brahms, becoming a faithful virtuoso by improvising "variations on the theme"; and the Dominican *contemplata aliis tradere,* "to communicate to others the fruit of one's contemplation and study," thus bringing together worship and scholarship while still distinguishing between them. The creed, its text and its history, is and must be the object of intense scholarly study and research, as the volumes of *Creeds and Confessions of Faith in the Christian Tradition* have demonstrated in what, I am sure, is at least sufficient, if not sometimes excessive, detail. But such research is inadequate if it does not come to terms with the *full* history of the creeds, of which their liturgical context has been an essential part.

But there is perhaps no scandal in the history either of such liturgical worship or of creedal profession that is more pervasive than the disjunction between the orthodox need for creed and the imperative of right action. The most shattering thunderbolts of the Hebrew prophets were reserved for that disjunction:

> Has the LORD as great delight in
> burnt offerings and sacrifices,
> as in obeying the voice of the LORD?
> Behold, to obey is better than sacrifice,
> and to hearken than the fat of rams,

Samuel warned (1 Sam 15.22). And standing squarely in that prophetic succession, Jesus told the following, altogether rabbinical story: "What do you think? A man had two sons; and he went to the first and said, 'Son, go and work in the vineyard today.' And he answered, 'I will not': but afterward he repented and went. And he went to the second and said the same; and he answered, 'I go, sir,' but he did not go. Which of the two did the will of his father?" (Mt 21.28–31). The "I go, sir" of the second stands for the prescribed formula set down in the orthodox tradition; what follows it, in five monosyllables (at least in English translation), *"but he did not go,"* has been the all too frequent outcome of the orthodox tradition. Therefore the expositors of the orthodox tradition—perhaps the most eloquent and most mordant of them all being Saint John Chrysostom, archbishop of Constantinople—have constantly warned that the outcome and expression of authentic orthodoxy, the second "great commandment," which is "like [the first]" (Mt 22.39), is "You shall love your neighbor as yourself." Through the centuries they have gone on warning—and the warning has gone on being needed, though not always heeded.

But that warning, necessary as it is, does not exhaust the meaning of this dimension of the need for creed. For pressed to its depths, the need for creed not only leads to, but actually presupposes, the commandment of love. "A new commandment I give you, that you love one another," Jesus said in his closing discourses (Jn 14:34). And *The Liturgy of Saint John Chrysostom* introduces the chanting of the *Niceno-Constantinopolitan Creed* with the formula: "Let us love one another, that with one mind we may confess Father, Son, and Holy Spirit, the Trinity one in essence and undivided."[53] It does not say, though that is what reasonably might have been expected, "Let us confess Father, Son, and Holy Spirit, that we may love one another." Rather, to quote Bishop Kallistos Ware's commentary on this portion of the Orthodox Liturgy,

> The Creed belongs only to those who live it. This exactly expresses the Orthodox attitude to Tradition. If we do not love one another, we cannot love God; and if we do not love God, we cannot make a true confession of faith and cannot enter into the inner spirit of Tradition, for there is no other way of knowing God than to love him.[54]

That is why although "faith [mentioned first, also as creed, the faith that is confessed, *fides quae creditur*], hope, love abide, these three, still the greatest of these is love" (1 Cor 13.13). That is also why *The Masai Creed* opens with the confession, "We believe in the one High God, who *out of love* created the beautiful world and everything good in it," and why this creed affirms that the purpose of the Incarnation of the Son of God was "showing that the meaning of religion is *love*," and that the content of Christian life and worship is to "live the rules of *love*, and share the bread together in *love*." For, paradoxically, we need creed also to cut creed down to size and to put creed in its proper place: it does "abide," yes, along with hope and love, "but the greatest of these is love." And that, too, is what the Church believes, teaches, and confesses by its Creed.

Notes

[1] At the urging of the editors and the publisher, I have decided to retain the original and personal flavor of the lecture in this article, in keeping with the celebratory character both of that event and of this volume.

[2] William James, *The Will to Believe, and Other Essays in Popular Philosophy* (reprint edition; New York: Dover, 1956). Most recently it has appeared as an appendix to Jon Boorstin's historical novel, *The Newsboys' Lodging-House, or The Confessions of William James* (New York: Penguin Books, 2003), 343–73.

[3] Jaroslav Pelikan, "Introduction" to William James, *The Varieties of Religious Experience* (1902), The Library of America Edition (New York: Vintage Books, 1990), xvi–xviii.

[4] Agnes von Zahn-Harnack, *Adolf von Harnack* (2nd ed.; Berlin: Walter de Gruyter, 1951), 416.

[5] References to creeds and confessions of faith are from: *Creeds and Confessions of Faith in the Christian Tradition*, Jaroslav Pelikan and Valerie Hotchkiss, eds. (4 vols.; New Haven: Yale University Press, 2003); abbreviated as *Creeds and Confessions of Faith*, followed by volume and page. *Credo*, the companion volume to the set, is cited separately. Unless otherwise identified, biblical quotations are from the Revised Standard Version.

[6] James, *Varieties*, 299; italics added.

[7] *The Journals of Father Alexander Schmemann 1973–1983*, trans. Juliana Schmemann (Crestwood, NY: Saint Vladimir's Seminary Press, 2000), 273 (under date of 20 October 1980); italics original.

[8] Jaroslav Pelikan, *The Christian Tradition: A History of the Development of Doctrine* (5 vols.; Chicago: University of Chicago Press, 1971–89).

[9] *Credo*, 538–85.

[10]James Turner, *Without God, Without Creed: The Origins of Unbelief in America* (Baltimore: Johns Hopkins University Press, 1985).

[11]Roger Hazelton, *Blaise Pascal: The Genius of His Thought* (Philadelphia: Westminster Press, 1974); *The Christian Tradition*, 4:349–50.

[12]Blaise Pascal, *Pensées* no. 418, trans. A.J. Krailsheimer (London: Penguin Books, 1966), 150–151.

[13]Gerald E. Myers, *William James: His Life and Thought* (New Haven: Yale University Press, 1986), 450–51.

[14]James, *Will to Believe*, 27.

[15]Quoted in Louis Menand, *The Metaphysical Club: A Story of Ideas in America* (New York: Farrar, Straus and Giroux, 2001), 436.

[16]James, *Varieties*, 36; italics added.

[17]James, *Will to Believe*, 9.

[18]*Creeds and Confessions of Faith*, 1:7.

[19]*Creeds and Confessions of Faith*, 1:29–31.

[20]James, *Will to Believe*, 9; italics added.

[21]*Oxford English Dictionary*, 7:1045.

[22]Claude Welch, *Protestant Thought in the Nineteenth Century* (2 vols; New Haven: Yale University Press, 1972–85), 1:31.

[23]Lionel Trilling, "Wordsworth and the Rabbis" (1950), *The Moral Obligation to Be Intelligent: Selected Essays*, edited and with an Introduction by Leon Wieseltier (New York: Farrar, Straus and Giroux, 2000), 180; italics added.

[24]Jaroslav Pelikan, "Foreword" to Etienne Gilson, *God and Philosophy* [1941] (Nota Bene edition; New Haven: Yale University Press, 2002), vii–xvii.

[25]Etienne Gilson, *Dogmatism and Tolerance* (New Brunswick: Rutgers University Press, 1952); Margaret McGrath, ed., *Etienne Gilson: A Bibliography* (Toronto: Pontifical Institute of Mediaeval Studies, 1982), no. 22.

[26]Ralph Waldo Emerson, *Poems*, "Give All to Love," lines 47–49, *The Selected Writings of Ralph Waldo Emerson*, edited by Brooks Atkinson (Modern Library Edition; New York: Random House, 1940), 775.

[27]Perez Zagorin, *How the Idea of Religious Toleration Came to the West* (Princeton: Princeton University Press, 2003).

[28]*Dignitatis humanae* (1965), *Creeds and Confessions of Faith*, 3:662–73.

[29]Hinrich Stoevesandt, *Die Bedeutung des Symbolums in Theologie und Kirche: Versuch einer dogmatisch-kritischen Ortsbestimmung aus evangelischer Sicht* (Munich: Christian Kaiser Verlag, 1970), 12.

[30]"The Articles of Faith of the Church of Jesus Christ of Latter-day Saints (Mormons), *Articles of Faith*, 1842," *Creeds and Confessions of Faith*, 3:256–58; *Tenets of the Mother Church, the First Church of Christ, Scientist* (1879/1892/1906), *Creeds and Confessions of Faith*, 3:370–71.

[31]*The Richmond Declaration of Faith of the Friends Yearly Meeting* (1887), *Creeds and Confessions of Faith*, 3:377–92. See also 3:136–48; 3:399–401.

[32]*The Washington Profession* (1935), *Creeds and Confessions of Faith*, 3:510; italics added.

[33]*Credo*, 304–5.

[34]John Courtney Murray, *We Hold These Truths: Catholic Reflections on the American Proposition* (Image Books edition; Garden City, NY: Doubleday), 102–25.

[35]*Declaration and Address* (1809), *Creeds and Confessions of Faith*, 3:219.

[36]*Credo*, 139–42; "Syndogmaticon" 8.13, *Credo*, 559.

[37]*The Sixty-Seven Articles of Ulrich Zwingli* (1523) 1, *Creeds and Confessions of Faith*, 2:209.

[38]Augustine *Against the Epistle of Manichaeus* v.6 (NPNF–14:131); *The Christian Tradition*, 4:262–74.

[39]*The Scots Confession* (1560) 18, *Creeds and Confessions of Faith*, 2:398.

[40]*The French Confession* (1559/1571) 3–4, *Creeds and Confessions of Faith*, 2:376.

[41]*Council of Chalcedon* (451) 25–27, *Creeds and Confessions of Faith*, 1:181; italics added.

[42]John Henry Newman, *An Essay on the Development of Christian Doctrine* [1878] (Reprint edition; Notre Dame: University of Notre Dame Press, 1989), 303.

[43]*Formula of Union of the Council of Ephesus* (431), *Creeds and Confessions of Faith*, 1:169.

[44]*The Christian Tradition*, 1:9. See Paul Valliere, *Modern Russian Theology: Bukharev, Soloviev, Bulgakiov: Orthodox Theology in a New Key* (Grand Rapids: William B. Eerdmans Publishing House, 2000), 379–80.

[45]Anthony-Emil Tachiaos, *Cyril and Methodius of Thessalonica: The Acculturation of the Slavs* (Crestwood, NY: Saint Vladimir's Seminary Press, 2001).

[46]*The Masai Creed* (c. 1960), *Creeds and Confessions of Faith*, 3:569; italics added.

[47]Eugene Hillman, *Toward an African Christianity: Inculturation Applied* (New York: Paulist Press, 1993), 30–32.

[48]*Creeds and Confessions of Faith*, 1:158–59; 162–63.

[49]*Creeds and Confessions of Faith*, 1:667–69.

[50]*Credo*, 179–81.

[51]*The Christian Tradition*, 2:183–98.

[52]James, *Will to Believe*, 9.

[53]*Liturgy of Saint John Chrysostom* II-D (*Creeds and Confessions of Faith*, 1:284).

[54]Kallistos Ware, *The Orthodox Church* (rev. ed.; Harmondsworth: Penguin Books, 1997), 207.

A Bibliography of the Works of Jaroslav Pelikan

COMPILED BY VALERIE HOTCHKISS

1946

THESES

"The Bible of Kralice." B.D. thesis, Concordia Theological Seminary, 1946.
"Luther and the *Confessio Bohemica*." Ph.D. diss., University of Chicago, 1946.

ARTICLES, ESSAYS, PUBLISHED LECTURES

"Luther after Four Centuries." *The Cresset* 9/4 (1946): 14–18.

REVIEWS

Boehmer, Heinrich. *Road to Reformation*. Translated by John W. Doberstein and Theodore G. Tappert. Philadelphia: Muhlenberg Press, 1946. In *The Cresset* 10/1 (1946): 57–58.

Casey, Robert Pierce. *Religion in Russia*. New York: Harper and Brothers, 1946. In *The Cresset* 10/1 (1946): 52–53.

Fales, Walter. *Wisdom and Responsibility*. Princeton: Princeton UP, 1946. In *The Cresset* 10/2 (1946): 67.

Voices of History. Compiled by Nathan Ausubel. New York: Gramercy, 1946. In *The Cresset* 10/1 (1946): 62.

Zweig, Friderike. *Stefan Zweig*. Translated by Erna McArthur. New York: Thomas Y. Cromwell Co., 1946. In *The Cressett* 10/2 (1946): 47–48.

1947

ARTICLES, ESSAYS, PUBLISHED LECTURES

"The Consensus of Sandomierz." *Concordia Theological Monthly* 18 (1947): 825–37.

186   ORTHODOXY & WESTERN CULTURE

"Natural Theology in David Hollaz." *Concordia Theological Monthly* 18 (1947): 253–63.
"The Spell of Saint Thomas." [Part 1]. *The Cresset* 10/8 (1947): 13–16.
"The Structure of Luther's Piety." *Una Sancta* 7 (1947): 12–20.

REVIEWS

Pfeffermann, Hans. *Die Zusammenarbeit der Renaissancepäpste mit den Türken.* Winterthur: Mondial Verlag, 1946. In *Journal of Religion* 27 (1947): 303–04.

1948

ARTICLES, ESSAYS, PUBLISHED LECTURES

"Luther's Attitude toward John Hus." *Concordia Theological Monthly* 19 (1948): 747–63.
"The Spell of Saint Thomas." [Part 2]. *The Cresset* 11/1 (1948): 12–17.

1949

ARTICLES, ESSAYS, PUBLISHED LECTURES

"History as Law and Gospel." *The Cresset* 12/4 (1949): 12–17 and 12/5 (1949): 19–23.
"Luther's Endorsement of the *Confessio Bohemica.*" *Concordia Theological Monthly* 20 (1949): 829–43.
"Luther's Negotiations with the Hussites." *Concordia Theological Monthly* 20 (1949): 496–517.

1950

BOOKS

From Luther to Kierkegaard: A Study in the History of Theology. St Louis: Concordia Publishing House, 1950; reprinted 1963.

ARTICLES, ESSAYS, PUBLISHED LECTURES

"Doctrine of Man in Lutheran Confessions." *Lutheran Quarterly* 2 (1950): 34–44.

"Form and Tradition in Worship: A Theological Interpretation." In *First Liturgical Institute, Valparaiso University*, 11–27. Valparaiso, IN: Valparaiso UP, 1950.

"The Marxist Heresy—A Theological Evaluation." *Religion in Life* 19/3 (1950): 356–66.

"The Origins of the Object-Subject Antithesis in Lutheran Dogmatics: A Study in Terminology." *Concordia Theological Monthly* 21 (1950): 94–104.

"Practical Politics." In *The Christian in Politics: Proceedings of the Institute of Politics*, edited by Alfred Looman and Albert Wehling, 9–34. Valparaiso, IN: Valparaiso UP, 1950.

"The Relation of Faith and Knowledge in the Lutheran Confessions." *Concordia Theological Monthly* 21 (1950): 321–31.

REVIEWS

Zwingli, Ulrich. *Zwingli-Hauptschriften*, v. 2, pt. 3 of *Der Theologe*. Edited by R. Pfister. In *Journal of Religion* 30 (1950): 140–41.

1951

ARTICLES, ESSAYS, PUBLISHED LECTURES

"Chalcedon after Fifteen Centuries." *Concordia Theological Monthly* 22 (1951): 926–36.

"Church and Church History in the Confessions." *Concordia Theological Monthly* 22 (1951): 305–20.

"The Temptation of the Church: A Study of Matthew 4:1–11." *Concordia Theological Monthly* 22 (1951): 251–59.

"Theology and Missions in Lutheran History." In *Proceedings of the Thirtieth Convention of the Atlantic District of the Lutheran Church, Missouri Synod*, 33–38. St Louis: Concordia Publishing House, 1951.

REVIEWS

Nigg, Walter. *Das Buch der Ketzer*. Zürich: Artemis, 1949. In *Journal of Religion* 31 (1951): 284–85.

1952

BOOKS

The Cross for Every Day: Sermons and Meditations for Lent. With Richard R. Caemmerer. St Louis: Concordia Publishing House, 1952.

ARTICLES, ESSAYS, PUBLISHED LECTURES

"Amerikanisches Luthertum in dogmengeschichtlicher Sicht." *Evangelisch-Lutherische Kirchenzeitung* 14 (1952): 250–53.

"The Eschatology of Tertullian." *Church History* 21 (1952): 108–22.

"In memoriam: Johann Albrecht Bengel, June 24, 1687 to November 2, 1752." *Concordia Theological Monthly* 23 (1952): 785–96.

"Some Anti-Pelagian Echoes in Augustine's *City of God*." *Concordia Theological Monthly* 23 (1952): 448–52.

"A Survey of Historical Theology." Mimeographed syllabus, Concordia Theological Seminary Mimeo Co., 1952. [Basic outline of *The Christian Tradition*, twenty years before publication of volume 1.]

1953

ARTICLES, ESSAYS, PUBLISHED LECTURES

"Some Word Studies in the *Apology*." *Concordia Theological Monthly* 24 (1953): 580–96.

REVIEWS

Dillenberger, John. *God Hidden and Revealed: The Interpretation of Luther's Deus Absconditus and its Significance for Religious Thought.* Philadelphia: Muhlenberg Press, 1953. In *Church History* 22 (1953): 343–44.

[World Council of Churches, Commission on Faith and Order]. *Intercommunion.* Edited by Donald Macpherson Baillie and John Marsh. London: SCM, 1951; New York: Harper, 1952. In *Lutheran Quarterly* 5 (1953): 222–23.

AUDIO/VISUAL RECORDINGS

"Martin Luther." Motion picture produced by Lothar Wolff. Research and screenplay by Allan Stone, Lothar Wolff, Jaroslav Pelikan and Theodore Tappert. Lutheran Film Associates, 1953. Video release by Vision Video, Worcester, PA, 1989.

1954

ARTICLES, ESSAYS, PUBLISHED LECTURES

"Four Questions at Evanston." *The American Lutheran* 37/7 (1954): 6–9.

REVIEWS

Cairns, David Smith. *The Image of God in Man.* New York: Philosophical Library, 1953. In *Church History* 23 (1954): 93–94.

Hyma, Albert. *Renaissance to Reformation.* Grand Rapids: Eerdmans, 1951. In *Church History* 23 (1954): 192.

Kähler, Ernst. *Karlstadt und Augustin: Der Kommentar des Andreas Bodenstein von Karlstadt zu Augustins Schrift De spiritu et litera.* Halle: Max Niemeyer, 1952. In *Archiv für Reformationsgeschichte* 45 (1954): 268.

1955

BOOKS

Fools for Christ: Essays on the True, the Good, and the Beautiful. Philadelphia: Muhlenberg Press, 1955. English imprint entitled *Human Culture and the Holy: Essays on the True, the Good, and the Beautiful.* London: SCM, 1959.

EDITIONS AND TRANSLATIONS

Luther, Martin. *Luther's Works.* American Edition. St Louis: Concordia Publishing House, 1955–69. General Editor for majority of volumes 1–30. [Individual volumes edited by Pelikan are listed for the year in which they appeared.]

Luther, Martin. *Selected Psalms I. Luther's Works*, 12. St Louis: Concordia Publishing House, 1955. Translations of Psalms 8, 19, 26, and 51 by Jaroslav Pelikan.

ARTICLES, ESSAYS, PUBLISHED LECTURES

"Doctrine of Creation in Lutheran Confessional Theology." *Concordia Theological Monthly* 26 (1955): 569–79.

REVIEWS

Rupp, Ernest Gordon. *The Righteousness of God.* New York: Philosophical Library, 1953. In *Journal of Religion* 35 (1955): 179–80.

1956

EDITIONS AND TRANSLATIONS

Luther, Martin. *Sermon on the Mount (Sermons) and The Magnificat. Luther's Works*, 21. St Louis: Concordia Publishing House, 1956. "Sermon on the Mount" translated by Jaroslav Pelikan.

ARTICLES, ESSAYS, PUBLISHED LECTURES

"Montanism and its Trinitarian Significance." *Church History* 25 (1956): 99–109.
"Tradition in Confessional Lutheranism." *Lutheran World* 3 (1956): 214–22. Published in German as "Die Tradition im konfessionalen Luthertum." *Lutherische Rundschau* 6 (1956–57): 228–37.

REVIEWS

Mossner, Ernest C. *The Life of David Hume*. Austin: University of Texas Press, 1954. In *Journal of Religion* 36 (1956): 50–51.

1957

EDITIONS AND TRANSLATIONS

Luther, Martin. *Selected Psalms II. Luther's Works*, 13. St Louis: Concordia Publishing House, 1957.
Luther, Martin. *Sermons on the Gospel of St John: Chapters 1–14. Luther's Works*, 22. St Louis: Concordia Publishing House, 1957.

ARTICLES, ESSAYS, PUBLISHED LECTURES

"Luther's Doctrine of the Lord's Supper." In *Proceedings of the Thirtieth Convention of the English District of the Lutheran Church, Missouri Synod*, 12–33. St Louis: Concordia Publishing House, 1957.
"Tyranny of Epistemology: Revelation in the History of Protestant Thought." *Encounter* 18 (1957): 53–56.

REVIEWS

Harbison, E. Harris. *The Christian Scholar in the Age of the Reformation*. New York: Charles Scribner's Sons, 1956. In *Journal of Religion* 37 (1957): 128.

Preus, Robert. *The Inspiration of Scripture: A Study of the Theology of the Seventeenth-Century Lutheran Dogmaticians*. Mankato, MN: Lutheran Synod Book Co., 1955. In *Church History* 26 (1957): 192–93.

Wentz, Abdel Ross. *Basic History of Lutheranism in America*. Philadelphia: Muhlenberg Press, 1955. In *Theology Today* 13 (1957): 558–59.

AUDIO/VISUAL RECORDINGS

"Inter-Church Relationships." Sound recording of panel discussion at Third Assembly, Lutheran World Federation, Minneapolis, 21 Aug. 1957. Minneapolis: Donald F. Rossin Co., 1957.

1958

BOOKS

More about Luther. Martin Luther Lectures, 2. With Regin Prenter and Herman A. Preus. Essay on "Luther and the Liturgy," 3–62. Decorah, IA: Luther College Press, 1958.

EDITIONS AND TRANSLATIONS

Luther, Martin. *Lectures on Genesis, Chapters 1–5. Luther's Works*, 1. St Louis: Concordia Publishing House, 1958.

Luther, Martin. *Selected Psalms III. Luther's Works*, 14. St Louis: Concordia Publishing House, 1958. Translations of "The Four Psalms of Comfort" by Jaroslav Pelikan.

ARTICLES, ESSAYS, PUBLISHED LECTURES

"Dogma" and "Dogmatics." In *A Handbook of Christian Theology: Definition Essays on Concepts and Movements of Thought in Contemporary Protestantism*, 80–85. New York: Meridian Books, 1958.

"Flying Is for the Birds." *The Cresset* 21/10 (1958): 6–9.

"Die Kirche nach Luthers Genesisvorlesung." In *Lutherforschung Heute*, edited by Vilmos Vajta, 102–10. Berlin: Lutherisches Verlagshaus, 1958.

"Luther on the Word of God." *The Minnesota Lutheran* 34/10 (1958): 16–25.

1959

BOOKS

Luther the Expositor: Introduction to the Reformer's Exegetical Writings. Luther's Works, Companion volume. St Louis: Concordia Publishing House, 1959. Published in Japanese; Tokyo: Seibunsha, 1959.
The Riddle of Roman Catholicism: Its History, Its Beliefs, Its Future. Nashville: Abingdon Press, 1959; London: Hodder & Stoughton, 1960.

EDITIONS AND TRANSLATIONS

The Book of Concord: The Confession of the Evangelical Lutheran Church. Translated and edited by Theodore G. Tappert in collaboration with Jaroslav Pelikan, Robert H. Fischer, and Arthur C. Piepkorn. Philadelphia: Muhlenberg Press; St Louis: Concordia, 1959; reissued 1967.
Luther, Martin. *Sermons on the Gospel of John, Chapters 6–8. Luther's Works*, 23. St Louis: Concordia Publishing House, 1959.

ARTICLES, ESSAYS, PUBLISHED LECTURES

"Ein deutscher lutherischer Theologe in Amerika: Paul Tillich und die dogmatische Tradition." In *Gott ist am Werk: Festschrift für Landesbischof D. Hanns Lilje zum sechzigsten Geburtstag*, 27–36. Hamburg: Furch-Verlag, 1959.
"Kerygma and Culture: An Inquiry into Schleiermacher's *Reden*." *Discourse: A Review of Liberal Arts* 2 (1959): 131–44.
"New Light from the Old World." *Christian Century* 76 (1959): 1182–83.
"Totalitarianism and Democracy: A Religious Analysis." In *God and Caesar: A Christian Approach to Social Ethics*, edited by Warren A. Quanbeck, 99–114. Minneapolis: Augsburg Publishing House, 1959.

INTRODUCTIONS AND FOREWORDS

Introduction to *Protestant Thought from Rousseau to Ritschl*, by Karl Barth. Translated by Brian Cozens. New York: Harper & Brothers, 1959.

1960

EDITIONS AND TRANSLATIONS

Luther, Martin. *Lectures on Deuteronomy. Luther's Works*, 9. St Louis: Concordia Publishing House, 1960.

Luther, Martin. *Lectures on Genesis, Chapters 6–14. Luther's Works*, 2. St Louis: Concordia Publishing House, 1960.

ARTICLES, ESSAYS, PUBLISHED LECTURES

"The Burden of our Separation." *Religion in Life* 29/2 (1960): 200–10.
"Catholics in America." *The New Republic* 142/12 (1960). [Issue devoted to account of symposium with John C. Bennett and Arthur Schlesinger, Jr.].
"Creation and Causality in the History of Christian Thought." *Pastoral Psychology* 10 (1960): 11–20. Also printed in *Issues in Evolution*, v. 3 of *Evolution after Darwin*, 29–40. Edited by Sol Tax and Charles Callender. Chicago: University of Chicago Press, 1960. Also reprinted in *Southwestern Journal of Theology* 32 (1990): 10–16.

REVIEWS

Ambrosius Catharinus Politus, 1484–1553: Ein Theologe des Reformationszeitalters: Sein Leben und seine Schriften. Edited by Joseph Schweizer. Munster: Aschendorf, [n.d.]. In *Archiv für Reformationsgeschichte* 51/1 (1960): 114–15.

1961

BOOKS

The Shape of Death: Life, Death, and Immortality in the Early Fathers. New York: Abingdon Press, 1961; London: Macmillan & Co., 1962; Westport, CT: Greenwood Press, 1978.

EDITIONS AND TRANSLATIONS

Luther, Martin. *Lectures on Genesis, Chapters 15–20. Luther's Works*, 3. St Louis: Concordia Publishing House, 1961.
Luther, Martin. *Sermons on the Gospel of St John: Chapters 14–16. Luther's Works*, 24. St Louis: Concordia Publishing House, 1961.

ARTICLES, ESSAYS, PUBLISHED LECTURES

"Cosmos and Creation: Science and Theology in Reformation Thought." *Proceedings of the American Philosophical Society* 105 (1961): 463–69.
"Luther's Attitude toward Church and Councils." In *The Papal Council and the Gospel: Protestant Theologians Evaluate the Coming Vatican Council*, edited by

Kristen E. Skydsgaard, 37–60. Minneapolis: Augsburg Publishing House, 1961. Published in German as "Luthers Stellung zu den Kirchenkonzilien." In *Konzil und Evangelium*, edited by Kristen E. Skydsgaard, 40–62. Göttingen: Vandenhoeck & Ruprecht, 1962.

"Overcoming History by History." In *The Old and the New in the Church: Studies in Ministry and Worship of the World Council of Churches*, edited by G. W. H. Lampe and David M. Paton, 36–42. London: SCM Press, 1961; Minneapolis: Augsburg Publishing House, 1961.

INTRODUCTIONS AND FOREWORDS

Introduction to *The Mission and Expansion of Christianity in the First Three Centuries*, by Adolf von Harnack. Translated and edited by James Moffatt. New York: Harper & Brothers, Torchbook Edition, 1961.

REVIEWS

Cannon, William R. *History of Christianity in the Middle Ages: From the Fall of Rome to the Fall of Constantinople*. New York: Abingdon Press, 1960. In *Religion in Life* 30/4 (1961): 625–26.

MEDIA

"What is Protestant-Catholic Dialogue Trying to Accomplish? Dialogue between Protestants and Catholics." Clifton E. Moore, Jaroslav Pelikan, John A. Hardon, Harold Schachern, Richard Philbrick. Originally telecast in 1961 on the NBC-TV series Frontiers of Faith, and released as a 16 mm. film by the National Council of the Churches of Christ in the U.S.A., Broadcasting and Film Commission. Released as a video in 1994.

1962

BOOKS

The Light of the World: A Basic Image in Early Christian Thought. New York: Harper, 1962.

ARTICLES, ESSAYS, PUBLISHED LECTURES

"The American Church and the Church Universal." *The Atlantic* 210/2 (1962): 90–94.

"Bergson among the Theologians." In *The Bergsonian Heritage*, edited by Thomas Hanna, 54–73. New York: Columbia UP, 1962.

"The Christian as an Intellectual." *Christian Scholar* 45 (1962): 6–11.

"The Early Answer to the Question Concerning Jesus Christ: Bonhoeffer's *Christologie* of 1933." In *The Place of Bonhoeffer: Problems and Possibilities in His Thought*, edited by Martin E. Marty, 145–65. New York: Association Press, 1962. Published in Korean by Han Kook Bai. Seoul, 1966.

"Fathers, Brethren, and Distant Relatives: The Family of Theological Discourse." *Concordia Theological Monthly* 33 (1962): 710–18.

"Issues That Divide Us: Protestant." In *Christians in Conversation*. Papers from a colloquium at Saint John's Abbey, Collegeville, Minnesota, 3–19. Westminster, MD: Newman Press, 1962.

"Karl Barth in America." *Christian Century* 79 (1962): 451–52.

"The New English Bible: The New Testament." *Criterion* 1 (1962): 25–29.

"The Protestant Concept of the Church: An Ecumenical Consensus." In *Proceedings of the Seventeenth Annual Convention [of the Catholic Theological Society of America]* (1962): 131–37.

"Religious Responsibility for the Social Order—A Protestant View." In *Religious Responsibility for the Social Order: A Symposium by Three Theologians* (Jaroslav Pelikan, Gustav Weigel, and Emil L. Fackenheim). New York: National Conference of Christians and Jews, 1962.

"Theological Library and the Tradition of Christian Humanism." *Concordia Theological Monthly* 33 (1962): 719–23.

INTRODUCTIONS AND FOREWORDS

Foreword to *The Impact of American Religious Liberalism*, by Kenneth Cauthen. New York: Harper & Row, 1962.

Preface and additional bibliography to *Protestant Thought before Kant*, by A. C. McGiffert. New York: Harper & Brothers, 1962.

Foreword to *The Structure of Lutheranism: The Theology and Philosophy of Life of Lutheranism Especially in the Sixteenth and Seventeenth Centuries*, by Werner Elert. Translated by Walter A. Hansen. St Louis: Concordia Publishing House, 1962.

1963

BOOKS

From Luther to Kierkegaard: A Study in the History of Theology. 2d ed. St Louis: Concordia Publishing House, 1963.

The Lutheran Reformation. With Jerald C. Brauer. [Chicago, 1963]. Produced as a syllabus by the Commission on College and University Work of the National Lutheran Council.

EDITIONS AND TRANSLATIONS

Luther, Martin. *Lectures on Galatians, 1535, Chapters 1–4. Luther's Works,* 26. Edited and translated by Jaroslav Pelikan. St Louis: Concordia Publishing House, 1963.

ARTICLES, ESSAYS, PUBLISHED LECTURES

"American Lutheranism: Denomination or Confession?" *Christian Century* 80 (1963): 1608–10.

"The Functions of Theology." In *Theology in the Life of the Church*, edited by Robert Bertram, 3–21. Philadelphia: Fortress Press, 1963.

"History of Christian Thought Bookshelf." ["Building a Basic Theological Library," pt. 5.] *Christian Century* 80 (1963): 711–12.

"John Osborne's Luther." *Christianity and Crisis* 23 (1963): 228–29.

"That the Church May Be More Fully Catholic." *The Catholic World* 198/1185 (1963): 151–56.

"The Vocation of the Christian Apologist: A Study of Schleiermacher's *Reden.*" In *Christianity and World Revolution*, edited by Edwin H. Rian, 173–89. New York: Harper & Row, 1963.

INTRODUCTIONS AND FOREWORDS

"The Basic Marian Idea." Introduction to *Mary, Archetype of the Church*, by Otto Semmelroth. New York: Sheed & Ward, 1963.

REVIEWS

Luther, Martin. *Luther: Lectures on Romans*, edited and translated by Wilhelm Pauck. Louisville: Westminster Press, 1961. In *Union Seminary Quarterly Review* 18 (1963): 173–75.

1964

BOOKS

Editorial Board. *A Library of Protestant Thought.* 14 vols. New York: Oxford University Press, 1964–72.
Obedient Rebels: Catholic Substance and Protestant Principle in Luther's Reformation. New York: Harper & Row, 1964; London: SCM Press, 1964.

EDITIONS AND TRANSLATIONS

Luther, Martin. *Lectures on Galatians, 1535, Chapters 5–6; 1519, Chapters 1–6. Luther's Works,* 27. St Louis: Concordia Publishing House, 1964. 1535 edition translated by Jaroslav Pelikan.
Luther, Martin. *Lectures on Genesis, Chapters 21–25. Luther's Works,* 4. St Louis: Concordia Publishing House, 1964.

ARTICLES, ESSAYS, PUBLISHED LECTURES

"American Lutheranism: Denomination or Confession." In *What's Ahead for the Churches,* edited by Kyle Haselden and Martin Marty, 187–95. New York: Sheed & Ward, 1964.
"In Defense of Research in Religious Studies at the Secular University." In *Religion and the University,* 1–19. *York University Gerstein Lectures.* Toronto: University of Toronto Press, 1964.
"Methodism's Contribution to America." In *History of American Methodism,* edited by Emory Stevens Bucke, 3: 396–614. Nashville: Abingdon Press, 1964.
"Mortality of God and the Immortality of Man in Gregory of Nyssa." In *Scope of Grace: Essays in Honor of Joseph Sittler,* edited by Philip J. Hefner, 79–97. Philadelphia: Fortress Press, 1964.
"A Scholar Strikes Back." *The Catholic World* 200/1197 (1964): 149–54.
"Thine Alabaster Cities Gleam—The Secularization of a Vision." *A.I.A. Journal* 42/2 (1964): 37–43.

INTRODUCTIONS AND FOREWORDS

Introduction to *Luther and Aquinas on Salvation,* by Stephen Pfürtner. New York: Sheed & Ward, [1964/65].

1965

BOOKS

The Christian Intellectual. Religious Perspectives Series, 14. New York: Harper & Row, 1965; London: William Collins, 1966.

The Finality of Jesus Christ in An Age of Universal History: A Dilemma of the Third Century. *Ecumenical Studies in History*, 3. London: Lutterworth, 1965; Richmond: John Knox Press, [1965].

EDITIONS AND TRANSLATIONS

Luther, Martin. *Lectures on Genesis, Chapters 38–44*. *Luther's Works*, 7. St Louis: Concordia Publishing House, 1965.

ARTICLES, ESSAYS, PUBLISHED LECTURES

"In memoriam: Paul Tillich." *The Cresset* 28/12 (1965): 24–25.

"*Justitia* as Justice and *Justitia* as Righteousness." In *Law and Theology Essays on the Professional Responsibility of the Christian Lawyer*, edited by Andrew J. Buehner, 87–98. St Louis: Concordia Publishing House, 1965.

"Theologian and Thinker [Albert Schweitzer]." *Saturday Review* 48/39 (1965): 21–22.

"Tradition, Reformation and Development." *Christian Century* 82 (1965): 8–10.

INTRODUCTIONS AND FOREWORDS

Introduction to *History of the Reformation: A Conciliatory Assessment of Opposite Views*, by John P. Dolan. New York: Desclés de Brouwer, 1965.

Foreword to *The Promise and the Presence*, by Harry N. Huxhold. St Louis: Concordia Publishing House, 1965.

1966

EDITIONS AND TRANSLATIONS

Luther, Martin. *Lectures on Genesis, Chapters 45–50*. *Luther's Works*, 8. St Louis: Concordia Publishing House, 1966.

Makers of Modern Theology. Edited and with introductions by Jaroslav Pelikan. 5 volumes. New York: Harper & Row, 1966–68.

ARTICLES, ESSAYS, PUBLISHED LECTURES

"Constitution on the Sacred Liturgy–A Response." In *The Documents of Vatican II*, edited by Walter M. Abbott, 179–82. New York: America Press, 1966.

"An Essay on the Development of Christian Doctrine." *Church History* 35 (1966): 3–12.

"Paths to Dialogue." In *1966 World Book Year Book*. Chicago: Field Enterprises Educational Corp., 1966.

"Relevance: The Preoccupations of Theology." In *Jesus Christ Reforms His Church: Proceedings of the Twenty-Sixth North American Liturgical Week*, 30–38. Washington, DC: Liturgical Conference, 1966.

"The Renewal of the Seminary in an 'Age of the Layman.'" [Commencement address, Episcopal Divinity School, Cambridge, MA, 9 June 1966]. *Una Sancta* 23/3 (1966): 4–11.

"Response to Constitution of the Sacred Liturgy." In *The Documents of Vatican II*. New York: Herder & Herder; Associated Press, 1966.

"Theology without God." In *Encyclopedia Britannica Year Book, 1966*. Chicago: Encyclopedia Britannica, 1966.

"Tradition, Reformation, and Development." In *Frontline Theology*, edited by Dean Peerman, 101–7. Richmond: John Knox Press, 1966.

INTRODUCTIONS AND FOREWORDS

Introduction to *The Reformation: Causes and Consequences*, by John A. O'Brien. Rev. ed. Glen Rock, NJ: Paulist Press, 1966.

AUDIO/VISUAL RECORDINGS

"Tolerance Is Not Enough." Sound recording produced by KUOM, University of Minnesota. Boulder, CO: University of Colorado, 1966.

1967

BOOKS

From Luther to Kierkegaard: A Study in the History of Theology, published in Japanese. Tokyo: Seibunsha, 1967.

EDITIONS AND TRANSLATIONS

Chrysostom, John. *The Preaching of Chrysostom: Homilies on the Sermon on the*

Mount. Edited and with introduction by Jaroslav Pelikan. Philadelphia: Fortress Press, 1967.

Luther, Martin. *The Catholic Epistles. Luther's Works*, 30. St Louis: Concordia Publishing House, 1967.

ARTICLES, ESSAYS, PUBLISHED LECTURES

"Absolution"; "Agnosticism"; "Agnus Dei"; "Anointing"; "Atheism"; "Atonement"; "Baader, Franz Xavier von"; "Bampton, John"; "Baptism, Christian"; "Barclay, Robert"; "Baur, Ferdinand Christian"; "Bible"; "Bidding Prayer"; "Biddle, John"; "Burnet, Thomas"; "Butler, Joseph"; "Case, Shirley Jackson"; "Catechism"; "Chalice"; "Chapel"; "Charity"; "Christianity"; "Communion, Holy"; "Confirmation"; "Congregation"; "Creationism and Traducianism"; "Dogma"; "Ernesti, Johann August"; "Eucharist"; "Excommunication"; "Exegesis and Hermeneutics, Biblical"; "Faith"; "Frommel, Gaston"; "Gichtel, Johann Georg"; "Grace"; "Hengstenberg, Ernst Wilhelm"; "Hope"; "Idolatry"; "Inspiration"; "Jesus Christ"; "Mary"; "Monophysites"; "Mysticism"; "Predestination"; "Religion"; "Sacrament"; "Sins, Seven Deadly"; "Theology"; "Trinity ." In *Encyclopedia Britannica*, 1967 edition.

"After the Monks—What? Luther's Reformation and Institutions of Missions, Welfare, and Education." *Springfielder* 31 (1967): 3–21.

"Confessions of Faith, Protestant." In *New Catholic Encyclopedia*, 1967 edition.

"Continuity and Order in Luther's View of Church and Ministry." In *Kirche, Mystik, Heiligung und das Natürliche bei Luther*, Vorträge des dritten Internationalen Kongresses für Lutherforschung, edited by Ivar Asheim, 143–55. Gottingen: Vandenhoeck & Ruprecht, 1967.

[Interview]. In *Theologians at Work*, by Patrick Granfield, 105–25. New York: Macmillan, [1967].

"Luther's Defense of Infant Baptism." In *Luther for an Ecumenical Age*, edited by Carl S. Meyer, 200–18. St Louis: Concordia Publishing House, 1967.

"Past of Belief: Reflections of a Historian of Doctrine." In *The Future of Belief Debate*, edited by Gregory Baum, 29–36. New York: Herder & Herder, 1967.

"Theology of the Means of Grace." In *Accents in Luther's Theology*, edited by Heino O. Kadai, 124–47. St Louis: Concordia Publishing House, 1967.

"Verius servamus canones: Church Law and Divine Law in the Apology of the Augsburg Confession." In *Studia Gratiana* 11 (1967): 1:367–88. Special issue, *Collectanea Stephan Kuttner*, edited by Alphons M. Stickler. Also published separately, Bonn, 1967.

REVIEWS

Dewart, Leslie. *The Future of Belief: Theism in a World Come of Age.* New York: Herder & Herder, 1966. In *Theological Studies* 28 (1967): 352–56.

1968

BOOKS

Spirit versus Structure: Luther and the Institutions of the Church. New York: Harper & Row, 1968; London: William Collins, 1968.

EDITIONS AND TRANSLATIONS

Interpreters of Luther: Essays in Honor of Wilhelm Pauck. Edited by Jaroslav Pelikan. Philadelphia: Fortress, 1968.

Luther, Martin. *Lectures on Genesis, Chapters 26–30. Luther's Works,* 5. St Louis: Concordia Publishing House, 1968.

Luther, Martin. *Lectures on Titus, Philemon, and Hebrews. Luther's Works,* 29. St Louis: Concordia Publishing House, 1968. Titus and Philemon lectures translated by Jaroslav Pelikan.

ARTICLES, ESSAYS, PUBLISHED LECTURES

"Adolf von Harnack on Luther" In *Interpreters of Luther: Essays in Honor of Wilhelm Pauck,* 253–74.

"After the Campus Turmoil: A Plea for Reform." *Panorama—Chicago Daily News,* 15 June 1968.

"Faculties Must Reassert Powers They Defaulted." *Los Angeles Times,* 16 June 1968.

"Jozef Miloslav Hurban: A Study in Historicism." In *Impact of the Church upon Its Culture: Essays in Divinity,* edited by Jerald C. Brauer, 2:333–52. Chicago: University of Chicago Press, 1968.

"Renewal of Structure versus Renewal by the Spirit." In *Theology of Renewal, Proceedings of the Congress on the Theology of the Renewal of the Church,* edited by L. K. Shook, 2:21–41. Montreal: Palm Publishers, 1968. Published in French as "L'Esprit et les structures selon Luther, étude sur 'La Captivite babylonienne de l'Église'." In *La Theologie du Renouveau,* edited by Laurence K. Shook and Guy-M. Bertrand, 1:357–74. Montreal: Éditions Fides, 1968.

"Wilhelm Pauck: A Tribute." In *Interpreters of Luther: Essays in Honor of Wilhelm Pauck,* 1–8.

INTRODUCTIONS AND FOREWORDS

Foreword to *The Church in the Churches*, by James O. McGovern. Washington, DC: Corpus Books, 1968.

Introduction to *The Church in the Modern World in the Words of Albert Cardinal Meyer.* Edited by Michael P. Dineen. Waukesha, WI: Country Beautiful, 1968.

1969

BOOKS

Development of Christian Doctrine: Some Historical Prolegomena. New Haven: Yale UP, 1969.

EDITIONS AND TRANSLATIONS

Luther, Martin. *Lectures on Isaiah, Chapters 1–39. Luther's Works,* 16. St Louis: Concordia Publishing House, 1969.

Twentieth-Century Theology in the Making. 3 volumes. Edited and with introductions by Jaroslav Pelikan. London: Fontana, 1969–70; New York: Harper & Row, 1971. [English edition of selections from the 2nd edition of *Die Religion in Geschichte und Gegenwart.*]

ARTICLES, ESSAYS, PUBLISHED LECTURES

"The Christian Religions." In *East Central Europe: A Guide to Basic Publications*, edited by Paul L. Horecky, 329–33. Chicago: University of Chicago Press, 1969.

"Theology and Change." In *Theology in the City of Man: Saint Louis University Sesquicentennial Symposium,* 375–84. New York: Cross Currents Corporation, 1969; reissued 1970.

INTRODUCTIONS AND FOREWORDS

Foreword to *The Anabaptists and the Czech Brethren in Moravia 1526–1628*, by Jarold Knox Zeman. Paris: Mouton, 1969.

Foreword to *Christus Victor: An Historical Study of the Three Main Types of the Idea of the Atonement*, by Gustaf Aulen. New York: Macmillan Company, 1969.

1970

EDITIONS AND TRANSLATIONS

Luther, Martin. *Lectures on Genesis, Chapters 31–37. Luther's Works*, 6. St Louis: Concordia Publishing House, 1970.

ARTICLES, ESSAYS, PUBLISHED LECTURES

"De-Judaization and Hellenization: The Ambiguities of Christian Identity." In *The Dynamic in Christian Thought*, edited by Joseph Papin, 81–124. Villanova: Villanova UP, 1970.

"Didakhe and *Diadokhe:* A Personal Tribute to Johannes Quasten." In Kyriakon, *Festschrift Johannes Quasten*, edited by Patrick Granfield and Josef A. Jungmann, 2:917–20. Munster: Verlag Aschendorf, 1970.

"Eve or Mary." In *Women's Liberation and the Christian Church*. Graymoor/Garrison, NY, 1970. [From conference sponsored by the Graymoor Ecumenical Institute, 11–12 November 1970].

"Law and Dogma: Some Historical Interrelations." In *Proceedings of the Canon Law Society of America, 31st Annual Convention*, edited by T. Gumbleton, et al., 69–77. Washington, DC: Canon Law Society of America, Catholic University, 1970.

"Luther, Martin"and "Lutherans ." In *World Book Encyclopedia*, 1970 edition.

"The Pope and the Jews." *New York Times*, 28 October 1970: 47. [Fifth anniversary of the Vatican II Declaration].

AUDIO/VISUAL RECORDINGS

"Tradition and Authority in the History of Christian Doctrine." Sound recording of a lecture delivered at Princeton Theological Seminary on 20 April 1970. Princeton, NJ: Princeton Theological Seminary Speech Studios, 1970.

"Women in Christian Theology." Sound recording of lecture delivered at Princeton Theological Seminary. Princeton, NJ: Princeton Theological Seminary Speech Studios, 1970.

1971

BOOKS

The Christian Tradition: A History of the Development of Doctrine, volume 1: *The*

Emergence of the Catholic Tradition (100–600). Chicago: University of Chicago Press, 1971.

Historical Theology: Continuity and Change in Christian Doctrine. New York: Corpus Books; London: Hutchinson, 1971.

ARTICLES, ESSAYS, PUBLISHED LECTURES

"Eve or Mary: A Test Case in the Development of Doctrine." *Christian Ministry* 2 (1971): 21–22.

"Historical Theology: A Presentation." *Criterion* 10 (1971): 26–27.

1972

EDITIONS AND TRANSLATIONS

Luther, Martin. *Notes on Ecclesiastes; Lectures on the Song of Solomon; Treatise on the Last Words of David. Luther's Works*, 15. Edited and translated by Jaroslav Pelikan. St Louis: Concordia Publishing House, 1972.

ARTICLES, ESSAYS, PUBLISHED LECTURES

"Dukedom Large Enough: Reflections on Academic Administration." *Concordia Theological Monthly* 43 (1972): 297–302. [An address at the inauguration of Robert V. Schnabel as president of Concordia College, Bronxville, NY, February 5, 1972].

INTRODUCTIONS AND FOREWORDS

Foreword to *Portrait of the Elder Brother: Jews and Judaism in Protestant Teaching Materials*, by Gerald S. Strober. New York: American Jewish Committee and National Conference of Christians and Jews, 1972.

1973

EDITIONS AND TRANSLATIONS

The Preaching of Augustine: Our Lord's Sermon on the Mount. Edited and with introduction by Jaroslav Pelikan. Translated by Francine Cardman. Philadelphia: Fortress, 1973.

ARTICLES, ESSAYS, PUBLISHED LECTURES

" 'Council or Father or Scripture': The Concept of Authority in the Theology
of Maximus Confessor." In *The Heritage of the Early Church: Essays in Honor
of the Very Reverend Georges Vasilievich Florovsky*, edited by David Neiman
and Margaret Schatkin, 277–88. *Orientalia Christiana Analecta*, 195. Rome:
Pontificale Institutum Studiorum Orientalium, 1973.
"The Liberation Arts." *Liberal Education* 59 (1973): 292–97.
"*Puti Russkogo Bogoslova*: When Orthodoxy Comes West." In *The Heritage of the
Early Church: Essays in Honor of the Very Reverend Georges Vasilievich
Florovsky*, edited by David Neiman and Margaret Schatkin, 11–16. *Orien-
talia Christiana Analecta*, 195. Rome: Pontificale Institutum Studiorum
Orientalium, 1973.
"Worship between Yesterday and Tomorrow." In *Worship: Good News in Action*,
edited by Mandus A. Egge, 57–69. Minneapolis: Augsburg Publishing
House, [1973]. Also printed in *Studia Liturgica* 9/4 (1973): 205–214.

AUDIO/VISUAL RECORDINGS

"The Sermon on the Mount and Its Interpreters" [Chrysostom, Augustine,
Luther]. *1973 Cole Lectures*. [Three lectures: "The Lordship of Christ";
"The Meaning of Discipleship"; "The Ethics of the Kingdom"]. Sound
recordings made at Vanderbilt University Divinity School, 1973.

1974

BOOKS

The Christian Tradition: A History of the Development of Doctrine, volume 2: *The
Spirit of Eastern Christendom (600–1700)*. University of Chicago Press, 1974.

ARTICLES, ESSAYS, PUBLISHED LECTURES

"Angel and Evangel [Rev 14:6–7]." *Concordia Theological Monthly* 45 (1974): 4–7.
"The Doctrine of *Filioque* in Thomas Aquinas and Its Patristic Antecedents:
An Analysis of *Summa Theologiae*, Part I, Question 36." In *Saint Thomas
Aquinas 1274–1974: Commemorative Studies*, edited by Armand A. Maurer,
1:315–36. Toronto: Pontifical Institute of Mediaeval Studies, 1974.
"Luther Comes to the New World." In *Luther and the Dawn of the Modern Era:
Papers for the Fourth International Congress for Luther Research*, edited by
Heiko A. Oberman, 1–10. Leiden: E. J. Brill, 1974.

"Paul M. Bretscher, Christian Humanist." *The Cresset* 37/9 (1974): 4.

REVIEWS

"Hazelton's Pascal: A Review Article." *Andover Newton Quarterly* 15 (1974): 145–148.

1975

ARTICLES, ESSAYS, PUBLISHED LECTURES

"Continuity and Creativity." *Saint Vladimir's Theological Quarterly* 19/3 (1975): 1–7. Also available in form delivered as commencement address at St Vladimir's Orthodox Theological Seminary, Crestwood, New York, May 24, 1975, http://www.jacwell.org/articles/1998-SPRING-Pelikan.htm.

1976

ARTICLES, ESSAYS, PUBLISHED LECTURES

"A Decent Respect to the Opinions of Mankind." *Scholarly Publishing* 8 (1976): 11–16.
"Quality and Equality." *The New York Times*, 29 March 1976: 29.
"The Research University and the Healing Professions." *Criterion*, Autumn 1976.
"The Ukrainian Catholic Church and Eastern Spirituality." In *The Ukrainian Catholic Church 1945–1975*, edited by Miroslav Labunka and Leonid Rudnytzky, 114–27. Philadelphia: St Sophia Religious Association of Ukrainian Catholics, 1976.
"We Hold These Truths to be Self-Evident: Reformation, Revolution, and Reason." In *The Historical Context and Dynamic Future of Lutheran Higher Education*, edited by J. Victor Hahn, 8–17. Washington, DC: Lutheran Educational Conference of North America, 1976.
"What Gibbon Knew: Lessons in Imperialism." *Harper's* 253/1514 (1976): 13–18.

REVIEWS

Our Common History as Christians: Essays in Honor of Albert C. Outler. Edited by John Deschner, et al. London & New York: Oxford UP, 1975. In *Perkins Journal* 29 (1976): 39–41.

AUDIO/VISUAL RECORDINGS

"Conditions of Christian Reconciliation." Sound recording. Kansas City, MO: National Catholic Reporter, 1976.

1977

ARTICLES, ESSAYS, PUBLISHED LECTURES

"Christianity," by H. H. Walsh, revised by Jaroslav Pelikan. In *A Reader's Guide to the Great Religions*, 2d rev. edition by Charles J. Adams, 345–406. New York: Macmillan Company and The Free Press, 1977.

1978

BOOKS

The Christian Tradition: A History of the Development of Doctrine, volume 3: *The Growth of Medieval Theology (600–1300)*. University of Chicago Press, 1978.

ARTICLES, ESSAYS, PUBLISHED LECTURES

"Historical Reflections on the Fortieth Anniversary of Saint Vladimir's Seminary." In *The Fortieth Anniversary of St Vladimir's Orthodox Seminary,* edited by Alexander Schmemann. Crestwood, NY: St Vladimir's Seminary, 1978.
"*Imago Dei*: An Explication of *Summa Theologiae*, Part I, Question 93." In *Calgary Aquinas Studies*, edited by Anthony Parel, 27–48. Toronto: Pontifical Institute of Mediaeval Studies, 1978.
"Lex orandi: The Dogma of Prayer in Historical Perspective." In *Conference II: The People of God at Prayer*, edited by Colman J. Barry. Collegeville, MN: Institute for Spirituality, St John's University, [1978]. Also available as a sound recording.
"The New Pope and the Old Schism." In *The New York Times*, 8 November 1978: A27.

1979

ARTICLES, ESSAYS, PUBLISHED LECTURES

"A First-Generation Anselmian, Guibert of Nogent." In *Continuity and Discontinuity in Church History: Essays Presented to George Huntston Williams*, edited by F. Forrester Church and Timothy George, 71–82. *Studies in the History of Christian Thought*, 19. Leiden: E. J. Brill, 1979.

"A Gentleman and a Scholar." *The Key Reporter* [Phi Beta Kappa] 45/2 (1979–80): 2–4.

"The Jewish-Christian Dialogue in Historical Perspective." *Bulletin of the American Academy of Arts and Sciences* 32/7 (1979): 18–30.

"Voices of the Church." In *Proceedings of the Thirty-Third Annual Convention [of the Catholic Theological Society of America]*, edited by Luke Salm, 1–12. The Bronx, NY, 1979.

"The Wisdom of Prospero." In *Minutes of the Ninety-fourth Meeting [of the Association of Research Libraries]*, 67–72. Washington, DC: ARL, 1979.

1980

ARTICLES, ESSAYS, PUBLISHED LECTURES

"Luther Comes to America." In *Encounters with Luther: Lectures, Discussions, and Sermons at the Martin Luther Colloquia 1970–1974*, edited by Eric W. Gritsch, 1:58–68. Gettysburg, PA: Institute for Luther Studies, 1980.

"The Research Library, an Outpost of Cultural Continuity." *Imprint of the Stanford Library Associates* 6/2 (1980): 5–10. [Address delivered at the dedication of the Green Library, Stanford University.]

"The Two Sees of Peter: Reflections on the Pace of Normative Self-definition East and West." In *The Shaping of Christianity in the Second and Third Centuries*, v. 1 of *Jewish and Christian Self-Definition*, edited by E. P. Sanders, 57–73. Philadelphia: Fortress Press; London: SCM Press, 1980.

AUDIO/VISUAL RECORDINGS

"The Place of Luther's Reformation in the History of Christine Doctrine." Sound recording of lecture given at a conference at the Lutheran School of Theology, Chicago, 19–24 October 1980.

1981

ARTICLES, ESSAYS, PUBLISHED LECTURES

"Negative Theology and Positive Religion: A Study of Nicholas Cusanus's *De pace fidei*." *Prudentia* supplementary number (1981): 65–78. [Aukland: University of Aukland, 1981].

"The 'Spiritual Sense' of Scripture: The Exegetical Basis for Saint Basil's Doctrine of the Holy Spirit." In *Basil of Caesarea: Christian, Humanist, Ascetic*, edited by Paul Jonathan Fedwick, 1:337–60. Toronto: Pontifical Institute of Mediaeval Studies, 1981.

INTRODUCTIONS AND FOREWORDS

Foreword to *The Christian Trinity in History*, by Bertrand de Margerie. Translated by Edmund J. Fortman. *Studies in Historical Theology*, v. 1. Still River, MA: Saint Bede's Publications, 1981.

1982

ARTICLES, ESSAYS, PUBLISHED LECTURES

"The Doctrine of the Image of God." In *The Common Christian Roots of the European Nations: An International Colloquium in the Vatican*, 1:53–62. [Rome: Tipo. Poliglotta Vaticana, 1982]; Florence: Le Monnier, 1982.

"From Reformation Theology to Christian Humanism." *Lutheran Forum* 16/4 (1982): 11–15.

"The Place of Maximus Confessor in the History of Christian Thought." In *Maximus Confessor, Actes du Symposium sur Maxime le Confesseur Fribourg*, edited by Felix Heinze and Christoph Schoenborn, 387–402. Paradosis: Études de litterature et de théologie ancienne, no. 27. Fribourg: Éditions Universitaires Fribourg Suisse, 1982.

"Special Collections: A Key into the Language of America." *Books at Brown* [Friends of the Library of Brown University] 29/30 (1982/83): 1–10.

"The Two Cities: The Decline and Fall of Rome as Historical Paradigm." *Daedalus* 111/3 (1982): 85–92.

INTRODUCTIONS AND FOREWORDS

Introduction to *Martin Luther: An Illustrated Biography*, by Peter Manns. Translated by Michael Shaw. New York: Crossroad, 1982.

Foreword to *The Secular Mind: Transformations of Faith in Modern Europe: Essays Presented to Franklin L. Baumer*, edited by W. Warren Wagar. New York: Holmes & Meier, 1982.

AUDIO/VISUAL RECORDINGS

"Darwin's Legacy." Recorded at the 18th Nobel Conference, Gustavus Adol-
phus College, 5–6 October 1982. St Peter, MN: The College, 1982.

1983

BOOKS

Scholarship and its Survival: Questions on the Idea of Graduate Education. Princeton: Carnegie Foundation for the Advancement of Teaching, 1983.

ARTICLES, ESSAYS, PUBLISHED LECTURES

"Darwin's Legacy." In *Darwin's Legacy: Nobel Conference XVIII, Gustavus Adol-
phus College,* edited by Charles L. Hamrum. San Francisco: Harper & Row,
1983.
"The Enduring Relevance of Martin Luther 500 Years after His Birth." *The
New York Times Magazine,* 18 September 1983, 42–45; 99–104.

INTRODUCTIONS AND FOREWORDS

Preface to *The Triads,* by Gregory Palamas. Edited by John Meyendorff. Translated by Nicholas Gendle. Classics of Western Spirituality. New York:
Paulist Press, 1983.

1984

BOOKS

The Christian Tradition: A History of the Development of Doctrine, volume 4:
Reformation of Church and Dogma (1300–1700). University of Chicago Press,
1984; reprinted in 1985 and 1989.
The Vindication of Tradition. Jefferson Lectures in the Humanities, 1983. New
Haven: Yale UP, 1984; reprinted in 1986.

ARTICLES, ESSAYS, PUBLISHED LECTURES

"The Aesthetics of Scholarly Research: An Address for the Sesquicentennial
of Tulane University." Delivered at the University convocation on Friday,
September 21, 1984. New Orleans: Tulane University, 1984.

"Scholarship: A Sacred Vocation." *Scholarly Publishing: A Journal for Authors and Publishers* 16/1 (1984): 3–22.

"Some Uses of Apocalypse in the Magisterial Reformers." In *The Apocalypse in English Renaissance Thought and Literature: Patterns, Antecedents, and Repercussions*, edited by C. A. Patrides and Joseph Wittreich, 74–92. Ithaca, NY: Cornell UP, 1984; Manchester: Manchester UP, 1984.

REVIEWS

John Paul II, Pope, and Andre Frossard. *Be Not Afraid.* Translated by J. R. Foster. New York: St Martin's Press, 1984. In *New York Times Book Review* 89/17 (22 April 1984): 12.

AUDIO/VISUAL RECORDINGS

"J. S. Bach, the Fifth Evangelist." Sound and video recording of the Women's Auxiliary Lecture delivered at Lutheran Theological Seminary, Philadelphia, 5 December 1984.

FESTSCHRIFT

Schools of Thought in the Christian Tradition. Edited by Patrick Henry. Philadelphia: Fortress Press, 1984.

1985

BOOKS

Comparative Work Ethics: Judeo-Christian, Islamic, and Eastern. With Joseph Mitsuo Kitagawa and Seyyed Hossein Nasr. Occasional Papers of the Council of Scholars, no. 4. Washington, Library of Congress, 1985.

Jesus Through the Centuries: His Place in the History of Culture. New Haven: Yale UP, 1985; New York: Perennial Library, 1987. Reprinted in 1999.

Maria: Die Gestalt der Mutter Jesu in jüdischer und christlicher Sicht. With David Flusser and Justin Lang. Freiburg: Herder, 1985. [English translation]. *Mary: Images of the Mother of Jesus in Jewish and Christian Perspective.* Philadelphia: Fortress Press, 1986.

Spirit of Medieval Theology. Etienne Gilson Series, 8. Toronto: Pontifical Institute of Mediaeval Studies, 1985.

ARTICLES, ESSAYS, PUBLISHED LECTURES

"Humanism: Two Definitions and Two Defenses." *Southern Humanities Review* 19 (1985): 193–202.

"Jesus, the Monk Who Rules the World." [Reprint from *Yale Review*, Spring 1985]. *Books and Religion* 13/7 (1985): 1–19.

"The Man Who Belongs to the World." [Excerpt from *Jesus through the Centuries.*] *Christian Century* 102 (1985): 827–831.

INTRODUCTIONS AND FOREWORDS

Introduction to *Maximus Confessor: Selected Writings*, edited by George Berthold. Classics of Western Spirituality. New York: Paulist Press, 1985.

Introduction to *Nature*, by Ralph Waldo Emerson [facsimile of first edition]. Boston: Beacon Press, 1985.

Foreword to and supplementary bibliography for *The Reformation of the Sixteenth Century*, by Roland Bainton. Boston: Beacon Press, 1985.

1986

BOOKS

Bach among the Theologians. Philadelphia: Fortress Press, 1986.

Evangelisches Kirchenlexikon. Edited by Erwin Fahlbusch, Jan Milič Lochman, John Mbiti, Jaroslav Pelikan, and Lukas Vischer. 5 vols. Göttingen: Vandenhoeck & Ruprecht, 1986–1997. English translation appearing as *Encyclopedia of Christianity*, Grand Rapids: Wm. B. Eerdmans Publishing Co.

Jesus Through the Centuries published in German as *Jesus Christus: Erscheinungsbild und Wirkung in 2000 Jahren Kulturgeschichte*, translated by Cornelia Hermanns. Cologne: Benziger, 1986.

The Mystery of Continuity: Time and History, Memory and Eternity in the Thought of Saint Augustine. Charlottesville: University of Virginia Press, 1986.

Scholarship Today: The Humanities and Social Sciences. With Jacques Barzum and John Hope Franklin. Three papers from a symposium sponsored by the Council of Scholars. Washington, DC: Library of Congress, 1986.

ARTICLES, ESSAYS, PUBLISHED LECTURES

" '*Determinatio Ecclesiae*' and/or '*communiter omnes doctores*': On Locating Ockham within the Orthodox Dogmatic Tradition." *Franciscan Studies* 46 (1986): 24, 37–45.

"King Lear or Uncle Tom's Cabin?" *The Teaching of Values in Higher Education*, 9–18. Washington, DC: Woodrow Wilson International Center for Scholars, 1986.

INTRODUCTIONS AND FOREWORDS

Foreword to *The Proper Distinction between Law and Gospel*, by C. F. W. Walther. St Louis: Concordia Publishing House, 1986.

REVIEWS

Maccoby, Hyam. *The Mythmaker: Paul and the Invention of Christianity*. San Francisco: Harper & Row, 1986; Weidenfeld & Nicolson, [n.d.]. In *Commentary* 82/5 (1986): 76–78.

1987

ARTICLES, ESSAYS, PUBLISHED LECTURES

"An Augustinian Dilemma: Augustine's Doctrine of Grace v. Augustine's Doctrine of the Church." The Saint Augustine Lecture, Villanova University, 1997. Published in *Augustinian Studies*, vol., 18:1–29.

INTRODUCTIONS AND FOREWORDS

"The Odyssey of Dionysian Spirituality." Introduction to *Pseudo-Dionysius: The Complete Works*, edited by Paul Rorem. Classics of Western Spirituality. New York: Paulist Press, 1987.

REVIEWS

"Speak of the Devil." Review of Jeffrey B. Russell, *The Devil* (Cornell UP, 1977); *Satan: The Early Christian Tradition* (Cornell UP, 1981); *Lucifer: The Devil in the* Middle Ages (Cornell UP, 1984); and *Mephistopheles: The Devil in the Modern World* (Cornell UP, 1986). In *Commentary* 83 (1987): 63–66.

1988

BOOKS

The Excellent Empire: The Fall of Rome and the Triumph of the Church. Rauschen-

busch Lectures, new series, 1. San Francisco: Harper & Row, 1988; reprinted 1990.
Jesus Through the Centuries published in Dutch. Kampen: Kok Agora, 1988.
Jesus Through the Centuries published in Italian. Bari: Gius Laterza Figli, 1988.
The Melody of Theology: A Philosophical Dictionary. Cambridge, MA: Harvard UP, 1988.
Paths to Intellectual Reunification of East and West Europe: A Historical Typology. [Princeton, NJ]: International Research and Exchanges Board, 1988.

ARTICLES, ESSAYS, PUBLISHED LECTURES

"Russia's Greatest Heretic, Lev Nikolayevich Tolstoy." The Archbishop Gerety Lecture at Seton Hall University, September 26, 1988. http://theology.shu.edu/lectures/russiaheretic.html.
"Sobornost and National Particularity in Historical Perspective." *Cross Currents* 7 (1988): 7–17.
"Writing as a Means of Grace." In *Spiritual Quests*, edited by William Zinsser, 85–101. Boston: Houghton Mifflin, 1988.

INTRODUCTIONS AND FOREWORDS

Foreword to *A Century of Church History: The Legacy of Philip Schaff*, edited by Henry W. Bowden. Carbondale: Southern Illinois UP, 1988.

1989

BOOKS

The Christian Tradition: A History of the Development of Doctrine, volume 5: *Christian Doctrine and Modern Culture (since 1700)*. Chicago: University of Chicago Press, 1989.
Jesus Through the Centuries published in French as *Jésus au fil de l'histoire: sa place dans l'histoire de la culture*. Paris: Hachette, 1989.
Jesus Through the Centuries published in Spanish as *Jesús a través de los siglos: su lugar en la historia de la cultura*. Barcelona: Herder, 1989.

ARTICLES, ESSAYS, PUBLISHED LECTURES

"How to Carry On Your Private Education in Public—And Get Paid for It." An address delivered on the occasion of the Second Annual Authors'

Dinner at the University of Alabama, 17 February 1988. [Tuscaloosa]: University of Alabama Press, 1989.

"Russia's Greatest Heretic [L. N. Tolstoy]." *Archbishop Gerety Lectures 1988–89*, 1–12. South Orange, NJ: School of Theology, Seton Hall University, 1989.

INTRODUCTIONS AND FOREWORDS

"The Church between East and West: The Context of Sheptyts'kyi's Thought." Introduction to *Morality and Reality: The Life and Times of Andrei Sheptyts'kyi*, edited by Paul Robert Magocsi. Edmonton: Canadian Institute of Ukrainian Studies, University of Alberta, 1989.

"Jefferson and His Contemporaries." Afterword to *The Jefferson Bible: The Life and Morals of Jesus of Nazareth*, by Thomas Jefferson. Boston: Beacon Press, 1989.

Foreword to *Martin Luther's Basic Theological Writings*, edited by Timothy F. Lull. Minneapolis: Fortress Press, 1989.

REVIEWS

Norwich, John J. *Byzantium: The Early Centuries*. New York: Viking, [1989]. In *Commentary* 88 (1989): 58–60.

1990

BOOKS

Confessor between East and West: A Portrait of Ukrainian Cardinal Josyf Slipyj. Grand Rapids: Eerdmans, 1990.

Eternal Feminines: Three Theological Allegories in Dante's Paradiso. New Brunswick, NJ: Rutgers UP, 1990.

Imago Dei: The Byzantine Apologia for Icons. Bollinger Series, 35, 36. New Haven: Yale UP; Princeton UP, 1990.

The World Treasury of Modern Religious Thought. Jaroslav Pelikan, editor; Clifton Fadiman, general editor. Boston: Little, Brown, 1990.

ARTICLES, ESSAYS, PUBLISHED LECTURES

"Canonica regula: The Trinitarian Hermeneutics of Augustine." In *Collectanea Augustiniana*, I, *Augustine: "Second Founder of the Faith*," edited by Joseph C. Schnaubel and Frederick Van Fleteren, 329–43. New York, Bern: Lang, 1990. Also in *Proceedings of the Patristic, Mediaeval and Renaissance Conference* 12/13 (1987–88): 17–30.

"Fundamentalism and/or Orthodoxy? Toward an Understanding of the Fundamentalist Phenomenon." In *The Fundamentalist Phenomenon: A View from Within; A Response from Without*, edited by Norman J. Cohen, 3–21. Grand Rapids, MI: W. B. Eerdmans, 1990; reprinted in 1991.

"Judaism and the Humanities: Liberation from History." In *The State of Jewish Studies*, edited by Shaye J. D. Cohen and Edward L. Greenstein, 255–67. Detroit: Wayne State UP, 1990.

"Newman and the Fathers: The Vindication of Tradition." In *Studia Patristica*, 18/4, edited by E. Livingstone, 379–390.

"Orthodox Theology in the West: The Reformation." In *The Legacy of St Vladimir*, edited by John Breck, 159–65. Crestwood, NY: St Vladimir's Seminary Press, 1990.

"*Philosophia* as a Woman: The Allegorical Vision of Boethius." *The Kathryn Fraser Mackay Lecture*, 1989. Canton, NY: St Lawrence University, 1990.

"Whose Bible? Second Thoughts on Listening to *Messiah*." Program notes for December 1990 issue of *Stagebill* for the Musica Sacra performance of Handel's *Messiah*.

INTRODUCTIONS AND FOREWORDS

Introduction to *The Varieties of Religious Experience*, by William James. New York: Library of America, 1990.

1991

BOOKS

Jesus, Not Caesar: The Religious World View of Thomas Garrigue Masaryk and the Spiritual Foundations of Czech and Slovak Culture. Westminster Tanner-McMurrin Lectures on the History and Philosophy of Religion at Westminster College, 3. Salt Lake City: Westminster College of Salt Lake City, 1991.

Jesus Through the Centuries published in Japanese. Tokyo: Shinchi Shobo, 1991 (reprinted in 1998).

ARTICLES, ESSAYS, PUBLISHED LECTURES

"Christian Mysticism East and West." *James I. McCord Memorial Lectures, Fall 1990*, 3–15. Princeton: Center of Theological Inquiry, 1991.

INTRODUCTIONS AND FOREWORDS

Foreword to *Life of Christ*, by Giuseppe Ricciotti. Library of Great Lives. Norwalk, CT: The Easton Press, 1991.

1992

BOOKS

The Idea of the University: A Reexamination. New Haven: Yale UP, 1992.

Jesus Through the Centuries published in Croatian. Zagreb: Graficki Zavod Hrvatske, 1992.

On Searching the Scriptures, Your Own or Someone Else's. Companion guide to *Sacred Writings* series edited by Jaroslav Pelikan (see below). New York: History Book Club, 1992.

EDITIONS AND TRANSLATIONS

Sacred Writings. Edited by Jaroslav Pelikan. New York: Book of the Month Club, 1992. Also Published by the History Book Club, 1992. 6 volumes.

Vol. 1: *Judaism: The Tanakh.* The New JPS Translation. Edited by Jaroslav Pelikan. New York: Quality Paperback Book Club, 1992.

Vol. 2: *Christianity: the Apocrypha and the New Testament.* From the Revised English Bible. Edited by Jaroslav Pelikan. New York: Quality Paperback Book Club, 1992.

Vol. 3: *Islam: the Quran* Translated by Ahmed Ali. Edited by Jaroslav Pelikan. New York: Quality Paperback Book Club, 1992.

Vol. 4: *Confucianism: The Analects of Confucius.* Translated by Arthur Waley. Edited by Jaroslav Pelikan. New York: Quality Paperback Book Club, 1992.

Vol. 5: *Hinduism, The Rig Veda.* Translated by Ralph T.H. Griffith. Edited by Jaroslav Pelikan. New York: Quality Paperback Book Club, 1992.

Vol. 6: *Buddhism: The Dhammapada.* Translated by John Ross Carter and Mahinda Palihawadana. Edited by Jaroslav Pelikan.

ARTICLES, ESSAYS, PUBLISHED LECTURES

"John Meyendorff, 1926–1992" [obituary]. *Christian Century* 109 (1992): 837.

"The Place of John Amos Comenius in the History of Christian Theology." *Communio viatorum* 34/3 (1992): 5–18.

"Unity and Reconciliation: The Historical Dialectic." [Address to General Board of National Council of Churches]. *Mid-Stream* 31 (1992): 123–128.

"The University's Secret Weapon." Address to the Charter Meeting of Friends of Yale University Press, 10 September 1992. New Haven: Friends of Yale University Press, 1992.

REVIEWS

The Anchor Bible Dictionary, 6 volumes. Edited by David Noel Freedman. New York: Doubleday, 1992. In *New York Times Book Review* 97 (20 December 1992): 3.

1993

BOOKS

Christianity and Classical Culture: The Metamorphosis of Natural Theology in the Christian Encounter with Hellenism. New Haven: Yale UP, 1993.
Jesus Through the Centuries published in Polish. Warsaw: Spoleczny Instytut Wydaw Znak, 1993.

ARTICLES, ESSAYS, PUBLISHED LECTURES

"The Historian as Polyglot." *Proceedings of the American Philosophical Society*, 137 (1993):659–68.

AUDIO/VISUAL RECORDINGS

"'And Alas, Theology Too': Goethe's *Faust* and the Christian Tradition." [Three lectures: "The Pantheistic Scientist"; "The Polytheistic Artist"; "The Monotheistic Moralist"]. Sound recording (3 cassettes) of the *Willson Lectures* presented at Southwestern University, Georgetown, TX, 30–31 March 1993.

MEDIA

"Public Poet, Public Critic." Part of *Soundings* (radio program) on "Education and Culture: East and West." With Nagayo Honma. Programs nos. 643–44. Research Triangle Park, NC: National Humanities Center, 1993.

1994

BOOKS

Bach among the Theologians published in Italian as *Bach teologo*. Piemme, 1994.
The Christian Tradition (5 vols) published in French. Paris: Presses Universitaires de France, 1994.

ARTICLES, ESSAYS, PUBLISHED LECTURES

"The Individual's Search for Truth—and Its Limitations." In *Individualism and Social Responsibility*, edited by W. Lawson Taitte. *Andrew R. Cecil Lectures on Moral Values in a Free Society*, 15. Dallas: University of Texas at Dallas, 1994.
"Orthodox Christianity in the World and in America." In *World Religions in America: An Introduction*, edited by Jacob Neusner, 131–50. Louisville: Westminster/John Knox Press, 1994.

AUDIO/VISUAL RECORDINGS

Christians of the East. [Video recording]. Yale Great Teachers Series. Florence, KY: Brenzel Publishing in cooperation with the Association of Yale Alumni, 1994.

1995

BOOKS

Das Bild in der Bibel: Bibelillustration von der Reformation bis zur Gegenwart. With Bernhard Bach. Munich: Claudius Verlag, 1995.
CD-Rom Version of *The Book of Concord: The Confessions of the Evangelical Lutheran Church*. Edited by Theodore Tappert. Contributions by Jaroslav Pelikan and others. Minneapolis: Augsburg/Fortress, 1995.
Faust the Theologian. New Haven: Yale UP, 1995.

ARTICLES, ESSAYS, PUBLISHED LECTURES

" 'Blut is ein ganz besondrer Saft: Am färbigen Abglanz haben wird das Leben.' The Aria 'Erwäge, wie sein blutgefärbter Rücken' in J. S. Bach's Saint John Passion." In *Das Blut Jesu und die Lehre von der Versöhnung in Werk Johann Sebastian Bachs*, edited by A. A. Clement, 205–13. Amsterdam: Royal Netherlands Academy of Arts and Sciences, 1995.

"Continuity and Development in Patristic Theology: The Relation between διακοχή and προκοπή in the Greek Fathers of the Fourth Century." In *Rightly Teaching the Word of Your Truth: Studies in Faith and Culture, Church and Scriptures, Fathers and Worship, Hellenism and the Contemporary Scene in Honor of His Eminence Archbishop Iakovos*, edited by Nomikos Michael Vaporis, 53–57. Brookline, MA: Holy Cross Orthodox Press, 1995.

"A Word from Plato about POK: A Laudatio for Paul Oskar Kristeller's Ninetieth Birthday." In *Paul Oskar Kristeller at Ninety*. New York: Columbia University, 1995.

INTRODUCTIONS AND FOREWORDS

Foreword to the *Heritage Institute Museum and Library: A Description,* by Robert A. Karlowich, E. Kasinec, I. V. Pozdeeva, et al. West Paterson, NJ: Diocese of Passaic, 1995.

AUDIO/VISUAL RECORDINGS

"Amnesia, An Occupational Disease of Professionals—and Its Antidote." New Haven: Video Production Services, Yale University School of Medicine, 1995.

"The Idea of the University in Action." President's Lecture Series, University of Montana. 1 sound cassette, 1995.

1996

BOOKS

The Idea of the University published in Japanese. Translated by Takao Taguchi. Tokyo: Hosei Daigaku Shuppankyoku, 1996.

Mary Through the Centuries. New Haven: Yale UP, 1996.

The Reformation of the Bible / The Bible of the Reformation. With Valerie Hotchkiss and David Price. New Haven: Yale UP, 1996.

ARTICLES, ESSAYS, PUBLISHED LECTURES

"Hebraica Veritas" (in German). *From Witness to Witchcraft: Jews and Judaism in Medieval Christian Thought,* 11–28. Edited by Jeremy Cohen. Volume 11 of Wolfenbüttler Mittelalter-Studien. Wiesbaden: Harrassowitz Verlag, 1996.

"Research as a Habit of Mind: A Catalog of Scholarly Virtues." Address to the First Annual University of South Carolina Research Banquet, December 5, 1996." Charleston, SC: University of South Carolina, 1996.
"Rhetoric and Beyond: Learning from the Greeks." *Fifth Annual Walter and Leonore Annenberg Distinguished Lecture in Communication.* Philadelphia: Annenberg Public Policy Center of the University of Pennsylvania, 1996.

FESTSCHRIFT

The Unbounded Community: Papers in Christian Ecumenism in Honor of Jaroslav Pelikan. Edited by William Caferro and Duncan G. Fisher. New York: Garland Publishing, 1996.

1997

BOOKS

The Illustrated Jesus Through the Centuries. New Haven: Yale UP, 1997.
Mary Through the Centuries published in Spanish. Madrid: PPC, 1997.
What Has Athens to Do with Jerusalem? Timaeus and Genesis in Counterpoint. Ann Arbor: University of Michigan Press, 1997.

ARTICLES, ESSAYS, PUBLISHED LECTURES

"Pernicious Amnesia: Combating the Epidemic." Speech at the Conferral of the Inaugural Jacques Barzun Award. Washington, DC: The American Academy for Liberal Education, 1997.
"The Predicament of the Christian Historian." Delivered at the Center for Theological Inquiry, Princeton Theological Seminary, April 1997. Published in *Reflections*, vol. 1 (1997) and at *http://www.ctinquiry.org/publications/reflections_volume_1/pelikan.htm*

1998

BOOKS

Jesus Through the Centuries published in Japanese. Tokyo: Kodansha, 1998.
Mary Through the Centuries published in Japanese. Tokyo: Seidosha, 1998.

ARTICLES, ESSAYS, PUBLISHED LECTURES

"A Conversation with Jaroslav Pelikan." Interview in *Initiatives in Religion* 7/1 (Winter 1998): 3–4.
"The Traditions that Divide, The Tradition that Unites." In *Ecumenism: Present Realities and Future Prospects,* edited by Lawrence Cunningham, 1–23. Notre Dame, IN: University of Notre Dame Press, 1998.

INTRODUCTIONS AND FOREWORDS

Foreword to *Religion and the Founding of the American Republic,* by James H. Hutson. Washington, DC: GPO, 1998.

REVIEWS

Bynum, Caroline Walker. *Resurrection of the Body in Western Christianity, 200–1336.* New York: Columbia UP, 1995. In *Catholic Historical Review* 84 (1998): 521–23.

MEDIA

"Religion and the American Republic." *Addresses on the Role of Religion and its relation to the American Colonies and the United States during the 17th–19th Centuries,* June 18–19, 1998. Chaired by Jaroslav Pelikan. With Mark A. Noll, Catherine A. Brekus, Michael Novak, Jon Butler, Rosemarie Zagarri, and James H. Smylie. Forum, Washington, DC. C-span video/CD; Product ID: 107529-1.

1999

BOOKS

Jesus Through the Centuries published in Korean. Soul-si: Tongyon, 1999.
Mary Through the Centuries published in German. Freiburg: Herder, 1999.
Mary Through the Centuries published in Italian. Roma: Citta Nuovà, 1999.

ARTICLES, ESSAYS, PUBLISHED LECTURES

"Christianity: The Western Church"; "Christian Theology." In *Encyclopedia of the Renaissance,* 6 vols., edited by Paul F. Grendler, 1:431–36; 1:441–45. New York: Charles Scribner's Sons, 1999.
"The Eastern Orthodox Quest for Confessional Identity: Where Does Orthodoxy Confess What It Believes and Teaches?" Fourth Annual James W.

Cunningham Memorial Lecture on Eastern Orthodox History and Culture, 6 November 1998. In *Modern Greek Studies Yearbook* (Vol. 14/15, 1998/1999), 21–36.

"The Predicament of the Christian Historian." In *Reflections: Center of Theological Inquiry*, 1:26–47. Reprinted in *Reformed Review* 52 (Spring 1999):196–211.

"Theology." In *Late Antiquity: A Guide to the Postclassical World*, edited by G. W. Bowersock, Peter Brown, and Oleg Grabar, 722–23. Cambridge, MA: Belknap Press of Harvard University Press, 1999.

INTRODUCTIONS AND FOREWORDS

Foreword to *Augustine Through the Ages: An Encyclopedia*, xiii–xiv. Edited by Allan D. Fitzgerald. Grand Rapids: Wm. B. Eerdmans Publishing Co., 1999.

REVIEWS

Kilmartin, Edward J. *The Eucharist in the West: History and Theology.* Collegeville, MN: Liturgical Press, 1998. In *Commonweal* 126 (1999): 26–28.

2000

BOOKS

Continuità e cambiamento della fede. Rome: Di Renzo, 2000.

Divine Rhetoric: The Sermon on the Mount as Message and as Model in Augustine, Chrysostom, and Luther. Crestwood, NY: St Vladimir's Seminary Press, 2000; London: Cassell, 2000.

The Illustrated Jesus Through the Centuries published in Portuguese. São Paulo: Cosac & Naify Edições, 2000.

Jesus Through the Centuries published in French. Paris: Hachette Littératures, 2000.

ARTICLES, ESSAYS, PUBLISHED LECTURES

"A Remembrance of Edward Hirsch Levi." *Bulletin of the American Academy of Arts and Sciences*, 53–5: 16–19.

"Zeit und Trinität in der christlichen Tradition." In *Am Ende des Millenniums, Zeit und Modernitäten: Castelgandolfo-Gespräche 1998*, edited by Krzystof Michalski, 3–23. Stuttgart: Klett-Cotta, 2000.

INTRODUCTIONS AND FOREWORDS

New preface to *Christianity,* by Roland Herbert Bainton. (Originally published as *The Horizon History of Christianity.* New York: American Heritage Publications, 1964.) Boston: Houghton Mifflin, 2000.

AUDIO/VISUAL RECORDINGS

"The Twentieth-century Recovery of the Eschatological Vision: Reflections for the Millennium of Messiaen's Quartet for the End of Time and Elgar's Dreams of Gerontius." In *Ratios and Radiance, Feathers and Faith: The Music of Olivier Messiaen.* Video recordings of the Brown Symposium 2000. Southwestern University, Georgetown, TX, 2000.

2001

BOOKS

Fools for Christ: Essays on the True, the Good, and the Beautiful. Reprint, Eugene, OR: Wipf and Stock Publishers, 2001.

ARTICLES, ESSAYS, PUBLISHED LECTURES

"Athens and/or Jerusalem: Cosmology and/or Creation." In *Cosmic Questions,* edited by James B. Miller, 17–27. New York: New York Academy of Sciences, 2001.

"Faust as Doctor of Theology." In Johann Wolfgang von Goethe, *Faust,* edited by Cyrus Hamlin, 586–98. 2nd ed. Norton Crtitical Editions. New York: W. W. Norton and Company, 2001.

2002

BOOKS

The Christian Tradition published in Chinese. Xianggang: Dao feng shu she, 2002.

Luther's Works on CD-ROM. Philadelphia: Fortress Press and St Louis, MO. Concordia, 2002. "This CD-ROM makes available the entire 55-volume set of Luther's Works, a magisterial translation project published jointly by Fortress Press and Concordia Publishing House in 1957." General editors: Jaroslav Pelikan and Helmut T. Lehmann.

ARTICLES, ESSAYS, PUBLISHED LECTURES

"Jacques Barzun." In *The A. W. Mellon Lectures in the Fine Arts: Fifty Years*, 105–6. Washington, DC: Center for Advanced Study in the Visual Arts, National Gallery of Art, 2002.

"Music as Metaphor." Keynote Address, Seventy-Seventh Annual Meeting of the National Association of Schools of Music. (Incorporating the Lecture, "The Decline and Fall of the Wotan Empire," Seattle Opera Symposium on the Wagner *Ring* Cycle, August 2001). In *Proceedings*, 1–14. Reston, VA, 2002.

"People of the Book—and of Books: The Book as Icon." Keynote Address, Commemorative Book, Dedication of the John G. Rangos Family Foundation Building, 26–29. Crestwood, NY: St Vladimir's Orthodox Seminary, 11 May 2002.

INTRODUCTIONS AND FOREWORDS

Foreword to *God and Philosophy*, by Etienne Gilson. 2nd ed. New Haven: Yale UP, 2002.

MEDIA

"The Russian Christ: The Silence of Jesus from Hesychasm to the Legend of the Grand Inquisitor" Lecture at the University of Illinois, April 19, 2002, and subject of radio interview on WILL-AM, FOCUS-580. Archived interview at http://www.will.uiuc.edu/am/focus/archives/02/020415.htm.

2003

BOOKS

Bach among the Theologians. Reprint, Eugene, OR.: Wipf and Stock, 2003.

Credo. Introductory volume to *Creeds and Confessions of Faith in the Christian Tradition*. New Haven: Yale UP, 2003.

Creeds and Confessions of Faith in the Christian Tradition, 3 volumes with CD-Rom of original language texts. Edited with Valerie Hotchkiss. New Haven: Yale UP, 2003.

ARTICLES, ESSAYS, PUBLISHED LECTURES

"Between Ecumenical Councils: The Orthodoxy of the Body of the Faithful." In *The Orthodox Parish in America*, edited by Anton C. Vrame, 93–103. Brookline, MA: Holy Cross Orthodox Press, 2003.

"Stewardship of Money in the Early Church: A Close Reading of *Who Is the Rich Man that Shall Be Saved?* by Clement of Alexandria." In *Good and Faithful Servant: Stewardship in the Orthodox Church*, edited by Anthony Scott, 13–26. Crestwood, NY: St Vladimir's Seminary Press, 2003.

INTRODUCTIONS AND FOREWORDS

Preface to *The Structure of Lutheranism: The Theology and Philosophy of Life of Lutheranism especially in the Sixteenth and Seventeenth Centuries*, by Werner Elert. Translated by Walter A. Hansen. Saint Louis: Concordia Pub. House, 2003.

AUDIO/VISUAL RECORDINGS

"Interpreting the Great Code: The Bible and the Constitution in the Church and in the Court." A 4-Lecture Series at the Yale Law School, New Haven, CT, April 2003. Video-recording at *http://www.law.yale.edu/outside/html/ Public_Affairs/videoarchive.htm*.

MEDIA

"The Need for Creeds" Hour-long program on *Speaking of Faith* hosted by Krista Tippett on National Public Radio, 2003. Outline, information on transcript, and audio recording of the program at *http://speakingoffaith.publicradio.org/programs/2003/09/19_pelikan/index.shtml*.

2004

BOOKS

The Christian Tradition, vol. 1, published in Romanian. Bucarest: Polirom, 2004.
Interpreting the Bible and the Constitution. New Haven: Yale University Press, 2004.

ARTICLES, ESSAYS, PUBLISHED LECTURES

"The Heritage of Heraclitus: John Archibald Wheeler and the Itch to Speculate." Delivered at a symposium in honor of John Archibald Wheeler, March 15–18, 2002. In *Science and Ultimate Reality: Quantum Theory, Cosmology, and Complexity*, edited by John D. Barrow, Paul C.W. Davies, and Charles L. Harper, Jr., 27–44. Cambridge: Cambridge UP, 2004.

"The History of the Christian Tradition: Laboratory of Universal History." Delivered 8 December 2004 at the Awards Ceremony for the 2004 John W. Kluge Prize in the Human Sciences. Washington, DC: The Library of Congress, 2004.

"Most Generations Shall Call Me Blessed: An Essay in Aid of a Grammar of Liturgy." In *Mary, Mother of God*, edited by Carl E. Braaten and Robert W. Jenson, 1–18. Grand Rapids: W. B. Eerdmans, 2004.

"The Otherworldly World of *Paradiso*." In *Dante Alighieri*, edited by Harold Bloom, 161–76. Philadelphia: Chelsea House Publishers, 2004.

"Who Do You Say That I Am—Not? The Power of Negative Thinking in the Decrees of the Ecumenical Councils." In *Who Do You Say That I Am? Confessing the Mystery of Christ*, edited by John Cavadini and Laura Holt, 17–31. Notre Dame, IN: University of Notre Dame Press, 2004.

INTRODUCTIONS AND FOREWORDS

Preface to *Cambridge Platonist Spirituality*. Edited and introduced by Charles Taliaferro and Alison J. Teply.

REVIEWS

"The Three Rings." Review of *The Monotheists: Jews, Christians, and Muslims in Conflict and Competition*. (2 vols.; Princeton: Princeton UP, 2003). In *Claremont Review of Books* (Fall 2004): 63–64.

2005

BOOKS

Reprint edition of *Jesus Through the Centuries* and *Mary Through the Centuries*. Bound together, with a new introduction by the author. New York: History Book Club, 2005.

Mary: Images of the Mother of Jesus in Jewish and Christian Perspective. Co-author with David Flusser and Justin Lang. Minneapolis: Fortress Press, 2005.

Whose Bible Is It? A History of the Scriptures through the Ages. New York: Viking, 2005.

ARTICLES, ESSAYS, PUBLISHED LECTURES

"The Great Unifier." On the death of Pope Paul II. *The New York Times,* April 4, 2005: A23.

"A Personal Memoir: Fragments of a Scholar's Autobiography." In *Orthodoxy &
   Western Culture: A Collection of Essays Honoring Jaroslav Pelikan on His Eightieth Birthday*, edited by Valerie Hotchkiss and Patrick Henry, 29–44. Crestwood, NY: St Vladimir's Seminary Press, 2005.

INTRODUCTIONS AND FOREWORDS

"The Press as an Institution of American Constitutional Democracy." In *The
   Press*, edited by Geneval Overholser and Kathleen Hall Jamieson, xvii–xxiv.
   New York: Oxford UP for the Annenberg Foundation Trust at Sunnylands,
   2005.
"The Public Schools as an Institution of American Constitutional Democracy." In *The Public Schools*, edited by Susan Fuhrman and Marvin Lazerson,
   xii–xxi. New York: Oxford UP for the Annenberg Foundation Trust at Sunnylands, 2005.

MEDIA

"Book Poses a Question: Whose Bible Is It?" Interview on National Public
   Radio, April 10, 2005. Audio recording at http://www.npr.org/templates/
   story/story.php?storyId=4584643.
"Whose Bible Is It?" A conversation with Pelikan about the history, evolution,
   and ownership of the Bible on WBUR-Boston. Aired on March 25, 2005.
   Audio recording at http://www.onpointradio.org/shows/2005/03/
   20050325_b_main.asp.

2006

BOOKS

Acts. *Brazos Theological Commentary on the Bible*. Grand Rapids, Mich.: Brazos
   Press, 2006.

Honorary Degrees

M.A.:
Yale University, 1961

D.D.:
Concordia College, Moorhead, Minn., 1960
Concordia Seminary, St Louis, 1967
Trinity College, Hartford, 1987
St Vladmir's Orthodox Theological Seminary, 1988
Victoria University, 1989
University of Toronto, 1989
University of Aberdeen, 1995

Litt.D.:
Wittenberg University, 1960
Wheeling College, 1966
Gettysburg College, 1967
Pacific Lutheran University, 1967
Wabash College, 1988
Jewish Theological Seminary of America, 1991

Hum.D.:
Providence College, 1966
Moravian College, 1986
University of South Carolina, 2001

L.L.D.:
Keuka College, 1967
University of Notre Dame, 1979

Harvard University, 1998
University of Regina, 1998

L.H.D.:
Valparaiso University, 1966
Rockhurst College, 1967
Albertus Magnus College, 1973
Coe College, 1976
Catholic University of America, 1977
St Mary's College, 1978
St Anselm College, 1983
University of Nebraska at Omaha, 1984
Tulane University, 1986
Assumption College, 1986
LaSalle University, 1987
Carthage College, 1991
The University of Chicago, 1991
Southern Methodist University, 1992
SUNY Albany, 1993
Florida International University, 1997
University of Pennsylvania, 2004
St Tikhon's Orthodox Theological Seminary, 2004
New York University, 2005

D.Theol.:
University of Hamburg, 1971
Charles University in Prague, 1999

Th.D.:
St Olaf College, 1972

S.T.D.:
Dickinson College, 1986

Dr.Sc.Hist.:
Comenius University, Bratislava, 1992

Sc.D.:
Loyola University of Chicago, 1995